SAILS
and the way they work

Derek Harvey

ADLARD COLES NAUTICAL
London

This edition published 2002 by Adlard Coles Nautical
an imprint of A & C Black (Publishers) Ltd
37 Soho Square, London W1D 3QZ
www.adlardcoles.co.uk

First published by Adlard Coles Nautical 1997
Reissued 2002

Copyright © Derek Harvey 1997

ISBN 0-7136-6212-3

A CIP catalogue record for this book is available from the British Library.

Typeset in 10½ on 13pt Galliard
Printed and bound in Great Britain by
The Cromwell Press, Trowbridge, Wiltshire

For details of the free computer aided design disk,
please turn to page 192

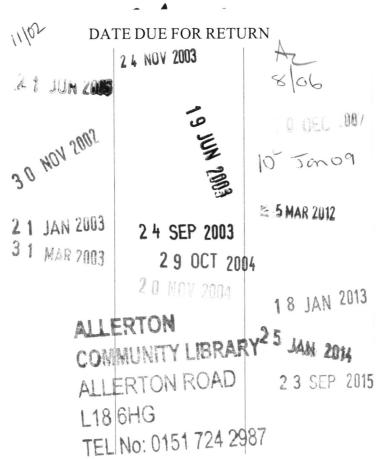

Other Titles of Interest

How to Trim Sails
Peter Schweer
ISBN 0 7136 3323 9

A practical introduction to getting the optimum from your sails. The most popular rig configurations found on today's yachts are described, and the correct standing rigging tensions are given for a variety of sailing conditions.

The New Book of Sail Trim
Edited by Ken Textor
ISBN 0 7136 4264 5

Here are 44 articles covering a wealth of information on sails and sail handling including trimming for maximum speed in light and strong winds; roll tacking; roll gybing; hiking and trimming for gusts; efficient deck layouts; mastering twin headstays and running backstays; using boom vangs and roller reefing headsails; and trimming fully battened mainsails.

Nicolson on Sails
Ian Nicolson
ISBN 0 7136 4468 0

This book is a treasure trove of sail tips and ideas for cruising and racing sailors alike. There's something here for everyone, from solving roller furling problems to checking sail twist, curing chafe to stopping leech flutter, fitting luff foil protectors to preventing hank wear.

Sail Performance: Theory and Practice
C A Marchaj
ISBN 0 7136 4123 1

Tony Marchaj explains the factors that affect sail power and concludes that the Bermudan rig, which dominates the contemporary sailing scene, is by no means the best available. This book marks a turning point in modern thinking on the subject.

Canvaswork and Sail Repair
Don Casey
ISBN 0 7136 5004 4

Here is all you need to tackle virtually any canvaswork project, from sails and sailcovers, flags, lee cloths and windscoops, to sprayhoods, cushion covers, boat covers and awnings – including Biminis. You'll save a lot of money and get exactly what you want in the process.

Contents

ACKNOWLEDGEMENTS

In preparing this book, I have needed to enlist the help of experts in various specialist fields. They have been generous with their technical advice and support, and I wish to express my appreciation and gratitude to all of them for so enthusiastically sharing their knowledge.

In particular I would like to thank my wise old friend 'Clarence' Austin Farrar, who has given unstintingly of his time, and without whose encyclopaedic knowledge of sails and sailing craft I would surely have run aground in any number of places. My thanks also to a valued Dutch colleague Nico Boon, enthusiastic yachtsman and archivist, for pointing out some of the peculiarities of his country's traditional boats; to John Parker, of Parker & Kaye Sailmakers, for helping me to understand the rapidly changing world of sail design and manufacturing in a major loft; T T Design's Tim Thornton, for his co-operation in providing the computer programs on which I have based the section on CAD; racing helmsman Stuart Eggledon, for showing me to some of the more subtle techniques of competitive sail trimming; that busy editor of *Boards* magazine, Bill Dawes, for taking the time to blue-pencil parts of the piece about windsurfers and updating me on their latest developments; Damon Roberts, of Carbospars, for explaining the finer points of the AeroRig and how it operates; the Junk Rig Association's Robin Blain, for steering me through the intricacies of Chinese sails and their controls; Adam Rice from Richard Hayward & Co, and Colin Appleyard of Hood Textiles, for their patience in answering my many queries on sailcloth performance; and from *Practical Boat Owner*, Audrey Diamond, who has so often and obligingly acted as a general information centre. Any remaining errors in the text must be down to me.

Lastly, but by no means least, a special thank you to Jane Dwyer for the little ink-and-wash sketches that decorate the final section of the book.

An example of the Aero Rig.

Introduction

With the current resurgence of interest in traditional concepts has come an awareness of what history has to teach us, and a growing realisation that most of the old ways of doing things are still relevant. In many of the smaller sailboats being built today, traditional forms and functions are blended with modern technology, such as in the combination of timber and time-honoured woodworking skills with the use of synthetic resins. Wooden vessels have become fashionable, but with labour costs as high as they are, people wanting the right craft at an affordable price are using these modern materials to build their own boats at home.

Yet there are comparatively few do-it-yourselfers who aspire to making their own sails, or to re-cutting old ones, which can save as much as three-quarters of their ready-made cost, and is essentially a fairly simple process compared with boatbuilding. The probable reason is that at first sight there seems to be more than a touch of professional magic in a well cut suit of sails, their design some sort of science that demands specialist skills and training. For sure this applies to most racing and other high-tech boats, but even in these cases, and despite the availability of improved materials and processes and the use of some mind-blowing computer programs, the old and proven methods of sailmaking should not be dismissed as obsolete. For today's high-tech sails are really no more than an amalgam of tradition and technology that owes as much to art as to science.

Most of us for whom sailing has become a way of life, and indeed anyone with more than a passing interest in the sea, can appreciate that the performance of a boat depends as much on the shape and size of her sails as on the form of her hull. Few can fail to admire the spectacle of sails in action, remembered in the paintings of bygone days as great clouds of straining canvas that combined such beauty with the power to drive a boat as fast as any engine, silently and tirelessly for hours and days on end. Needing no fuel and very little maintenance, wasting no resources and preserving the ecology – only borrowing the breeze, so to speak, and returning it intact – sails are a source of natural energy that costs nothing to use and can be relied on to get us home sooner or later, whatever the distance.

Almost any yachtsmen can make their own sails, given the right design, a measure of determination and perseverance, plenty of patience and the use of a sewing machine. At this point I must offer an apology to the ladies. To keep referring to 'yachtsmen and yachtswomen' would be tedious and cumbersome, 'yachtsperson' looks awkward, and 'yachtspeople' isn't any better. So, with no disrespect intended, yachtsmen it will be.

Workable sails can be made out of just about any old bits of material, so long as they are sufficiently strong and durable. Cotton and flax served us well enough for hundreds of years and occasionally still do, although nowadays synthetic cloths are much to be preferred. Another of the great attractions of home sailmaking is that it requires no special talents, just some advice and guidance before attempting it for the first time. The oldest practitioners of the art – for art it undeniably is, though not such a black one as we are sometimes led to believe – have long maintained that you can't learn it from books. In fact you can, as I hope to show you here, although every form of art has its trickier bits and the design and making of sails is no exception.

For example, every one of them needs a certain amount of draft or fullness in the right places before it can assume the sort of curvature that will enable it, when filled with wind, to drive effectively. The depth and extent of this draft and its whereabouts represent vital, and to a large extent interdependent, design parameters, their relationship to one another under varying operating conditions affecting the overall performance of the sail. It is easy enough to cobble together a few bits of cloth that will move the boat while the wind is more or less astern. History tells us that long before cloth was invented, all you had to do to go sailing was to weave some papyrus reeds into a piece of matting and hang it up on a pole. Add a few ropes made from plaited creepers or animal hide to prevent the whole thing from falling down and you were in business. It was a long time before someone discovered that their vessel could actually make limited progress to windward if the sail was angled to suit the direction of the breeze, with an overall size and degree of fullness that could be adjusted according to how hard it was blowing – too little of either and the sail would lose some of its drive, too much and it could quickly overpower the boat.

The skills needed to design and make sails and to use them to best advantage have evolved very gradually, refined through trial and error by generations of seafarers all over the world. This book is not the place for a detailed history of sail: there are enough learned and fascinating volumes on the subject for those interested in it. But given some account of what went before, it is easier to appreciate the functioning of a modern sailplan and the logic behind its design – to realise just how far man has progressed in harnessing the ocean winds, and how slow and at times difficult has been the process. So I have written at some length about the early forms of boat and their rigs, and the ways in which they came to be developed and refined over the centuries.

In the far distant days of prehistory, it was reward enough for the sailor to be able to stay afloat while he paddled his raft or drifted before the wind. Thousands of years were to pass before he began to strive for more speed and the ability to sail to windward, which meant being able to round the next headland before the tide turned against him, or to claw off a lee shore in a storm instead of being driven on to it. It spelled profits for the merchantmen, success as often for the pirates as for the navy trying to outrun them – or even survival on a long voyage before the food ran out; and in recent times, the difference between winning and losing races. For racing has become the real spur to the development of more efficient hulls, sails and gear, much to the benefit of cruising sailors. Seaworthiness apart, most of us experience the occasional urge to outsail any similar boat within range, even if we are not racing; and always we value the ability to climb upwind. Like money in the bank, we may not need it immediately, but it's nice to know it's there.

Nevertheless there are still those of us, it must be said, who are inclined to take their sails for granted, content to fit them at the beginning of the season and, except for routine hoisting and trimming, to ignore them until laying-up time. But to do this is to forgo much of the potential interest and enjoyment of sailing. A grasp of the fundamental principles of the aerodynamics of sails and the way they *really* work provides the incentive to take more care with their settings and to get the best out of them, whatever the weather and sea conditions. I trust that what I have included on these subjects will provide some useful pointers.

I have also described in some detail a number of the better known rigs, explaining the reasoning behind their particular layout and the way they behave and can be made to handle. Every sailor has his own personal preferences, and not everyone will agree with my assessments of their respective merits and disadvantages. However, these notes should serve to highlight the salient features of each configuration and the performance that can be expected from it.

For much the same reasons, and of course to enable the enterprising amateur to loft and cut a suit of sails, I have outlined, step by step, how they are designed, firstly using the traditional rule-of-thumb methods that have served generations of sailmakers; and then, since more often than not these days someone in the family has a computer, how to enlist its help in the design process, using the set of simple programs referred to later. The general purpose sails that can be produced by either method, and following the procedures outlined in the section on practical sailmaking, will be suitable for the majority of dinghies, dayboats and small cruising craft.

Larger sails are by no means impossible for the ambitious and determined amateur, but they can pose problems with their sheer bulk and the space needed for handling them; while to be competitive, high performance racing sails demand the use of advanced design equipment, know-how, and manufacturing processes that are beyond the reach of most of us, to say nothing of the cost and frailty of the exotic materials involved (although I have included descriptions of them so as to complete the picture). Such sails are best left to the commercial lofts with their essential expertise, experience and facilities. It is to such professionals that I am greatly indebted for the advice that a number of them have given me, and for their readiness to discuss what I imagined might be trade secrets. Far from perceiving my efforts as any sort of a threat, however slight, to their livelihood, they proved to be as keen as I am to further the cause of sailing and to encourage newcomers to the sport. For that has been my other purpose in writing this book.

'A man doesn't learn to understand a thing unless he loves it.' – Goethe

The Four Stages of Sail

PREHISTORY

Sails still power countless thousands of small working boats throughout the Third World, their use encouraged by development agencies with self-help schemes for fishermen who cannot afford an engine or its fuel. Around the coasts and estuaries of the great seafaring nations, however, the survival of sail is for the most part due to the rapid growth of yachting after World War II into an altogether more egalitarian pursuit – more aptly known nowadays as boating – open to ordinary family sailors and the less well-off sportsmen and women, instead of the fortunate few.

It was the Victorians, reacting to the expense, over-elegance and social tophamper of their somewhat effete style of yachting, who first recognised that the smaller and simpler the boat, the greater the fun and sense of freedom it could provide. It is often assumed that yachting began in Britain, back in the days when yachtsmen were still gentlemen who wore reefer jackets and gave the orders. In fact it was the 17th century Dutch who started it. Then, as now, the Netherlands, with its vast network of inland waterways, hosted the largest fleet of small boats anywhere in the world. Some of these were known as *jachts*, which meant light, fast sailing craft; and from them are descended, through some 300 years of refinement, the dinghies and most of the cruising and racing sailboats of today.

Papyrus rafts

But to trace the beginnings of sail itself, we need to look back a further 5000 years or so, through the primordial mists of prehistory, to the land of the Pharaohs. Boats, in the form of simple rafts made from bundles of papyrus reeds, are believed to have existed long before that, dating back to at least 20000 BC on the evidence of tomb discoveries. They were lightweight, more or less unsinkable until the reeds became waterlogged and the boat had to be dried out ashore, and were particularly quick and easy to build. Indeed

Fig 1.1 An early Egyptian ship dating from around the 20 000 BC. Note the A-frame mast, multiple backstays, and the steersmen aft. 2000 years were to elapse before axial rudders were invented by the Chinese.

watercraft like these, but shaped as canoes, are still used today by fishermen in the Arabian Gulf, for example, and along the Red Sea coasts.

Around the time that the Egyptians were learning to cross lakes and rivers, and even to travel along the coasts on what were little more than mats of vegetation, so too were the men from Mesopotamia and the Middle East, and before long the same sort of thing was happening on the south coast of China. But here the logical material would have been bamboo which grows widespread throughout Asia. Not only is it very strong, light enough to float well clear of the water, with airtight compartments providing enough reserve buoyancy to carry people and goods, but strips of the outer skin make good lashings for tying the bamboos together into the shape of a boat.

Much later on, around 4000 BC, archaeological evidence from coins and cave paintings show that larger, more seaworthy trading craft voyaged the length of the Gulf and out into the Indian Ocean, helped by the regional currents and winds that are seasonal and reliable in strength and direction. These were probably rafts, or raft boats with shaped bows, flat bottomed and broad beamed in the interests of load carrying and stability, and with rudimentary sheltered accommodation which would have increased their windage and hence their downwind progress.

However, no one seems to have thought of sails for another thousand years or so, and it is likely that they first evolved on the River Nile, as did so much of the early boatbuilding. The majority of the ancient civilisations tended to cluster around the lakes and navigable rivers that provided food and water, and well as facilities for irrigation and transport. In the case of the Nile, the river flowed north, while for most of the year the prevailing winds conveniently blew south, so boats were able to drift down and sail back up.

Most of the earlier vase paintings of boats had included men with paddles and steering oars, and sometimes with war shields. They gave no indication of any mast or sail. But it is easy to imagine that when one or more shields were raised on poles to support canopies or to act as banners, as they would have been during religious ceremonies and state occasions, someone noticed that they also helped to move the boat before the wind. So in this or some similar way, sailing was probably invented by accident.

Skin boats

While rafts and their derivatives remained for centuries the most widely used form of watercraft, there is evidence that several altogether different species had evolved in other parts of the ancient world. The first of these were the skin boats. Rock carvings from as far afield as Siberia and Central Asia indicate that inflated animal skins were often used as personal buoyancy aids for short journeys such as river crossings, or with a number of them lashed together to form a fisherman's raft – surely the forerunners of today's inflatable dinghies and RIBs? Alternatively the hides were stretched, probably after they had been tanned, over a framework of bones or wickerwork to produce a light, resilient structure capable of surviving some hard knocks. The result was the dumpy little one-man vessel we recognise today in Wales and parts of India as a coracle, or the longer, canoe-shaped Irish curragh, the Eskimo fisherman's uniak, and the Alaskan kayak.

It would be unrealistic to suggest any accurate sequence into which these fragments of historical guesswork might have fitted into the complex overall jigsaw of human evolution. The precise nature of many of the materials used must remain a matter for conjecture, based on their indigenous availability, for reed, bamboo and skins were, of course, perishable. They soon rotted away, and hence did not show up in archaeological excavations.

Bark boats and dugouts

Not so the prehistoric wooden vessels, the bark boats and dugouts, well preserved examples of which have been discovered in old harbours from which the sea has receded, and in peat bogs, marshes and burial mounds in appropriately wooded areas of the northern hemisphere and South America.

Bark boats were made by stripping a continuous roll of bark, like peeling an apple, from a tree such as birch and forming it into a boat shape. The ends were then tied together and the shape maintained by inserting a strengthening framework of twigs lashed together inside it – the reverse, in fact, of the skin boat process. They were particularly efficient craft for forest travel, being light enough to be carried overland for long distances, easily repaired and capable of supporting quite heavy loads in shallow water. But their flexibility and vulnerability to damage placed restrictions on their size, and they never progressed much beyond the canoe stage.

On the other hand dugouts, the fourth main root of boatbuilding, had by far the widest influence on it. They were limited only by the size of the tree from which they were to be hollowed out, a skilled process using axes or adzes, or by lighting a carefully controlled fire along the middle of the log. Some of the surviving examples are crude and heavy, others light and graceful shells that look as though they were fashioned from thin planks. Indeed, where the tools and skills existed to make planks from logs, the large seagoing dugouts had their topsides built up by sewing or pegging on a series of planks so as to increase the freeboard.

Even in planked ships, a dugout log often served as a central keel member. By far the most spectacular example of this technique is to be seen in the earliest preserved ship ever found, the great Royal Ship of Cheops, which on the evidence of scrolls dates back to 2600 BC. It was discovered in an Egyptian pyramid a few years ago, lying dismantled in an air- and watertight grave. Built mainly of Lebanese cedar and fastened by lashings and pegs, the ship has been reassembled and now stands towering some 26 ft (8 m) above its keel line, 140 ft (43 m) long and weighing around 40 tons, its advanced form of construction an impressive tribute to the naval architects of that era.

The first sails

Although the Cheops ship relied solely on oarsmen for her stately progress, contemporary Egyptian hieroglyphics had begun to show some vessels sprouting a mast, with a yard carrying a rectangular sail, tall and narrow and not unlike a shield in profile. It was probably made from palm fronds woven into a tight, strong matting, while the mast appears to have been a bipod with multiple backstays in order to spread the load evenly across the papyrus hull, and set well forward on it. This configuration would only have enabled it to sail downwind, and it wasn't long before masts appeared nearer to amidships. Sails were shown sheeted diagonally, inferring that the boat could crab across the wind, and they became wider and lower – presumably in the interests of stability, which would occasionally have been threatened with the old high ones if, as seems likely, these shallow, flat bottomed boats carried no ballast. Sideways drift was resisted by bracing one or more paddles, or a long steering oar, against the lee side of the vessel.

Centreboards

The first people to use purpose-made leeboards were probably the Chinese, who are thought to have originated the idea of pushing a wooden blade down through the bottom bamboos of their rafts to act as an adjustable centreboard. It proved highly effective, and within a few hundred years seafarers from a number of other countries had made the discovery for themselves. From then on it was only a matter of time before they evolved the sophisticated technique of steering a course by installing a series of daggerboards at intervals along the centreline. Adjusting their individual projections had the effect of varying the hull's centre of lateral resistance in relation to the centre of effort of the sail, so that sailing balance could be maintained by holding up the bows to the wind, leeway reduced, and the raft manoeuvred, all at the same time.

Centreboards with elaborately carved handles, excavated from ancient graves in Peru, lend credence to the hypothesis put forward by Thor Heyerdahl, and demonstrated with the famous raft *Kon-Tiki* in which he sailed and drifted the thousands of miles from the westernmost tip of the South American continent to the South Sea Islands, that the Peruvians were among their first settlers. It is generally accepted, however, that the majority of them originated in Burma and Indo-China, starting to migrate eastwards around 2000 BC, with successive generations of families moving through the Philippines and Marianas into Polynesia, eventually settling the Hawaiian islands soon after the beginning of the Christian era.

Others travelled south-eastwards, via Indonesia, to colonise Fiji and the islands of Melanesia, later fanning out across the South Pacific to Tahiti, Samoa and beyond, to the Marquesas and even as far as Easter Island. But here the trail of identifiable Asian relics – pottery, tools, fish hooks and spearheads – seems to have ended, so whether any of these great travellers ever reached South America will probably never be known.

An important factor that would have made these open sea voyages less dangerous than they are today is that the sea levels at that time were considerably lower, and consequently the distances they had to sail were very much shorter. Nevertheless theirs were gigantic feats of navigation and seamanship, and even taking advantage of ocean currents that can run at 20–30 miles a day in those regions, sailpower and the ability to follow some sort of predetermined track would have played a vital part in their survival.

Outrigger canoes

It was the Melanesians who found that by placing a large log under one side of a raft so as to lift it partially clear of the water, its drag was reduced and it became easier to paddle. In due course the log became a dugout, connected by cross-poles to a slender outrigger log which acted both as a float and a balance weight, and later gave the boat enough stability to carry a sail. Thus was born the outrigger canoe, the proa, which is still used by the fishermen and traders of Africa and Central Asia, as well as throughout the Pacific. Relying to such an extent on the agility of its crew to keep the outrigger just skimming the waves by scrambling from side to side to balance every gust of wind, capsizes are commonplace. But those waters are warm and a proa remains afloat even when swamped. Manoeuvring it is another energetic process, for since it must always present its outrigger side to the wind, tacking can only be achieved by sailing backwards, with the bow becoming the stern after the tack of the sail and its supporting spars have been walked to the opposite end of the boat.

The Polynesians did things differently. They used a matched pair of logs, subsequently dugouts, and replaced the raft by flexible crossbeams that allowed some 'give' between the two hulls as they moved with the waves. The

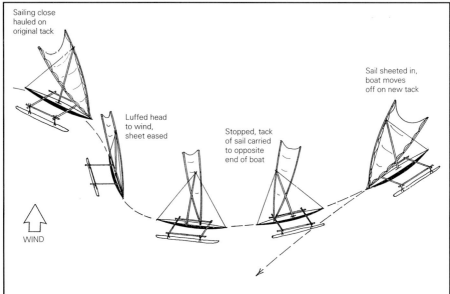

Sailing close
hauled on
original tack

Sail sheeted in,
boat moves
off on new tack

Luffed head
to wind,
sheet eased

Stopped, tack
of sail carried
to opposite
end of boat

WIND

Fig 1.2 A proa is tacked by sailing it backwards and carrying the rig to the opposite end of the boat.

resulting double canoe was as stable as a raft, but was naturally much faster and easier to steer. Some are known to have been over 100 ft (30 m) long, great sailing vessels with topsides built up by wash strakes to increase the freeboard, and with roofed shelters for their hundreds of passengers.

A third multihull configuration was introduced much later by people arriving from Malaya. Their hulls were teak planked and shaped so as to be reasonably stable without any exterior support. But they must have come across some of the proas left behind by their predecessors, for they improved the seaworthiness of their boats by fitting a float on either side, their double-outrigger craft being the forerunners of the modern trimaran.

All these types played their parts in the colonisation of the vast Pacific regions, while single-hulled vessels continued to evolve in Egyptian waters and throughout the Mediterranean, as well as in parts of Northern Europe. Rafts were becoming more boat-shaped and boats better proportioned, built with planks as the tools and technology became more generally available during the Bronze Age, and rounder in the bilge instead of being flat bottomed. By this time, about the only major difference between a boat and a well developed raft was that whereas the boat derived its buoyancy from its displacement as a watertight whole, the free-flooding raft depended on the individual buoyancy of its logs or reeds.

Once again it seems to have been the enterprising Chinese who led the field, with a unique school of boatbuilding that has survived to this day. Sampans and the larger trading vessels, the junks, were in effect plank-built copies of their bamboo rafts, distinguished by a particularly deep fore-and-aft rocker, the sheer line sweeping up from amidships to a high, broad transom stern matched by another, smaller transom at the bow, with the waterline beam much wider aft than forward – in general shape not unlike a modern pram dinghy.

Axial rudders

To the Chinese too must go the credit for inventing the axial rudder. Shortly before 100 BC, one of them must have discovered that rotating a vertical lee-board to and fro on its axis resulted in additional steering control; for pottery models began to include boats with a rudder, hung in a trunk through the hull at the stern, or in an after compartment, and controlled by rope tackles. As if this were not enough, they went on to add a balance area ahead of the rudder axis, so as to ease the work of the helmsman and reduce turbulence – all this more than a thousand years before Western carvings showed ships with any form of rudder at all, other than the conventional steering oars.

A further example of Chinese originality during this period was the introduction of alternative positioning for the masts when two or more were to be stepped. By means of a row of heel sockets, the masts could be staggered athwartships (instead of having them all in a fore-and-aft line) and raked longitudinally like the spines of a fan, so as to avoid the blanketing of one sail by another. These remained salient features, along with the accentuated sheer, of sampans and junks through the ages. Nor after a time did they continue to use conventional oars for propulsion when the wind dropped. They originated that ingeniously simple labour-saving device, the self-feathering oar or *yuloh*, and for their inshore warships the first paddlewheels, which were worked by treadmills. This was followed by the copper sheathing of hulls, long before the practice was adopted in Europe, and by the most famous Chinese maritime contributions of all, the magnetic compass and the sextant. What a nation of innovators they must have been!

DEVELOPMENT: TRADING SHIPS AND FISHING VESSELS

As advances in boatbuilding techniques led to refinements in hull forms, they were paralleled by some far-reaching improvements in the design and layout of their sails, all of them derived from the basic squaresail that to this day remains an extremely effective downwind shape. Only the ways in which it has been set and handled, and the material from which it has been made, have changed it significantly in four thousand years.

Among the most detailed drawings of ancient square rigs yet discovered are those of Peruvian rafts dating from about AD 100 . They show a bipod mast supported by stays, usually with a yard suspended at its midpoint from the top of the mast and controlled by braces. Sheets ran aft from the clews, with tack lines forward. Some carried the yard on a crossed pair of sheerlegs, while others dispensed with the yard altogether and simply lashed the head corners of the sail to the tops of the sheers.

Planked hulls

With the introduction of planked hulls in the Mediterranean and Gulf regions, the bipods were replaced by single pole masts with shrouds, some having cleats up either side to allow them to be climbed, since the standing rigging would have been too light for this and a ladder impractical. The sail, still a crude affair made of matting, was furled on its yard by brail lines running through rings.

Tilting yards

With such a sail trimmed diagonally across the boat, limited progress could sometimes be made with the wind just forward of the beam. But more often than not, continuous rowing was necessary to maintain way, even on a broad reach – until it was found that by tilting the yard so as to peak its trailing end well above the masthead, and tacking the opposite foot down to the deck, the sail developed slightly more drive. As it turned out, this was to be a momentous discovery, one in which lay the origins of the fore-and-aft rig; for it couldn't have been long before someone tried going one better by sliding the yard across the mast to give less sail ahead of the mast and more behind it, instead of projecting equal areas on either side. The result was a further improvement in performance, leading to the evolution of the lugsail in its various forms.

Chinese junks

One of these was adopted by the Chinese, but with typical inventiveness they came up with the idea of dividing the sail into a lattice of separate panels, each of which could be individually sheeted, reefed, or replaced when it became worn or damaged. By the time Chinese maritime affairs reached their peak around the 15th century, this industrious nation operated a huge fleet of vessels rigged in this way, some of them 500 ft (150 m) ocean-going giants, that was more advanced than any in

Fig 1.3 A 19th century Burmese junk, showing how the designs of the ancient Egyptian ships influenced the rigs of the Far East.

Europe. The junk sail, as it is commonly known, has not altered significantly since those days. Nor, on the other hand, has it ever found much favour elsewhere in the world, despite its many virtues, probably because although it is extremely simple to use, it is comparatively complex to assemble.

Crab claw and lateen sails

Similarly derived from the basic square sail, two other types of rig evolved in parallel, but quite independently of one another, and both are still quite widely used. Even in the far-off days before the birth of Christ, it was recognised that the wind tends to be stronger aloft than at sea level where, as we now know, surface friction slows it down. The first to take advantage of this were the Pacific voyagers and fishermen who rigged their sail with its widest part at the top to catch the wind, and the narrow end on deck, where incidentally it offered the least obstruction to crew and cargo. Known nowadays as the 'crab claw', for its shape, the sail is laced between two slender, curved spars, lashed together where they meet at the bow, angled obliquely upwards past a short mast from which it hangs on a halyard, and terminating in a short, sharply concave leech. It is an exceptionally fast and weatherly rig, but it was not until the 18th century that it was brought to the attention of the Western world, following one of the great voyages of discovery by Captain Cook, who reported that his powerful 12 knot ships were easily outrun by these primitive local craft.

The other early and better known interpretation of the 'wind aloft' principle is the Arabian lateen, the world's first true fore-and-aft sail, that was introduced around the 8th century and is still the dominant feature of the Nile, Red Sea and Gulf dhow and feluccas. Although nowadays known to be rather less efficient than the crab claw, it was simple to make, as well as being light and easy to handle – at least in the smaller sizes – and has always been one of the most graceful of all rigs. It consists of a loose-footed triangular sail, with its luff laced to a long, curved yard running up from the bows at an angle of about 45 degrees and slung about a third of its length from a short, forward-raking mast.

Right from its inception, the main disadvantage of this sail was always the size of the yard. When lowered, it extends a most inconvenient distance beyond the stern of the boat, resulting in frequent entanglements and shouting matches in a crowded harbour. As the boats grew larger, the yard became correspondingly heavier and more unwieldy, so the sail was divided between two masts, as on the Mediterranean tartana, and later on between three masts. These vessels, known as *caravels*, formed part of the Spanish Armada fleet, some of them carrying a mixed rig with a couple of squaresails on the foremast to improve downwind sailing. The hulls themselves were built for speed and manoeuvrability, with smooth skinned carvel (edge-to-edge) planking that slipped easily through the water.

Fig 1.4 The Northern European tartana was rigged with a couple of lateens, each with a brailing line for shortening sail quickly in gusty weather.

Square-riggers

Meanwhile, up in the northern waters bordering the Atlantic and North Sea, the squaresail is known to have been used by seafarers since the dawn of the Viking Age in the 7th century. Their boats were sturdier and double-ended with pointed bow and stern, and were clinker built, each plank overlapping the one below like rows of roof tiles, and riveted to it and to the ribs. This shape, form of construction and rig were well suited to the hard climate and rough seas of the North, and were first beached on the English coasts as raiders crewed by Viking warriors. They later formed the basis of the growing fleet of merchant vessels trading out of Germany to the Baltic ports and to England, itself soon to become a major seafaring nation. Then as seaborne trade developed between the northern and southern states of Europe during the 14th century, their ships began visiting the Mediterranean, and the seamen and shipwrights of each region were quick to appreciate the advantages of each other's rig and methods of building.

The northerners adopted carvel planking for their larger vessels, clinker construction being impracticable, and the mizzen squaresail was replaced by a lateen which they found more effective for keeping the ship's head up into the wind. The southerners, for their part, began substituting square sails for lateens on their main and foremasts, some of whose huge yards needed as many as 50 men to change sails when the weather blew up. The square-rigged ships, with their shorter yards and more easily managed canvas that could be reefed, required smaller crews, much to the benefit of running costs. They also fitted stern rudders instead of the steering oars or side rudders they had relied on until now. The resulting ships, generally referred to as *carracks*, laid the design foundations for future ocean-going vessels.

Mizzen and foresails were at first quite small, functioning more as steering aids than to help drive the ship. But as trade flourished, the pursuit of greater hold capacity and higher speed led to progressive increases in sail area, calling for a stronger and more complex web of standing rigging. It also required a bowsprit with stout stays to take the strain of the foremast whenever the sails were taken aback in a flukey headwind. The bowsprit in turn became steadily longer and more prominent, and sprouted a small yard and sail of its own – often two on the big ships, each with a square spritsail. Masts grew taller, with topmasts to carry additional sails and a small semi-circular platform where they were joined, the 'top', in which a lookout or an armed marksman could be stationed. At about this time, the use of reef points went out of fashion in favour of bonnets, the lower portions of which were made detachable by unlacing them one after another as the wind freshened. It was a slow and laborious process, and it is surprising that it took as long as 200 years for reef points to be reintroduced.

By the 15th century, some of the carracks voyaging from Europe into the newly discovered trading areas were as large as 1500 tons, able to carry heavy cargoes and armed with cannon for defence against the growing number of privateers and pirates, and the fleets of Arab traders who not unnaturally resented the competition and interference with their own long-established commerce. These were the ships in which Christopher Columbus crossed the Atlantic to find America, later making the first crossings of the Pacific in both directions, rounding the Cape of Good Hope to India, the East Indies and China, and completing the first circumnavigation of the world.

Seaworthy they must have been, but they were still extremely limited in their windward capability. The theoretical aspects of sail performance had yet to be recognised, and their design was very much a hit-or-miss affair, the main object being simply to set as large a spread of canvas as possible. Sails were by now generally made from a coarsely woven flax reinforced with a rope hem, a combination that had proved much stronger and more durable than the cloths of hemp or ramie hitherto used by sailmakers. No one attached any importance to the way that flax sails stretched so readily and lost their shape. It didn't much matter on a run, but the combination of such an inefficient rig and a bulky, broad-beamed and bluff-bowed hull meant that these ships were unable to steer closer than about 80° towards the wind. As a result, the choice of open sea routes was largely dictated by the prevailing trade winds, and seafarers were often forced to wait several weeks for a favourable slant before they could make a passage in narrow waters.

Fierce rivalry between the European countries to secure a share of the expanding world trade led to an almost permanent state of undeclared war in distant seas, hence the development of specialised warships. Powerful but ponderously large, some of them over 2000 tons, 200 ft (60 m) long and 50 ft (15 m) in the beam, they were notable for the tall forecastles and even loftier sterncastles that were superimposed on their sheer lines. These housed several additional decks, with as many as 100 heavy cannon ranged along them and another 100 or so smaller guns in the castles, the exaggerated tumblehome

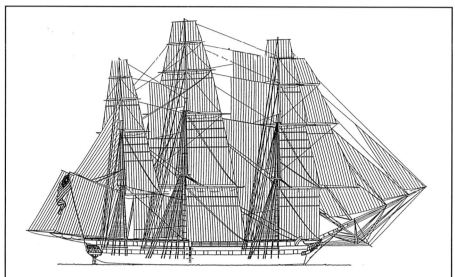

Fig 1.5 The powerful 52-gun American frigate *Constitution*, later known as *Old Ironsides*, with her cathedral of sail and complex rigging. Built in 1797, she was restored in 1930 in Boston, where she remains on exhibition.

of their topsides being necessary to provide a reasonably stable gun platform. They were lavishly rigged too, with anything up to five sets of squaresails – main, topsail, topgallant, royal and skysail – on each of the three masts, with additional 'studding' sails set outside the squaresails in moderate weather. Main yards were often 100 ft (30 m) long, while a mainmast could measure as much as 40 in (102 cm) in diameter where it passed through the middle deck, with the tip of its gilded truck soaring 200 ft (60 m) above the water.

Gaff rigs and galleons

During the 16th and 17th centuries, staysails began to appear between the masts, in the form we know today as the gaff rig. Space being very restricted by the complex web of standing and running rigging, those parts of the lateen rig located ahead of the mast had been removed to produce a more compact and easily managed quadrilateral sail suspended from a gaff yard. The mizzen 'spanker' also sported a lower boom to spread the sail out, whereas the staysails were loose-footed. It was the Dutch who were the first to introduce these on big ships, although fore-and-aft rigs had long been a feature of their small inshore craft, as we shall see later. As a further refinement, most big ships now sported two or more triangular sails on their forestays, which made the process of tacking in light airs or rough seas somewhat less uncertain. The total area of all these sails was by now approaching 100 000 sq ft (9300 sq m), although they could seldom all be set simultaneously, as some would be blanketing others. Surprisingly, these ships often carried only one sailmaker. He must have had to work hard in heavy weather to keep up with repairs.

With the exception of the large and prestigious vessels operated by the East India Company, the majority of merchantmen, though generally less than half the size of their naval counterparts, were none the less beamy and bulky to satisfy demand for increased cargo space. They were corresponding-ly slow, despite the veritable cathedral of canvas they were given to drive them, and they went to windward like a sack of potatoes. Naval constructors paid scant attention to the need for finer underwater lines, or to considering sail area in relation to stability. As a result these magnificent ships, tender and topheavy from their excessive weight and windage aloft, were on occasion blown over on to their beam ends and would lie wallowing and pinned down at a 90° angle until the gale abated, sometimes remaining in this undignified position for days on end. Their buoyant wooden spars prevented them from rolling any further, provided that all ports and hatches had been closed and effectively sealed, which was not always the case.

Furthermore they were agonisingly slow to manoeuvre, and so were their naval counterparts. In the course of the battles that followed the spread of war to European waters, it was found that a faster and more nimble vessel, armed with long range guns, could sometimes get in among the heavyweights and wreak havoc before they could turn to bring their massive broadside of cannons to bear, let alone land a boarding party. Such were the famous galleons with which the British defeated the Spanish Armada, supported by the smaller frigates and corvettes which served as the scouting cruisers and maids-of-all-work to the warring fleets. Nevertheless the great ships-of-the-line such as HMS *Victory*, with their formidable firepower, were still the aristocrats, and continued to play vital strategic and deterrent roles right through to the dawn of the steamship era at the beginning of the 19th century.

Improvements in hull design

This period saw a number of significant advances in the design of rigs and hulls, notably in the gradual departure from the traditional 'cod's head and mackerel tail' underwater shape – bluff bows with the greatest beam forward of amidships, tapering to a long, easy run aft. Instead, following the then cur-rent American practice, hulls began to feature sharper bows with a slightly hollow entry, and the point of maximum beam aft of amidships.

The consequent improvement in the sailing qualities of merchant ships was soon to prove of value to the immensely profitable trade in opium between India, where it was grown under an East India Company monopoly, and China, whose entrepreneurs accepted it in payment for tea and silk. These ships had to be able to beat against the monsoon while on passage from India, and then to race back to Europe or America in order to be first with the annual tea crop. The traditional piled-up fore-and-aft castles had been replaced by flush decks and long, slim hulls, and these sleek vessels became known as 'clippers', after the little American trading schooners, which were undisputedly the fastest ships in the world, with their fine lines, steeply raked masts, and the fore-aft rig that the Dutch settlers had earlier brought with them to America. (Indeed, so good was the sailing performance of these schooners, especially to windward, that Britain bought a number of them for service as armed coastguard cutters.)

Clippers and windjammers

Until now, ships had been constructed entirely of wood. But the decline in American commercial shipbuilding that followed the financial depression and the Civil War left the way clear for the advancement of this industry in Britain. One result was the development of composite hulls, with wooden planking on an iron framework, used on the famous fleet of tea clippers such as the *Cutty Sark*, fast and weatherly vessels that proved capable of averaging 300 miles a day – call it 12 knots – for a week or more at a time. Another such vessel, *Thermopylae*, could make 7 knots in airs so light, it was said, that they wouldn't blow out an unshielded candle on deck. For all their grace and beauty, however, these fine-lined hulls sacrificed cargo capacity for speed. The building of the larger clipper ships that were to follow them, some of them four-masters, was boosted by the discovery of gold in California and Australia, and the demand for the fastest possible passages to each; and by the introduction of transatlantic passenger services. One Boston-built clipper, *Sovereign of the Seas*, made the all-time sailing ship record for the crossing between New York and Liverpool in 13½ days, during which she is reputed to have touched an astonishing 22 knots during moments of surfing – no mean achievement for a modern racing yacht, let alone for a 2000 ton passenger ship 150 years ago.

Towards the end of the 19th century, sail was no longer able to compete economically on the most favoured routes with the steamships, which although not always as fast in terms of top speed, were not constrained by wind direction and could invariably make shorter passages, besides requiring smaller crews and less maintenance, and could carry larger cargoes.

Nevertheless sheer size counted for much, and there followed the building of the biggest sailing ships in history, the 'windjammers'. Many of them were some 300 ft (91 m) long and displaced over 4000 tons, with iron – and later steel – hulls, steel spars and standing rigging, and winches for working the braces and hoisting the sails. The latter were divided up into a multiplicity of comparatively small units for ease of handling, and the mixture of fore-and-aft and squaresails was spread out over four or five masts. In the last days of sail, a typical four-masted barque could set some 50000 sq ft (4650 sq m) of canvas, and fully laden could carry it in winds of up to force 5 close-hauled, or force 7 when running before, progressively shortening sail to leave just the topsails and lower courses in a force 10. What a stirring sight they must have made, thundering along in a huge cloud of spray, main decks awash to the rails. But it became almost commonplace for men to be washed overboard when the ship was pooped by a sea boarding from astern, or to be torn from the rigging when she heeled over in a broach, twin terrors always in the minds of helmsmen steering before a gale.

A number of these leviathans were still in commission at the outbreak of World War II, but although only a few are afloat today, serving as youth training ships, most of them are funded, together with a few more modern vessels, by governments of maritime nations that rightly regard them as prestige symbols. And already our environmentally conscious age has seen the first pollution-free ships in service. These are a pair of 3000-ton four-masted

Fig 1.6 *Star Clipper*, a modern 3000-ton four-masted barquentine, built as a luxury cruise ship and carrying 170 passengers in air-conditioned cabins.

barquentines, capable of 17 knots and each carrying 170 passengers in air-conditioned cabins. Inertial water ballast systems reduce rolling, and using electrically powered capstans and winches, all sails can be set or furled in two minutes with only six of the crew on deck. Economics dictate that we shall never see a large scale return to commercial sail, but it is encouraging to find that there is once more a place for it, albeit a small and specialised one, on the high seas.

PROGRESS

Down through the ages, despite the wealth of experience gained in the design and usage of all forms of sail, the squaresail has remained the most reliable and effective for downwind working. But its windward performance and manoeuvring capabilities have always been very limited compared with most types of fore-and-aft rig. This was recognised as long ago as the 16th century by the Dutch, whose vast network of narrow canals and rivers and shallow coastal channels encouraged them to develop a handy rig for their small craft. Squaresails were far too clumsy for tacking in and out of small harbours, and insufficiently close-winded to allow a vessel to lay its course in a confined inland waterway, while the Mediterranean lateen with its lengthy yard was unsuitable for the boisterous, squally North Sea. So they came up with their own form of quadrilateral sail, with one edge laced to the mast and stretched diagonally by a spar – the sprit – placed between the tack and the peak, from which it was controlled by a vang, plus a sheet from the clew, both ropes being held by the helmsman in a small boat.

Spritsails

The Dutch were not, as it happened, the originators of the spritsail. It was used in ancient times by fishermen along the coasts of Greece and elsewhere in the Mediterranean, and survived into the mid 20th century in parts of India and South East Asia, and in America where it became popular on small pleasure craft. In Holland, it was supplemented by one or more of the triangular fore-sails that were to inspire the use of staysails on square-rigged ships, and by hinged leeboards that were lowered for beating to windward or swung up in shallow water and when running downwind. The resulting combination of sprit rig and leeboards can still be seen today on the few surviving Thames barges.

Dutch sloops

On their larger boats, whose sprits had become correspondingly longer and more difficult to control, the Dutch replaced the sprit with a spar along the top of the sail, the gaff, with jaws at one end to embrace the mast, often adding a square topsail for downwind working. This easily managed rig became the standard wear for the multitude of small craft that were used throughout Holland for the transport of goods and for day to day transport, as well as on the fast purpose-built *jachts* that were regularly paraded at regattas and took part in sham fights. It was one of these, the *Mary*, that was presented in the year 1660 by the Dutch East India Company to King Charles II on his return to the English throne from Holland, where he had been living in exile following certain difficulties with one Oliver Cromwell, and where he had made many friends and become an enthusiastic sailor.

The dawn of yachting

He and his brother, the Duke of York, were so delighted with their new play-thing that they and a number of other English gentlemen ordered several more to be built in their local yards – but with less beam, deeper draught and fixed keels – and before long they had begun racing against one another. By the middle of the following century, yachting had become a popular sport among the wealthy in Britain. Their boats were large and prestigious, luxury versions of naval brigs and revenue cutters, as big as 250 tons and some 170 ft (52 m) overall, and drawing 15 ft (4.5 m) or more. Many of them were in fact conversions of ex-government craft, while others were discreetly purchased from smugglers, whose vessels could be relied on to be just as fast, if not faster than those on the side of the law. Indeed, boats for both types of customer were often built side by side in the same yard. Also at around this time, some specialist and rather more scientifically based design techniques were being applied to privately funded yachts, as distinct from the traditional Admiralty style of naval architecture which still tended to concentrate on strength and seaworthiness. This meant that the new yachts were often able to show a clean pair of heels to their opposite numbers in Revenue service. So it wasn't long before the government were having their cutters built like yachts, sometimes on the same stocks, the main difference being that the yachts were usually rigged as yawls or ketches, while the revenue cutters were single-masted, with a huge spread of canvas on extra long spars.

Rig design revolution

By the 1850s, the square topsail had given way to a triangular sail which filled the space between the mast and the gaff, and the clew of the mainsail was often held out by a boom on to which it could be lowered and furled, instead of being brailed up to the mast and gaff for stowage. Brailing lines were still employed, however, on the upper part of the sail for reefing, with one or more rows of reef points lower down. Fiddle blocks had by now come into general use for tensioning the various lifts, runners, vangs, downhauls and headsail sheets, and for the mainsheet which worked from an iron 'horse'. Smooth carvel planking took the place of clinker-building and lead weights, bolted to the keel, replaced the traditional gravel ballast. Taken overall, it can be said that this was probably the period in history of the greatest progress ever made in small craft design.

Similar two-masted rigs were to be seen on many fishing and coastal trading vessels, with only the smaller inshore boats, French as well as British, and the smugglers carrying contraband across the Channel, continuing to set a single loose-footed lugsail, while the Thames watermen preferred spritsails, as on the big barges. The Dutch, for their part, stayed with their bulbous shoal-draught hulls, but they now gave their mainsails a taller and more triangular shape by replacing the long straight gaff with a short curved one. No topsail was needed, there was less weight aloft, and they found that the new rig gave them considerably more drive to windward. This was mainly due to the increase in aspect ratio (see p.56), although it was another 100 years before this particular cause and effect was recognised, in the design of aircraft wings.

Racing measurement rules

The upward spiral of power and size was halted, for the time being, by the imposition of a series of club regulations outlawing the use of special additional sails, only the normal rig being permitted. In due course, the newly formed Yacht Racing Association introduced a formula for measuring the effective tonnage and sail area of each boat.

But measurement systems have seldom led to the development of wholesome hull shapes. At first they penalised beam, which resulted in excessively narrow 'plank-on-edge' boats that needed a veritable lead mine in their keels to prevent them from toppling over. Next the rule makers sensibly tried limiting waterline length in relation to sail area, with no limit on beam. This produced a succession of stiff and weatherly boats that were not unduly ballasted, but featured some almost grotesque overhangs at bow and stern. And in quite recent times, one of the internationally recognised measurement systems produced some freakishly flared hulls that relied for much of their stability on their exaggerated midships beam. These specialist and ill-mannered racing machines not only cost a small fortune and required an expert crew of 'hired assassins' to drive them, but proved totally unsuitable for ordinary sailing. Not surprisingly, there was a widespread welcome to one of the current formulae which encourages the building of user-friendly boats that can be used for family cruising, as well as for racing.

American schooners and sandbaggers

Meanwhile, back in mid-19th century America, the fast and weatherly schooner rig, favoured both by pilots who needed its speed to get the business and by the slavers to avoid capture, was also chosen by the majority of well-heeled yachtsmen. Others preferred to base their boats on the famous Hudson River sloops, beamy shoal-draught centreboarders which were particularly close-winded, sporting a huge, tall mainsail and short gaff. This was supplemented by a single large headsail, usually club-footed to make it self-tacking and easier to handle in the confines of a narrow river. These craft were considerably over-canvased, but it didn't matter very much because they were not intended for going to sea.

At the same time, two other types of boat were becoming fashionable among the less wealthy sportsmen. The first of these were known as 'sandbaggers'. Only 20–30ft (6–9m) on the waterline, but twice that overall, with extremely long bowsprits and main booms to tension their generous spread of canvas, they relied on a disproportionately large and active crew to keep them upright by sitting along the weather rail, and humping heavy sandbags from side to side when tacking. The other was the cat boat, an essentially American development that has remained justly popular to this day for its sheer ease of handling. It featured a simple, self-tending rig, with a single gaff sail on a mast set right forward in the bows, where incidentally it did not interfere with the accommodation.

It is interesting to note that by now a number of the larger American yachts, schooners as well as sloops, were equipped with sail tracks and slides much like those used today, and mechanical winches on the halyards. One or two even featured a lightweight hollow mast and boom, built up like a barrel with staves secured by a series of iron hoops.

Cotton sails

The most far reaching innovation, however, was the use of cotton sailcloth instead of the traditional flax. Around the time of the American Revolution, weaving was no more than a cottage industry in Britain until productivity was so improved by three successive English inventions that it became a factory-based system. These were the flying shuttle which greatly increased the speed at which weavers could work, the spinning jenny which was able to spin several threads at once, and the power loom which was needed to keep pace with the mounting output of yarn. The new spinning technique also made it possible to work with cotton fibre, which has a shorter staple than flax, and a range of fine new fabrics were developed, using Egyptian cotton which was – and still is – the best quality available anywhere in the world. But this source was disrupted for a time by the Napoleonic wars and the Battle of the Nile at the end of the 18th century, and America became the prime supplier. And it was the Americans who were the first to recognise the advantages of cotton cloth for sailmaking.

While flax has a much greater resistance to rot than cotton, and is considerably stronger and less inclined to tear, it is more flexible and slippery and it stretches more readily, so that the sails soon become baggy. This is of no importance to square-riggers, and the flexibility of flaxen sails makes them easier to handle than cotton ones, which tend to become stiff and unyielding when they are wet. But the ability of cotton fore-and-aft sails to hold their shape began to win races in America; and it attracted world attention in 1851 when the schooner *America* crossed the Atlantic on her own bottom and handsomely trounced the pick of the British fleet in a Royal Yacht Squadron race around the Isle of Wight.

Her success was at first credited to her fine, sharp lines and light displacement. But it didn't take long for the experts to realise that her superior speed was due largely to her close-fitting suit of cotton sails, with both main and headsail laced to booms and cut so that they set tight and flat. They were also considerably less porous than the stretchy, loose-footed windbags of her rivals, which suffered from excessive draught in all the wrong places and were consequently at a hopeless disadvantage on windward legs. Although the majority of British yachtsmen lost no time in changing to cotton, it seems their sailmakers had not learned their lesson properly, for in the absence of any notable racing successes during the next few years, they reverted to flax and didn't go back to cotton until the turn of the century.

YACHTING DEVELOPS AS A SPORT

Although by now the era of the great clipper ships was drawing to a close as steamships took their place, big racing yachts were still being built for millionaires and syndicates of wealthy sportsmen, along with some splendidly appointed showpieces for Europe's crowned heads and senior statesmen. The royal yacht *Britannia*, for example, carried some 9000 sq ft (837 sq m) of sail, and hoisting her main took 14 crew on the halyard, including the steward and ship's cook. In those days yachting was a strictly seasonal activity, and the paid hands would usually go back to the fishing boats in the winter. There were, however, signs that the sport was no longer being confined to the rich and famous. A growing number of sailing enthusiasts with more limited financial resources had taken to converting a small working boat for their purposes, or having a yacht built on similar lines. There was a wide variety of types and rigs for them to choose from, depending on whether they were content to cruise or wanted to go racing.

The ketch rig

The ketch rig was generally preferred for cruising on account of its ease of handling, and the ability to jog along in heavy weather under headsails and mizzen, while schooners were invariably faster but not as handy for a small crew. The yawl, which seems incidentally to have been a British development, also became fashionable as a halfway stage between a schooner and a single masted cutter or sloop, combining the glamour and power of one with the convenience of the other. The same applied, of course, to the ketch. Technically, the only difference between it and a yawl was that its mizzen was stepped forward of the rudder post, whereas the yawl's was aft of it. In reality it was more of a question of the relative sizes of their mainsails, the yawl being essentially a ketch with a larger main and smaller mizzen. It was also, under the racing measurement rules, accorded a particularly favourable rating compared with the other rigs, often enabling it to win races on handicap, even though in some cases the tiny mizzen was seen by some as little more than a rule-bending appendage on the stern of a cutter.

Two types of fishing ketch that were particularly popular in 19th century Britain for conversion into yachts were the Brixham Trawler and the Lowestoft Drifter, powerful sea-keeping 60 footers, deep draughted and massively built, and notable for their forward raking masts and very large staysails. The Brixham skippers had a reputation for setting a topsail even over a double-reefed main, reckoning that the topsail steadied the gaff in a seaway. The Lowestoft boats, distinguished for their boomless mainsail and the boomed mizzen which overhung the stern, would set narrow jackyard topsails on both masts, but only in light weather.

Among the cutter-rigged working craft most favoured for private use were the Bristol Channel pilot cutters, generally somewhat smaller than the two ketches, but fine seaboats renowned for their speed and manoeuvrability. They had shallow, self-draining cockpits which were a good safety feature despite offering the crew very little protection from the weather, and they were possibly the first to feature roller reefing gear on their main booms. Another was the Thames bawley, a shoal-draughted fisherman not unlike the flat-bottomed Thames trading barge, with an enormous bowsprit and a boomless mainsail supported by an equally long gaff instead of the barge's sprit, both boats shortening sail by means of brails, a technique inherited, like their flat bottoms, from the Dutch.

Lugsails

There were also large fleets of low-priced 'luggers' from which anyone looking for a boat to convert for cruising could pick up a bargain. Owing its origins to the earliest squaresail, their simple, handsome rig had been favoured by generations of inshore fishermen, lifeboatmen and smugglers, and may still be seen on some knockabout dinghies today. It consisted of a big quadrilateral sail, often loose-footed, bent on a yard that hung obliquely from the mast, with about a third of its length projecting forward of it. On the basic dipping lug, the tack was hove down and hooked to the stemhead, both sail and yard having to be lowered, dipped from one side of the unstayed mast to the other when going about, and re-hoisted. With its luff set well clear of the mast's disturbed airflow, it was a powerful lifting sail, but it was hard work for the crew in strong winds and difficult in the dark. This led to the development of a variant known as a standing lug which proved to be less efficient but much easier to handle, its tack being secured near the foot of the mast, so that only the heel of the yard needed to be dipped round it. Both types were (and still are) widely used, and luggers of all shapes and sizes, the larger ones usually rigged as ketches, worked the length of the North Sea coasts of England and Scotland, and out of the fishing ports on both sides of the English Channel.

The fishing fleets

It was natural for craft of nearby nations to influence each other, especially where they congregated on common fishing grounds, with each country, and sometimes even individual localities in those countries, adapting the rigs to suit their own requirements.

The Dunkirk and Boulogne herring drifters, for example, were powerful gaff ketches that bore a strong resemblance to the Ramsgate and Lowestoft trawlers; and many of the Belgian and Breton luggers, the *Chasse-Marées*, were built on similar lines but sported highly individualistic rigs of their own, with a mizzen and mainmast plus a foremast perched precariously on the stemhead, all three raked in a curious jumble of conflicting angles which looked quaintly eccentric, to say the least, but happened to suit local working practices.

Dutch boats, for their part, remained largely unaffected by any local seafaring influences because of their unusual working conditions, which were not mirrored elsewhere. A unique combination of extremely shallow and often treacherous coastal sea areas, and the need to navigate the national network of inland waterways, had produced a range of highly distinctive vessels that were widely admired but never copied. Shoal draughted, most of them plump and rounded like well fed ducks, they were all equipped with leeboards for working to windward, and even the smaller boats and their yachting counterparts were roomy enough for the skipper and his family to live aboard in considerable comfort. Some were also fitted with comparatively tall rigs to catch more of the wind above the river banks, with tabernacle-mounted masts that could be quickly lowered using an 'A' frame.

Further south, along the Atlantic seaboard of Spain and throughout the Mediterranean, the lateen sail had long since spread from Egypt to become the standard rig on virtually all small craft, while in northern waters the fishing fleets of the Shetland islands, which for several centuries were part of the Norsk kingdom, had inherited the double-ended hulls and simple squaresails of their Norwegian counterparts. (Strange to relate, the sturdy double-ended hulls and powerful gaff rigs of the later Norwegian lifeboats owed much of their development to a British naval architect, Colin Archer, who had migrated across the North Sea to settle in the port of Larvik. He was later to become world famous for his yachts, which were themselves based on his lifeboat designs.) In the same way, Breton and Portuguese seamen, longlining for cod off the Newfoundland Banks, learned much from the American schooners working there out of Gloucester and other Maine ports.

The Bermudan rig

At that time, these fast and weatherly vessels, together with the majority of the smaller American boats, were still gaff-rigged. Around the turn of the century, however, a handful of enterprising yachtsmen on either side of the Atlantic began to experiment with a sail that had for many years been used in ships' boats by Britain's merchant marine and her Royal Navy. Known on account of its shape as a 'leg-o-mutton', it was in effect an enlarged version of a loose-footed triangular foresail, but this one had its luff laced to the mast. The resulting rig met with only limited success, and might have remained a rarity were it not for a train of events that had begun down among the islands of Bermuda more than 200 years previously.

Their schooners, it transpired, had been rigged like this ever since its introduction by a shipload of English people who had settled there and founded what was to become a prosperous and fast growing colony. But it took time, and the development of a trading route westwards across to Chesapeake Bay, for the rig to be seen and adopted by the locals for their famous 'bug-eye' schooners; and for its reputation to spread up the eastern seaboard of America.

Despite a number of racing successes, however, the jib-headed (Bermudan) or 'Marconi' rig – so named after the Italian radio pioneer whose early wireless masts were tall, elaborately stayed wooden spars – was slow to catch on, being disapproved of in the somewhat sniffy yachting circles and completely ignored by designers. This state of affairs persisted until the period of World War I, when the new science of aerodynamics was first applied to sail design, and wind tunnel experiments in America demonstrated the superiority to windward of the jib-headed sails over the quadrilateral

Fig 1.7 An 18th century Dutch schooner, with boomed mainsail sheeted to a horse.

rigs of the day. (If anyone had thought to include the seemingly primitive junk and crab claw rigs in their comparisons, they would have been in for a few surprises, because contemporary tests have shown that on certain points of sailing, both can actually beat the Bermudan, as it is known in Britain.) Be that as it may, by the 1920s, Bermudan rigs were becoming accepted as essential for racing, although the traditional gaff rigs were still preferred for cruising by the majority of yachtsmen who considered that sailing to windward was a laborious, wet and uncomfortable penance to be avoided at all costs, even if it meant waiting for a change in the weather. (So what's new?)

Cross-cut sails

Three other developments in sail design were to have a profound influence on the performance capabilities of yachts. The first was not so much a change in the shape of sails as in the art of making them, the way they were cut. It had long been known that sail cloth, like any other, stretched most readily along the warp, with correspondingly little elongation across it when under stress. But no one understood this behaviour sufficiently to take proper advantage of it. So when during the 1850s American designers attempted to reduce sail stretch by laying their cloths in line with the boom instead of, in time honoured fashion, parallel to the leech, the results were disappointing. The sails still became baggy when it blew, and the idea might have been

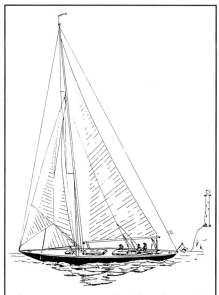

Fig 1.8 Cross-cut mainsail and mitred headsails on a 12 metre Bermudan cutter of the 1920s.

dropped altogether had not someone thought of running the cloths at right angles to the leech. This really worked. Cross-cut sails, as they were known, were found to hold their shape under conditions that would have stretched even the heaviest of vertically sewn canvas. Although still rather too radical to be trusted for *America*'s challenge, the new method gradually won acceptance by sailmakers, due largely to the pioneering efforts of that legendary American genius Nat Herreshof, and cross-cut sails are still favoured for most of today's cruising rigs.

Mitred headsails

Meanwhile an alternative approach to the problem of stretch was being tried in Britain. As far back as 1825 Matthew Orr, a Scottish sailmaker, had devised what he called his Angular Method of cutting in which two sets of cloths, one laid parallel to the leech and the other to the foot, were joined together by a diagonal seam which bisected the angle of the clew. Although this produced a marked improvement in the set of the sail, and 'Scotch-cut' jibs later became quite fashionable, it missed the essential purpose of cross-cutting. It was left to another of yachting's great names, the Cowes sailmaker Thomas Ratsey, to come up with the idea of diagonally seamed sails with cloths *perpendicular* both to the leech, which was no longer liable to curl and could even support an area of roach with the aid of battens, and to the foot, which could now be tensioned to good effect. Patented by Ratsey in 1897, the new cut proved particularly suitable for the huge gaff mainsails of the day, and his 'mitred' headsails remained a popular option for many years.

Spinnakers

The second development in this historic trio, the spinnaker, is believed to have come from the traditional practice by Thames barge skippers of poling out their big fore-staysails when the wind was free in light weather. First seen on the yacht *Sphinx* during a regatta at Cowes in 1866, it took the form of a gigantic triangular sail shaped like a balloon jib, with a definite luff and leech, which meant that its tack could not be alternated. As if the monster wasn't already awkward enough to handle, the international rules required that its sheet be led inside the lee shrouds, which made it almost impossible to gybe without lowering it to the deck and resetting it on the opposite side. Added to this, the spinnaker pole had to be enormously long, and ended up so near the water that it was liable to dunk the foot of the sail whenever the boat rolled, with the result that the foreguy would break, allowing the pole to be carried aft and snapped across the weather shrouds. Nevertheless these sails proved so powerful and effective downwind that they continued to be used right up until 1927, when a Swedish racing skipper, Sven Salén, devised the modern parachute spinnaker. It was seamed down its middle, with an identical luff and leech, with a broad head that lifted it well clear of the deck, and it was by now sheeted outside the shrouds, following a relaxation of the rules. It also featured a wide foot, which enabled it to be set ahead of the forestay on a comparatively short pole.

Genoas

Today's yachtsmen owe a lot to that Swede. For to Salén (also in 1927, as it happened) must go the credit for an entirely new form of sail for close-hauled working, the genoa, so called after he had first used it at a regatta in Genoa. Diagonally cut and very flat, it was a true deck hugger, with a low clew sheeted right aft, abreast of the cockpit, and trimmed outside the shrouds, which in consequence were set as far inboard as possible without threatening the structural security of the rig. This resulted, however, in a tendency for the middle sections of the mast to bow sideways, leading in turn to the development of multiple spreaders to keep it in column.

With the gathering momentum of civil and military aviation in the years leading up to World War II, and the consequent advancement of aircraft research, the early 1930s saw renewed interest in the behaviour of sails in their various shapes and combinations, and their influence on one another. From wind tunnel tests on aircraft components and by studying the contours of birds' wings, technicians came up with a number of theories to explain the behaviour of sails and how to improve their efficiency including, for example, the way in which the mainsail was affected by jib overlap. This became known as the 'slot effect', which was for many years misunderstood, and wrongly credited with much of the genoa's potency. It took today's computer technology, allied to the science of fluid dynamics as applied to ships' bottoms, to discover the truth about why sails work and how to make them work better. Some of the facts turned out to be stranger than fiction. Indeed, in the light of the new knowledge, it came as a surprise that some of the rigs of past centuries should have functioned as well as they did, all things considered. It also explained why a few of them were so effective. The ancients must have guessed a thing or two about airflow that we have only just discovered.

Chapter 2

How Sails Work

'A very queer thing is the wind', wrote John Masefield. Queer indeed. You can feel it, hear it, measure it, even lean against it sometimes, but you can't actually see it. Which is why, compared with those of other prime movers, the underlying principles of sailpower may seem difficult to grasp. Some are admittedly quite complex, but unfortunately many of the traditional explanations are either flawed or far too superficial, with the result that how sails *really* work is easily misunderstood. And without a fundamentally correct understanding of how they take energy from the wind to drive a boat, little else in sailing makes sense. Even in the seemingly obvious case of a downwind squaresail, for example, it is misleading to visualise it as simply an obstruction in the path of the wind, and being blown along before it. There is rather more to it than meets the eye, especially if additional sails are set or there are other boats in the vicinity, let alone with fore-and-aft rigs, and the local aerodynamics become a lot more complicated than that when sailing to weather. Airflow patterns, to be clearly interpreted, need a series of explanatory diagrams, and too much back-to-the-classroom theorising in a book like this is liable to stop the average reader dead in his tracks. Nevertheless, with such a choice of confusing and sometimes conflicting explanations available to a sailor, it's about the only way to avoid getting some entirely wrong ideas about airflow and its behaviour.

It is not actually wrong to visualise a sail full of wind being driven along by air pressure on one side and some sort of suction on the other. But that's only part of the propulsion process. The picture is incomplete, because it doesn't show *why* the relative pressures are different and hence, more importantly, *how* they can be altered so as to control the boat.

SPEED VS PRESSURE

The force that the wind exerts on a rig depends on the sail area, the density of the air, which varies slightly with the seasons, and the square of the windspeed – twice the speed gives twice the flow, as well as twice the force: double double. The path followed by a stream of air meeting an obstruction, or passing through a restriction, is often at odds with what commonsense suggests would be its logical direction. Its real-life behaviour can be demonstrated in a wind tunnel, using smoke or wool tufts, or simulated in an open channel of water by sprinkling aluminium powder on to the surface so as to follow its movement. On paper, the most convenient way of depicting this is by drawing a series of imaginary lines – streamlines – to represent the direction of the air at various points in the flow field, and varying the distance between the lines according to the speed of the air between them. Because the flow will always stay between adjacent streamlines, it has to speed up where their spacing narrows in order to get through the smaller area and conversely must slow down as they open out.

The spacing also denotes pressure. As long ago as 1738, a far-sighted Swiss professor named Daniel Bernoulli established one of the primary laws on which all aerodynamic principles are based. He discovered that in any fluid, the sum total of pressure plus velocity remains constant, meaning that if air moves faster, its pressure is reduced, and if it decelerates, its pressure rises. So when the streamlines are spread far apart, speed is low and pressure is high. And vice versa: like closely packed isobars on a weather map, close spacing signifies low pressure and strong winds.

Squeezing the end of a hosepipe might give the impression of increasing the pressure in it. It does so, but only upstream. Pressure actually falls at the outlet, where the water has to flow faster to pass through the restriction. Try dangling a spoon between finger and thumb near the flow from a tap. As you bring the back of the spoon close to the stream of water, it will suddenly be drawn towards it as if to a magnet, because the surrounding air, moving with the water, accelerates rapidly as the spoon approaches and its pressure falls. This 'venturi effect', as it is termed, is even more strikingly demonstrated, sometimes in more ways than one, when two vessels pass one another too closely, or if one is moored too near to the other, and they are forcibly sucked together by the acceleration of the water rushing between their hulls. It also enables birds to fly.

AIRFLOW AND LIFT

A bird's wing surfaces are suitably curved for the purpose, but even a flat plate can develop a certain amount of lift. Paper darts can fly, as we know, flat sails can drive a boat upwind, and a sheet of plywood in a windy street can carry a man clean off his feet. Although crude and inefficient compared with a proper three-dimensional aerofoil, the flat plate acts on an airstream in much the same way, and, without the complications of additional dimensions such as camber and twist, which we will come to later, the process is easier to visualise and to illustrate in a diagram.

Most sailors carry a picture in their mind's eye of sails blown into their curvature and driven along by the pressure of the wind on one side, helped

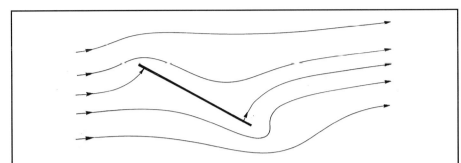

Fig 2.1 Airflow across a flat plate, showing the stagnation streamlines, upwash at the leading edge and flow reversal at the trailing edge, assuming the air had no viscosity. It has not been deflected by the plate, so it could not have exerted any force on it.

by a certain amount of suction on the other. (In fact, the reverse is true, as we shall see.) Fig 2.1 shows how the airstream might behave with our flat plate angled like a sail going to windward. The flow along either side of it is divided by a central streamline leading to the spot where it meets the plate, slightly below its forward edge. This is the so-called 'stagnation' point, where its velocity is lowest and therefore, per Bernoulli, its pressure is highest. The forward stagnation point is matched by another one near the trailing edge, with its own mirror-image streamline. The flow above the forward stagnation streamline is forced up and around the leading edge – a movement known as 'upwash' – and, constrained by the streamlines above it, accelerates, losing pressure as it does so. It then gradually slows down as the influence of the plate diminishes and the streamlines open out, which in turn induces a flow reversal around the trailing edge. The air that has flowed below the plate turns sharply back on itself and moves *upstream* to fill the void under the stagnation streamline before rejoining the departing column of air.

BOUNDARY LAYER

Notice how the airstream in Fig 2.1 has left the plate at the same angle as the one it arrived at. Bearing in mind Newton's well known Third Law of Motion, which states that for every action there has to be an equal and opposite reaction, this means that since the flow has not been deflected by the plate, it could not have exerted any force on it. Under these circumstances, the paper dart could not have flown and the boat would still be stationary.

All this is what *might* have happened if the air had no viscosity, which in this context we can look on as 'stickiness'. Air is considered to be a fluid, and all fluids have a certain amount of viscosity and are affected by friction. Spray water on to a sail and some of it will stick to the cloth. Air behaves in the same way though to a lesser degree. Seen diagrammatically (Fig 2.2), a thin but

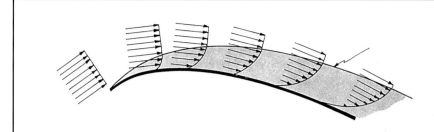

Fig 2.2 The boundary layer. Since air has a certain amount of viscosity, it is affected by friction. This causes the air next to the sail to stick to it and be carried along with it. But as each succeeding layer slides over its neighbour it moves faster, until at the outer edge of the boundary layer, viscosity has no further effect and the air flows freely with the mainstream.

very significant layer of it sticks to the sail and is carried along with it, moving forwards against the main airstream. Next to this 'attached' slice of the flow is another and then another, in succeeding layers, each moving slightly faster than its inner neighbour as it slides over it, their relative friction decreasing until the boundary is reached where viscosity has no further effect and the air flows freely. In reality the transition is stepless, with a steady acceleration taking place across the thickness of the boundary layer from zero velocity relative to the plate, to full speed across it, in a steady state known as laminar flow.

STARTING VORTEX

One of the more peculiar laws of physics is that although air flows in an orderly fashion while it accelerates into a low pressure area, it is liable to misbehave if it is slowed down too abruptly by friction, or a sudden change of direction, or by too severe a rising pressure gradient. The flow will then cease to be laminar and will separate from the surface that was supporting it, departing in an undisciplined series of swirls and eddies. This occurs, for example, along the upper surface of the plate whenever its angle becomes too steep, a phenomenon known as stalling. It is also what happens to the boundary layer stream under the plate trying to make the sudden U-turn around the trailing edge. It slows suddenly and begins to skid outwards, only to run slap into the flow along the upper surface and break away from the plate altogether, spinning off in a swirl of air called a 'starting vortex'.

As a result, it has failed to fill the void under the stagnation streamline, and since the necessary air has to come from somewhere, still more – in the form of upwash – is diverted around the leading edge from under the plate, or an aerofoil as in Fig 2.3. There is now a much greater volume of air passing along the upper surface than below it, as evidenced by the way the forward

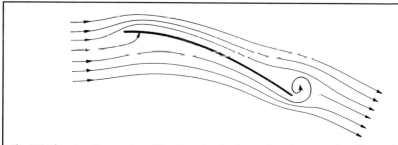

Fig 2.3 The starting vortex. The flow in the boundary layer under the trailing edge of the aerofoil has failed to make the sharp turn and has developed a curling vortex. The streamlines remain equidistant and parallel to one another, indicating that the columns of air above and below the stagnation streamline are at the same pressure as each other and travelling at the same speed (the Kutta condition). However, they have been deflected downwards and consequently the foil is developing lift.

stagnation point has been shifted aft. Yet although the flow is no longer symmetrical, it has adjusted itself to leave the trailing edge with its streamlines equidistant and parallel to each other, indicating that the air above and below the stagnation streamline doesn't mix, it is all at the same pressure and travelling at the same speed.

This process of adjustment constitutes one of the fundamental principles of aerodynamics known as the 'Kutta condition', after the scientist who discovered it at the beginning of this century. Note also that the column of air leaving the foil is no longer travelling in the direction it was when it approached. It has been deflected downwards and consequently the foil is developing lift. However, not all the lift is derived from this linear flow. Some is due to an additional and often unrecognised type of flow called 'circulation'. Neither can cause lift on its own. Each relies on the other to help create lift, and both are needed to satisfy the Kutta condition.

CIRCULATION

Circulation begins soon after the starting vortex has been swept off the trailing edge into the clean air downstream. As the vortex revolves, it transfers some of its energy to the surrounding air, acting on it in the manner of one gearwheel meshing with another (Fig 2.4), and starting a general airflow circulating *in the opposite direction*. Action and reaction again. This counter-circulation grows to surround the entire foil, effectively adding to the upwash and the speed of the air along the upper (leeward) side and decreasing it on the other, with a correspondingly larger pressure differential between them and hence increased lift. The concept of circulation started out as a purely mathematical corollary to Kutta's theory, but it has been proved to occur in reality.

Try it for yourself in the bath. Sprinkle some talcum powder on to a few

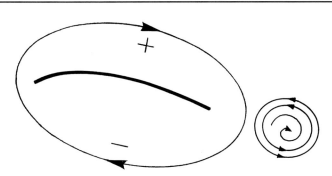

Fig 2.4 Circulation. As the Kutta condition becomes established and the stagnation points move counter-clockwise around the foil, the starting vortex is shed downstream. As it revolves, it transfers some of its energy to the surrounding air, acting on it in the manner of one gearwheel meshing with another. The resulting counter-rotation increases the speed of the flow to leeward and decreases it to windward, the increased pressure differential across the foil adding to its lift.

inches/centimetres of water and use a scrap of card as the foil, preferably bent – or cut, for example, from a yoghourt carton – so that it is cambered like a sail. It will work better that way, a curved foil being much more effective than a flat one. Draw the card very gently along the length of the bath, lift it out, and you will see it has left a starting vortex revolving at one end. Then slowly but surely another, larger swirl will start to counter-rotate at the other, one 'gearwheel' driving the other.

Note also the measurable time lag before the vortex spins up to speed, and the rather longer delay before it gets the circulation going. It explains why, in the case of a sailing boat, anything that disturbs the aerodynamic equilibrium, such as an abrupt helm movement or vigorous sail trimming, will result in a loss of speed until the boat has settled down under the new aerodynamic conditions. The larger the chord of a sail – the straight line distance between its luff and leech – the greater the circulation and the longer it takes for it to build up speed and for the lift to develop. This is most apparent in light airs, when delicate handling is one of the marks of a good sailor. Unfortunately there isn't anything he can do about it in heavy weather, because while the boat is rolling and pitching, the airflow is too unstable for any worthwhile circulation to develop.

CAMBER

Camber is the fore-and-aft curvature of a sail relative to its chord, the straight line between luff and leech. Compared with a flat plate, a cambered sail is able to persuade the flow to remain attached to the leeward surface for a greater distance before breaking away. That distance is determined by the maximum

depth of the camber and its location, its incidence or angle of attack presented to the approaching airstream, and its relative speed. These are the three
principal factors governing the amount of lift, that is to say the power, that a
sail can develop.

The precise way in which it does it has been variously and often incorrectly
explained. The most popular misconception is the one about the air having
to travel farther around the leeward side and hence having to go faster to
catch up with the windward part of the stream at the trailing edge. It *does* in
fact travel farther and faster. But if you think about it, this can't be due to the
thickness of the sailcloth, which is little more than a membrane measuring virtually the same along either side. Not so for a comparatively thick aircraft
wing, with its flat underside and pronounced camber across the upper surface.
But since aircraft can fly upside down, given an adequate angle of attack, the
physical measurements can't make any difference in that case either. The reasons are in fact aerodynamic, rather than geometric, as evidenced by the
streamlines we looked at earlier. The Kutta condition specifies only that the
speed and pressure of the two flows off the trailing edge are the same. Indeed,
if it were possible to watch two leaves arriving simultaneously at the leading
edge, the leeward one would actually leave the trailing edge ahead of its partner, although their speeds by then would be the same.

Generally speaking, the deeper the camber – the fullness, or *draft* in sailmakers' terms – and the greater the angle of attack, the more wind is deflected and the more power the sail will develop. This makes the boat more lively
and responsive, less liable to be stopped by a wave, and helps it to accelerate
out of a tack. But simply increasing either of them doesn't always make the boat
go faster, because the fore-and-aft location of the draft also affects the behaviour of the airstream. Draft is usually expressed as a percentage of the chord
across any particular section of the sail. Hence a 1-foot maximum draft in a
10-foot chord would be rated as 10%, representing a fairly flat sail that would
be effective in a fresh breeze, whereas 20% is reckoned to be full, and would
be a powerful shape suitable only for light airs. This is why.

Laminar flow is established as soon as the sail is filling. This occurs at an
angle of attack of around 10° and is maintained up to about 25°, which represents a typical broad reach. Beyond that, the falling pressure gradient along
the lee side becomes too steep and any further increase in angle reduces the
upwash and moves the separation point forward and around to the weather
side. Some of the air then fails to make the increasingly sharp turn around the
luff, especially when it is moving slowly in light winds, and lifts slightly away
from it, forming a 'separation bubble', a sort of artificial thickness over which
the subsequent airstream is able to pass more easily. This part of the sail has
become stalled. However, the flow subsequently re-attaches further aft, so
that the rest of the sail is still driving the boat. What happens next is that as
the sail is angled still further, the bubble begins to extend downstream

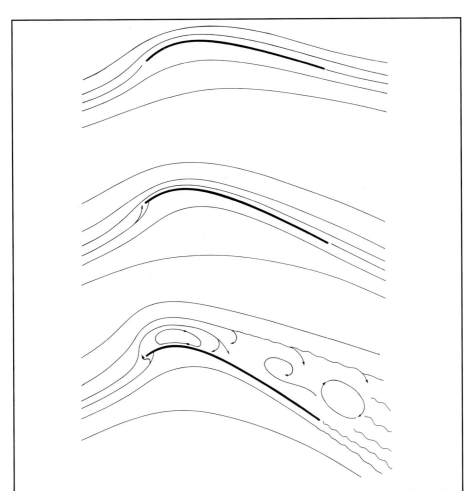

Fig 2.5 Angle of attack. Central stagnation streamline divides air passing either side of a sail. Streamlines on the leeward side become closer together, depicting accelerating flow and falling pressure, while windward streamlines open out as flow decelerates and pressure rises. *Top:* Sail at 25°: moderate lift. *Centre:* Sail at 35°: maximum lift, flow still attached. With further increase in angle, the airflow will begin to separate from the sail in the region of maximum camber, but will re-attach downstream without appreciable loss of lift. *Bottom:* Sail at 45°: stall has set in, with reversed flow vortex inside separation bubble, random eddies and large turbulent wake. Severe loss of lift and increase in drag.

towards the leech, collecting more stagnant material from the boundary layer. The flow remains attached for the time being and the power of the sail continues to increase (Fig 2.5).

The final limit of laminar flow is reached at a certain critical combination of angle, the depth of the draft and its position. As a particular angle is approached, there is a tendency for the air, after it passes the draft point – the crown of the hill, so to speak – to once again detach and fly off at a tangent instead of decelerating smoothly. This leads to the formation of another separation bubble, which is dragged along behind the leech as a band of dead air, wasting energy. With any further increases in angle and hence in lift, this secondary bubble extends rapidly forwards, the airflow over it becoming increasingly turbulent, until finally it joins up with the luff bubble and bursts. The sail has become completely stalled *at that level* and power decreases suddenly. Conditions are usually different higher up, because of 'twist' (page 48).

WIND ANGLE

The phenomenon known as upwash around the luff (the same thing occurs underwater with the keel) actually begins some distance ahead of it. The diversion of the streamlines is not instantaneous. Nature decrees that they follow a curved path rather than make any sudden sharp changes in direction. Consequently the airstream, warned in this seemingly mystical way of the sail's impending arrival, starts to bend in anticipation; and given the correct angle of incidence, the soft cloth develops a firm and powerful belly. Too large an angle causes the sail to stall, even though it remains full and apparently drawing; too small, and there is insufficient upwash to maintain any worthwhile pressure differential across the sail, with the result that it starts to collapse, losing what little drive it may have had.

This all-important angle is the *apparent* direction of the wind acting on the sail. It is the wind felt by the crew of a boat moving through the water; or to be more accurate, moving 'across the ground'. If it was merely stemming the tide, the strength as well as the direction of the wind experienced by those on board would be the same as if the boat was lying motionless at anchor. That would be the true wind.

The apparent windspeed is composed of these two vectors, true windspeed and boatspeed. Travelling directly into the wind, as when motoring, has the effect of adding the speeds together: eg true windspeed 10 knots, boatspeed 4 knots, apparent windspeed 14 knots. Running downwind, one is subtracted from the other, so the crew will now only experience 3 knots across the deck. Throughout the range of headings in between, the apparent windspeed and its direction will vary between the two extremes, and are easily determined by drawing a simple vector diagram such as one of those in Fig 2.6, using a protractor to plot the angle, with the length of each line proportional to speed. It can be seen that except when the true wind is dead ahead or astern, the apparent wind is always forward of the true wind; and when beam-reaching or close-hauled, it has a higher speed than the true wind.

The differential can be observed even on a slow dinghy, but it increases with speed and reaches dramatic proportions on the fastest boats, the ocean racing multihulls. Nearing their maximum speeds of well over 30 knots,

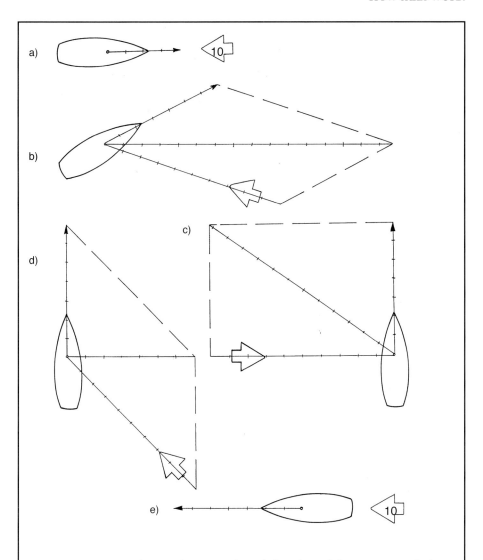

Fig 2.6 Apparent wind. How the strength and direction of the apparent wind vary with the speed and heading of the boat. True wind is constant at 10 knots.

a) Boatspeed 4 knots, true wind ahead, apparent wind 14 knots ahead

b) Boatspeed 7 knots, true wind at 45°, apparent wind 15.7 knots at 27°

c) Boatspeed 7 knots, true wind abeam, apparent wind 12.4 knots at 65°

d) Boatspeed 7 knots, true wind at 135°, apparent wind 7 knots abeam

e) Boatspeed 7 knots, true wind astern, apparent wind 3 knots astern which they can easily achieve in a fresh breeze by continuously heading up as they accelerate and draw their apparent wind forward, these greyhounds find themselves continuously sailing into storm force winds, having added most of their own speed to that of the true wind. They have also drawn the apparent wind so far forward that they are obliged to sail exceptionally close to it – within 20° or less – in order to make good as high a speed as possible in the direction of the true wind, which is probably blowing from around 40°. The ultimate limit of speed to windward is reached when the wind is drawn so far forward that the boat simply cannot point high enough and the helmsman has to bear away.

Most good boats will beat to weather at 30° or less to the apparent wind, but still only tack through 80° on the compass. However, if the true wind stays constant and boatspeed increases, then so will the apparent wind, producing a header; which is why it usually pays to tack on a header instead of bearing away. But if boatspeed remains the same and true wind increases, the apparent wind will free. Conversely, as the true wind draws aft, the apparent wind will decrease until both are dead astern, which is usually the slowest point of sailing. From here, it needs only a small change in direction or boat heading to make a big difference to the apparent wind angle, increasing its strength and restoring boatspeed. The fastest boats, whatever the direction of the true wind, necessarily spend much time beam-reaching or beating.

TWIST

The windspeed in free air increases with its height above the water, where normally it is slowed by surface friction, in the same way that it varies through the boundary layer of a sail. Rough or gusty conditions break up the sea's boundary layer and obliterate much of its surface friction. In a calm sea the wind gradient between sea level and the masthead of the average cruising boat can be as much as 50%, even more with tall masts. But because the wind senses the approach of the boat, the freestream is already lifting and accelerating by the time it reaches the sail. The result of this upwash is that the actual speed difference between deck and masthead is much less than expected, but it can still be as much as 10%. Consequently the apparent windspeed is also greater at the masthead than at deck level and has in turn shifted aft, producing a vertical twist of some three to five degrees. The closer-winded the boat, the less is the apparent wind twist. Nevertheless, the lower part of the sail can be beating, or even stalled, while the top is still close-reaching.

This wind twist has to be accommodated by letting the head of the sail fall away in relation to the foot (Fig 2.7), the object being to present the optimum angle of entry all the way up. In matching the apparent wind, allowance has also to be made for the increase in depth-to-chord ratio needed to offset the loss in area and lift as the sail narrows towards the head. This becomes even more necessary in the case of a fractional rig, where the part of the mainsail which extends above the jib is not influenced by any downwash from it. If the angle-of-attack were to remain constant, the airflow over the increased camber would tend to separate and stall that part of the sail. The sailmaker caters for all this by building in a certain amount of twist as well as draft. Nevertheless, under increasing load the sails, if left to themselves, will always twist more than necessary and have to be restrained by mainsheet or vang tension on the boom, and by correct tensioning of the headsail sheets and lead blocks. This in turn affects the airflow on to the mainsail and the circulation around it; which brings us to the much misunderstood matter of the way in which these two sails work together.

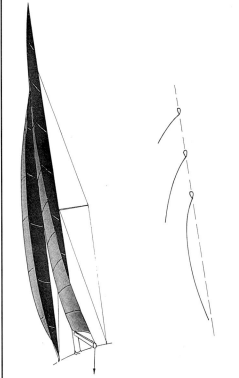

Fig 2.7 *Left:* Twist in a mainsail and jib, viewed from astern. Pulling down the boom would tighten the leech and reduce the twist. *Right:* Mainsail shape near the head, in the middle, and near the foot.

THE SLOT

For a long time it was thought that the jib's prime function, apart from helping to drive the boat, was to increase the power of the mainsail. There is no doubt that most boats really come alive when a headsail is hoisted. This was supposed to create a venturi between the sails which accelerated the airflow on to the main, increasing the suction along its lee side and revitalising the flow where it might be starting to separate (although if you think about it, a partial vacuum in the venturi would be more likely to cause the jib to collapse into the gap). The traditional interpretation of the slot effect nevertheless looks fairly logical at first glance, and many sailors still accept it. But recognition of the principle of circulation a few years ago changed the entire concept of sail interaction.

Every sail is now known to be surrounded by its own individual circulation, each of which has the effect of simultaneously slowing the airflow to windward, increasing the degree of downwash, and of accelerating it on the

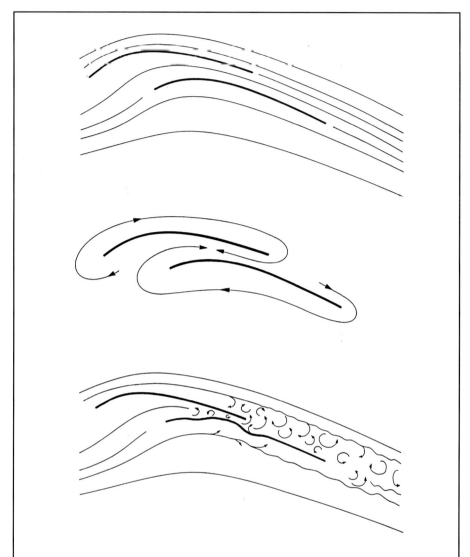

Fig 2.8 The slot. *Top*: Airflow in the slot, without circulation. *Centre*: Circulation around each sail accelerates the flow to leeward and slows it to windward, increasing their combined power, although the flows in the slot are opposed. *Bottom*: Over-sheeted jib backwinds the main and spoils both their flows.

lee side, adding to the upwash. However, these circulations tend to cancel each other out in the slot, where they are moving in opposite directions (Fig 2.8). The result is that instead of increasing the flow across the mainsail, the slot actually *reduces* it. It also brings the apparent wind further ahead of the main, which consequently requires closer sheeting, not only for it to draw properly, but because it directly affects the efficiency of the overlapping jib, which relies to some extent on the main's localised high speed flow to satisfy its own Kutta condition.

At the same time the jib, operating within the circulation of the main, benefits from the resulting increase in upwash, some of which had already formed as the freestream divided ahead of the sail. More of the air that would otherwise have passed through the slot is deflected by the combined circulation fields into the lee of the jib, increasing the speed of the air past it and giving it a gratuitous lift to windward as it draws the apparent wind aft. The boat can now be pointed closer to the wind without the jib luffing. However, if the slot is left too open, as by undersheeting the jib, much of its effect will be lost as each sail tends to act independently; too narrow, and an over-sheeted jib will dump its exhaust stream on to the lee side of the main and backwind it. The optimum sheeting angle depends on the pointing ability of the hull and the relative areas of the jib and main. It could be as low as 6° on a fast, light-displacement boat with a high performance rig and a small jib, whereas on a typical mid-displacement cruiser with a large head-sail it would be around 12°, the actual minimum angle being dictated by the siting of the sheet blocks.

In practice, it is often found that some backwinding close to the luff, where a non-rotating mast will already have caused quite a lot of disturbance, has little or no effect on performance, provided the airflow remains attached across the rest of the sail, especially in the leech area where much of the power is generated while sailing to windward. Racing in heavy weather while hard on the wind, more than half the mainsail can be allowed to collapse as the boom is trimmed out in the gusts, because the leech continues to drive the boat and helps it to point up. The normal cruising procedure – taking a reef in the interests of comfort and to ease the strain on the boat – would reduce the all-important leech area and with it, several degrees of pointing ability.

Under normal conditions and correctly trimmed, with the main suitably shaped by means of the draft controls described earlier and sheeted in at a narrower angle than the jib, each sail complements the other. In effect, all that the forward part of the mainsail does is to connect the after part to the mast. The two should act as a single foil extending from the jib luff to the mainsail leech, with a virtually uninterrupted flow across their lee sides. Nevertheless *it's the mainsail that increases the power and effectiveness of the jib*, rather than the other way round.

Sailors on the old square-riggers could hardly have realised this, let alone the reasons for it. But it was common knowledge, on a ship beating to windward, that as each sail was 'put to sleep', it would end up sheeted more tightly than the one ahead, the yards fanning out progressively and their angle decreasing by as much as 25° between the forward and after masts.

SAIL FORCES

The total reaction force exerted by a sail as it deflects the wind is angled between that of the arriving and departing airstreams, but except when running dead downwind, only a part of it is directed forwards to drive the boat. The remainder of the thrust is sideways, at right angles to the line of travel and to the mast, heeling the boat and producing leeway. The heeling effort is balanced by the weight and leverage of the keel, and/or by that of the crew out on the weather rail, while leeway is resisted by the keel and rudder. In the downwind case, the sail simply catches the wind and pushes the boat along without heeling it or trying to drive it sideways, converting all the energy it has extracted into thrust, but doing so very inefficiently with the airstream tripping over the edges of the sail and tumbling along behind it without creating any useful suction. On all other points of sailing, the

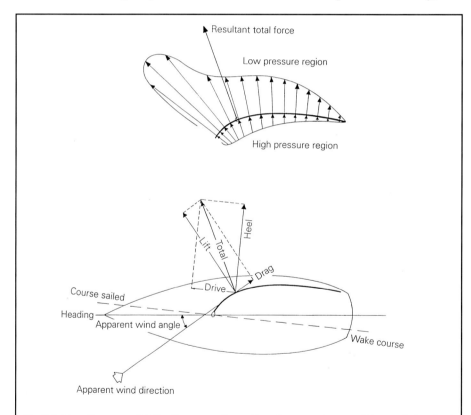

Fig 2.9 *Top*: Pressure distribution over the sail surfaces under conditions of attached flow, showing how most of the lift is developed on the lee side of the sail and is concentrated close to the leading edge. Large arrow denotes the resultant total force, acting through the centre of effort. *Bottom*: Relationship between the driving and heeling forces produced by the sail, and its lift/drag ratio.

heeling force grows larger and larger as the boat is turned closer to the wind, reaching a maximum when sailing close-hauled of about four times the driving force.

In real life this drive is greater than might be expected from the diagrams, because as soon as the wind is brought round off the stern, the sail begins to act as an increasingly powerful aerofoil instead of a mere windscoop. Consequently most boats are about as fast beating as they are when running, despite the effort wasted in extra drag when the boat is heeled and crabbing through the water instead of going where it is pointed; and all reach their top speed on or near a beam reach (surfing excepted: a boat may touch two or three times its theoretical maximum while riding the crest of a wave).

There is another way of looking at the forces acting on a sail – or on a combination of two or more, which we can treat as a single large sail for the purpose of these explanations. The total force exerted through the centre of effort of the sail can be split into a lifting force at right angles to the apparent wind, and another directly downwind, representing the drag of the sail (Fig 2.9). The higher the ratio of lift to drag, the greater is the useful drive of the sail and the smaller its tendency to heel the boat and make leeway. Likewise, the wider the range of angles through which a sail can maintain high L/D ratios, the greater its all-round efficiency and scope.

There are two ways of getting more power from a sail. The first and seemingly the more effective is simply to increase its angle-of-attack by oversheeting it, or by turning the boat away from the wind without easing the sheet, and steering too low a course. Either will have the effect of increasing the upwash on to the luff and pulling in more air from windward, speeding up the leeward flow. Widening the angle also increases the overall deflection of the flow and the corresponding amount of lift this has generated, always provided that it has managed to remain attached.

The second and more subtle way of increasing power is, as we have seen, to turn the wind through a greater angle by deepening the camber of the sail, either by trimming it in, or by easing the outhaul, halyard or backstay – or in the case of a headsail, by moving the sheet lead forwards. (More about these forms of camber control later.) Increasing the camber cleans up the airstream by providing a more gentle introduction to the sharp bend around the luff; but as we have seen, too much camber will cause the flow to separate.

An additional and largely unrecognised factor that influences sailpower is air temperature: the colder the air, the denser it becomes, and this in turn affects the pressure it exerts on the sail. Fifteen knots of wind in the winter can carry as much weight as 20 knots on a summer's day – which is why, often without realising the reason for it, the sailor finds that his boat needs to be reefed at lower windspeeds in cold weather. It is also a fact, as indicated in Fig 2.9 (*bottom*), that any increase in drive can only be achieved at the expense of a certain amount of added drag, and the whole art of the sail trimmer lies in encouraging one, which is relatively easy, while minimising the other, which is not.

Drag is difficult to visualise, because it is composed of three separate elements: form drag, frictional drag, and induced drag.

FORM DRAG

Any obstruction in the path of a moving fluid, wind or water, causes form drag. An obviously streamlined shape can normally be expected to have a lower drag coefficient than a blunt or boxy one; but shapes can be misleading, especially the slippery looking ones. A circular section such as a mast (or even a rope) is one of the worst, because as soon as the airflow passes the mid point, it separates into a bubble of disturbed air behind the offending profile. This is the major reason why a headsail, with only a wire or a slender foil supporting its luff, is so much more efficient to windward than a mainsail. A pear-shaped or aerofoil section is better for a mast, but the efficiency of a mainsail can be considerably improved by allowing the mast to rotate until it assumes the correct angle of attack to the apparent wind (Fig 2.10). It then provides a smooth entry for the airflow across the leading edge of the sail and its heavily cambered forward area, where much of the drive is developed. This can be further increased by deliberately over-rotating the mast by means of the 'spanner', a lever fixed to it near the heel and angled to and fro by control lines, or on big boats by hydraulic actuators.

The fore-and-aft depth of the mast section on high performance multi-hulls and some of the largest racing monohulls can amount to 10% or more of the overall chord of the mainsail, with an aspect ratio (see p.56) approaching that of a glider wing, hence the term 'wingmast'. As such, it is a highly efficient aerofoil that can develop a powerful driving force of its own. But as it cannot be reefed, problems can arise in heavy weather – notably with the jumbo sizes used on some ocean-racing multihulls – because its movement cannot be sufficiently damped for it to be safely left to feather into the wind. The risk is that it will oscillate so violently as to cause damage and eventually

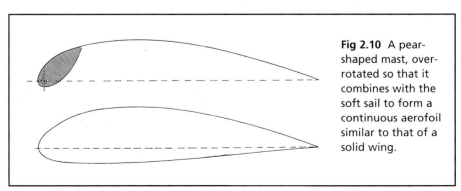

Fig 2.10 A pear-shaped mast, over-rotated so that it combines with the soft sail to form a continuous aerofoil similar to that of a solid wing.

flutter itself to destruction, so it has to be stabilised by allowing it to develop some lift. Consequently a huge wingmast can be a dangerous liability in extreme weather conditions, the boat being forced to continue driving on at high speed, regardless of the heavy seas and virtually unable to slow down (except by towing the anchor cable or a collection of long warps – another example of form drag, though hardly a typical one!). Even a dinghy's rotating mast should be removed when the boat is left unattended.

The separation referred to earlier also occurs when a sail is over-sheeted or given too much camber. The gradient across the lee side becomes too steep for the flow to remain attached and to slow down sufficiently to satisfy the Kutta condition. So instead of slipping smoothly off the leech, it breaks away to form another bubble of turbulent air which is trailed along in the wake of the sail, holding it back. However, form drag becomes progressively less of a dragon as the wind comes aft of the beam, until by the time the boat is running, it has changed its role from being a retarding force to providing virtually all the forward drive – though very inefficiently, as we saw earlier. So the more form drag above the waterline the better when sailing downwind. (Not so for the submerged parts of the hull, because their form drag continues to rise as the square of their speed through the water: double the boatspeed and form drag quadruples, hence the incentive to underwater streamlining.)

On the other hand, by looking on reaching as a cross between beating and running, the reason why beam-reaching is the fastest point of sailing becomes apparent: the total thrust of the sail is then angled most closely in line with the direction of travel, combining maximum drive and only moderate form drag and heeling force.

FRICTIONAL DRAG

Of the three types of drag, this has the least effect on a sail. As its name implies, it is caused by the friction of the air flowing past the sailcloth, with the various seams, stitches and wrinkles superimposed on its surface texture. These irregularities break up the smooth laminar flow in the boundary layer, making it turbulent, and the energy it takes to fuel this disturbance represents frictional drag. Strange as it may seem, however, this energy is well spent; for this small degree of turbulence is actually more of a help than a hindrance. Not only is it better able to withstand rapid rises in pressure but separation, when it occurs, is smoother than with laminar flow, whose breakaway is sudden and drastic and more likely to result in stalling. In other words, turbulent flow is more forgiving. This is the probable explanation for one aspect of the performance of a junk's sails. It is certainly the reason for the small projecting feathers on the leading edges of a bird's wing, for example, and the purpose of the dimples on a golf ball. They create turbulent flow.

Water being five times as viscous as air, turbulent flow is all too easy to create to excess below the waterline. Theoretically a small amount, as produced by a shark's skin, reduces friction; but a weedy bottom can ruin a yacht's performance. The reason why a porpoise is capable of occasional bursts of speed in excess of 40 knots is believed to be its extraordinary ability to detect and regulate the change from laminar to turbulent flow, and to alter the texture of its skin and reshape its body accordingly.

Yet despite the significant part played by frictional drag in the performance of a sail, its contribution to total air drag is relatively small. Even when going to windward, frictional and form drag together account for scarcely a quarter of the total. All the rest is induced drag, the biggest bogey of them all.

INDUCED DRAG

Look on it as a largely unavoidable evil, caused directly by the process of generating lift. In the case of a sail, this depends on there being a pressure difference between the windward and leeward sides. With nothing to prevent vertical flow, a certain amount of air is bound to leak across from one side to the other, streaming up and over the head of the sail and under the foot, and spiralling off downwind in two energy-consuming vortices. Lift has been obtained at the expense of the considerable amounts of energy lost in these vortices, which prevent the windward and leeward streamlines from closing up at the trailing edge, and induced drag is the measure of maintaining such an unhealthy flow. With an aircraft wing, the transverse flow is all outwards, the fuselage forming an effective seal at one end, so the vortices trail from the wing tips. The heavier the aircraft, the more violent are the vortices. Those from a jumbo, to cite an extreme example, can extend like twin tornadoes for several miles astern. Their centres may revolve at over 18000 rpm and they contain fearsome amounts of disruptive energy, representing much of the effort in creating two hundred tons or so of lift (and to be strictly avoided, therefore, by any other aircraft in the vicinity).

Wing 'fences' on heavy aircraft serve to restrict the spanwise flow and subsequent losses, and some boats have winglets on the bottoms of their keels for this purpose. Using the deck itself as an end plate, low-cut genoas are nearly always carried in racing, despite the total loss of forward visibility which requires a look-out to be stationed beside the forestay during close-quarters manoeuvring. Wide booms are also occasionally fitted on racing boats, but they have never become popular because given the depth needed to resist the vertical bending stresses, they are massive and somewhat cumbersome.

ASPECT RATIO

The profile of the sail itself has a significant effect on induced drag. The taller the sail, the greater will be the volume of air it influences; and the longer the luff in relation to the foot – the aspect ratio or AR, as it is known – the smaller the area of foot and head compared with the leech, and the shorter the frontiers across which air can escape vertically. The resulting reduction in induced drag for the same amount of lift makes the sail more efficient for beating to windward, although excessive AR only increases the heeling force without adding much more to the drive, and requires a heavier, thicker and draggier mast with stronger rigging. On the other hand, a short, broad sail of the same area is better for beam to broad reaching, partly because its greater induced drag is no longer a handicap, beginning to drive the boat as soon as the apparent wind is abaft the beam; and also because the lower AR sail can develop a greater total force before it stalls, with more of this usable in practical terms, since heeling is no longer a limiting factor. This may explain why the square-riggers were unchallenged under these conditions.

The scale of ratios we are discussing range from an average top figure of around 3.0 for the mainsail of a Bermudan rigged racer, that is to say with a luff length three times that of the foot, down to 1.0 or even less for a gaff cruiser. These are what we may call sailors' measures, and are widely used to describe AR, but they take no account of roach, the area beyond the straight line between clew and head produced by convex curvature of the leech. Aerodynamicists and some yacht designers define AR as the square of the luff length divided by the sail area. This allows for roach, and a similar, rather less accurate figure can be arrived at by dividing the luff length by the mean chord (the fore-and-aft length halfway up). Clearly, for a straight-sided triangular sail the resulting number would be twice that of the simple sailor's version, so be careful to check the form of usage when making comparisons.

The application of roach is usually restricted to mainsails, because the battens which are needed to support it cannot, in the case of a jib, be tacked past the mast – except in the case of narrow headsails, and these offer only limited potential to exploit it. One effect of roach is to provide a slight increase in sail area, which under the majority of racing rules is 'free', since it is not measured. Its primary purpose, however, is to reduce tip vortices. Curved leeches, supported by full length battens, have been a feature of Chinese junks and sampans for 2000 years, but not until World War II was the existence of tip vortices recognised, let alone their cause and effect. It was R J Mitchell, designer of the legendary Spitfire, who first realised that one way to minimise them was to introduce an elliptical curve into the trailing edge of a wing. This inhibited the spanwise flow across every section of it, and the resulting reduction of induced drag turned out to be of the order of 20–30%, with every section of the wing having the highest ratio of lift to induced drag for a given area and aspect ratio.

To achieve this on a soft sail, the sailmaker juggles with a combination of draft and twist. The lowest part of the sail, having the longest chords, is the area with the greatest lift potential and the highest induced drag. So in some designs, one is sacrificed in order to minimise the other and improve the over-all lift:drag ratio. This is done by reducing the draft in the vicinity of the boom. The middle of the sail, say half to three-quarters of the way up, is usually given the highest angles of attack and plenty of camber; and the top, where the heeling force is greatest and the chords are short, is given even more camber, with twist to match, so as to maximise what lift is left up there after the vortex losses from the head of the sail. The effect of these variations in camber, superimposed on the planform of the sail, is to give it a more elliptical pattern of lift by – as it were – compressing its bottom areas and extending its top.

Alternatively, the draft-to-chord ratio can be kept constant from head to foot, so that it presents the same relative curvature throughout its height; or the same fullness may be carried all the way to the top, so as to get as much power as possible from the unproductive upper part of the sail.

DRAFT CONTROL AND SAIL TRIM

Within limits, the further aft the draft point, the greater the camber that the air at any given windspeed can be persuaded to follow without total separa-tion, the more of the sail will be doing useful work and the greater its drive. Conversely the stronger the wind, the less camber it will tolerate. Just to com-plicate matters, there is a third factor in the equation: both the fullness of the sail and the location of its draft point affect the profile of its all-important

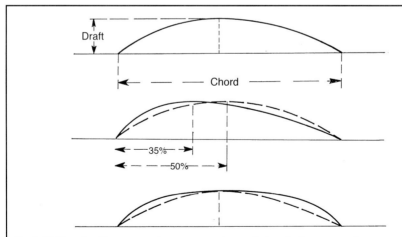

Fig 2.11 *Top*: Draft expressed as a percentage of chord. It can vary from around 10% on a mainsail flattened for strong winds, to as much as 20% for a full headsail in light airs. *Centre*: Draft position. Forward at 35% with a well-rounded luff is easier to helm. Draft aft at 50% gives a finer entry for higher pointing, but is prone to stalling in rough water. *Bottom*: Two sails with the same draft ratio and position. One has a flat entry, the other a fuller luff.

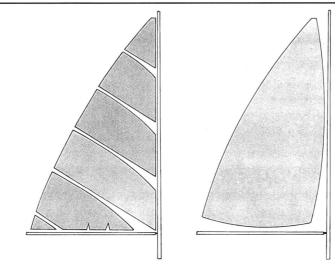

Fig 2.12 Sail shaping by broadseaming and edge rounding. *Left*: One seam of each panel is made convex, so that when it is sewn to its straight-edged neighbour, fullness is forced into the sail. *Right*: This is also achieved by cutting the luff and foot in a convex curve, so that when either is set on a straight spar, the surplus material sags into the body of the sail.

leading edge (Fig 2.11). Opinions differ on the optimum shape. A draft-aft profile tends to produce a sharp, flat entry for the airstream, requiring the sail to be set at a correspondingly small angle of attack and allowing the boat to point high. But such a sail is unforgiving and needs skilful helming in rough seas and blustery winds when pitching and rolling play havoc with the airflow, because the further aft the draft, the rounder the leech and the greater the chances of stalling the sail. A draft-forward shape, on the other hand, with a more coarsely rounded luff, increases lift and reduces drag with a flatter leech section. This sail is less prone to stalling, which is a big advantage in rough water when precise helming becomes difficult, but at the same time it produces increased heeling forces and can soon be overpowered in strong winds.

If no expense is to be spared, the racing yachtsman may have a number of specialist sails to meet these conflicting requirements, whereas general purpose cruising sails are a compromise, typically with the point of maximum draft positioned at around 40% aft of the luff. Their optimum settings for varying wind strengths and sea states can only be found by trial and error, but fortunately draft doesn't require the constant trimming that sheets do, and is often ignored altogether on cruising boats without any serious consequences. Nevertheless optimum performance cannot be achieved without giving it some attention.

Draft is built into a sail using the techniques shown in Fig 2.12. Firstly, the sailmaker cuts one edge of the cloth panels in a convex curve, so that when it is sewn to the straight edge of the adjacent one, a process known as 'broadseaming', fullness is forced into the sail. The depth and location of the draft is determined by the width, length and positioning of these seams, and additional darts may be put in where localised fullness is needed. He also cuts a convex curve into both the luff and the foot of a mainsail, when this is to be fixed along a boom, so that when either is straightened along its supporting spar, the extra material sags into the sail to increase the draft. On a boomless sail, foot curve is simply a means of increasing area.

Headsails have to be treated differently. They are normally cut with little if any broadseaming, because they can so easily be given extra draft by easing the sheet. More importantly, all headstays sag to some extent, even on a stiff mast with a powerful backstay adjuster and despite any amount of mainsheet tension. This pushes extra material into the front of the sail, making it fuller. The stronger the wind, the more the headstay sags and the greater the draft becomes, which is just the opposite of what is wanted for windward working. To help counter this, the luff can be given a *hollow* profile, amounting to slightly less than the anticipated sag, so as to produce sufficient draft to suit the weather conditions – a certain amount of fullness in a light airs genoa, for example, flat as a board for a storm jib. Tightening the halyard decreases the draft and draws it forward. Increasing the backstay tension has a similar effect, straightening the luff and flattening it by pulling some of the sag out of the headstay.

Roller genoas naturally become fuller from the surplus cloth as they are rolled down. So they are cut extremely flat in their forward areas usually with tapered padded luffs, fatter in the middle than in the ends to compensate for this, and their reefing gear should if possible be fitted with independent tack and head swivels to reduce both draft and area simultaneously. At the same time, correct fore-and-aft positioning of the sheet lead block is crucial. Its traveller car needs to be moved progressively forward with every few additional turns of the reefing drum in order to maintain the geometrically correct sheeting angle and roughly equalise the foot and leech tensions. However, as the breeze freshens, the upper part of the leech can be opened so as to spill wind and de-power the sail, and the foot flattened to reduce any back-winding of the main, by shifting the car slightly further aft.

Camber stripes in a contrasting colour, sewn on to the sail and running from luff to leech, help to indicate the depth of the draft and its position. They add interest but are not essential. Telltales certainly are, because they show you with considerable accuracy whether you are pointing even a fraction too high or low. Wool tufts are best, threaded through the sail and knotted either side, and placed about a foot (30 cm) back from the luff at approximately a quarter, half and three-quarters of the way up. It is useful to have an additional set further back, for use when the forward ones are rolled away. If the top telltale breaks before the bottom one, the sheet lead needs to come forward, and vice versa. If the windward woollies start lifting, you are too high and the sail is losing its drive; fall too far off the wind and the leeward ones will begin to flutter as a stall warning. Both sets should be streaming out smoothly at either side of the sail.

The shape of the mainsail, besides affecting its own performance, has a profound influence on that of the headsail, because of the action of the 'slot' between them, and the most powerful control over that shape on a masthead rig is the mainsheet. Besides using it in conjunction with the traveller to adjust the sail's angle to the wind, increasing the sheet tension tightens the leech, reduces twist and improves pointing ability, at the same time decreasing the draft and moving it aft. If hard pressed when beating in windy conditions, the leech should if possible be kept tight by letting the traveller down to leeward, instead of easing the mainsheet. Unfortunately traveller controls are usually much less convenient to handle than the sheet; but by setting the traveller a little way below the centreline, the sheet can be played in a gust without losing too much leech tension, and the boat will continue to point up. Conversely, the traveller can be pulled up to windward in light airs so as to centre the boom, using only light sheet tension in order to *open* the leech and maintain attached airflow.

The kicking strap or vang, as it is increasingly known, provides an alternative means of closing the upper leech by pulling down the boom, particularly useful on boats without a traveller. On a run, with the boom right out, the traveller ceases to have any effect and the vang (or a line temporarily rigged as a preventer) is the only means of restraining it from swinging upwards and allowing the upper leech to twist so far forward that the entire sail becomes unstable and the boat begins to roll with increasing violence. The vang also reduces the mainsheet load, although when this is most needed – in beating to weather in a freshening wind-sheet tension usually makes the vang's contribution minimal. Instead, any further flattening of the mainsail under these conditions is made primarily by increasing its luff tension with the halyard, or alternatively by using a downhaul through an eyelet in the leech, known as

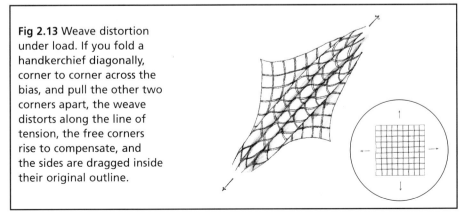

Fig 2.13 Weave distortion under load. If you fold a handkerchief diagonally, corner to corner across the bias, and pull the other two corners apart, the weave distorts along the line of tension, the free corners rise to compensate, and the sides are dragged inside their original outline.

the Cunningham, fitted a short distance above the tack. The draft will have been blown aft by the wind. Distorting the cloth by stretching the luff pulls this draft forward again and reduces its depth, because the cloth has been cut on the bias. (Try this with a handkerchief by folding it diagonally, corner to corner, and holding it by the other two corners (Fig 2.13). As you pull them apart the weave a trough appears along the 'luff' of the handkerchief, and the free corners rise to compensate.)

Unless the sail has to some extent become permanently stretched through maltreatment or years of hard work, use of the Cunningham is only necessary when racing, when the head of the sail will already have been hoisted as far as a black band painted on the mast. Another band is located at the tack, and a third on the boom at the clew. These three mark the legal limits to which a sail may be extended. Exceeding them in a race would provide an unfair advantage by stretching the sail beyond the area prescribed for that class of boat.

To some extent the process of stretching a sail and moving its draft occurs automatically when sailing. As the wind strengthens and increases the tension in the sheet, the resulting loads are less in the middle and frontal areas of the sail, so these stretch less than the leech and the draft returns forward – which is exactly what is required. Draft can also be varied by tensioning the foot with the outhaul. Slackening it moves the draft forward and increases it without affecting the leech to any extent. The effect of this is necessarily confined to the lower part of the sail, but since this is where most of its power comes from, the outhaul provides a convenient secondary means of camber control. It is even more effective if the sail is provided with a 'shelf foot', which is an extra panel of cloth sewn into the bottom of the mainsail. This allows the sail to move away from the boom when the outhaul is eased, adding local draft, and to fold up as the outhaul is tensioned. Another way is to pull down a small 'flattening reef' with a cringle a little way up the leech. As with the headsail, telltales are essential to monitor the behaviour of the main, in this case being placed along the leech and preferably between the battens, so as to avoid any stitching on which they might snag. As long as all these telltales can be kept streaming, the tighter the leech can be and the better the boat will point, for it's the aftermost part of the mainsail that has the greatest effect on windward performance. Tighter, but not 'hooked' through ever-zealous tightening of the leech line. If a leech is fluttering, the leech line should be tightened only just enough to stop it and no more. And try to remember to let it out again when the wind lightens. For if it is never eased, the sailcloth inside the tabling is liable to stretch slightly, causing the permanent hook from which old sails so often suffer. In the case of a fluttering headsail leech, first check whether you can stop it by adjusting the sheet lead, and hence the leech tension, before tweaking the leech line.

To sum up, the general rule is to strap everything in tight and flatten the sails when it's blowing hard, ease the tensions to give them more fullness and twist in lower windspeeds, or for some extra drive in choppy water, and tighten up a little in a very light breeze because the slow moving air is liable to break away from a heavily cambered sail.

All these techniques of draft adjustment rely to a large extent on stretching the woven fabric from which most cruising sails are made. Nevertheless this lack of stability is the sail designer's worst enemy, because it makes it impossible for him to forecast the precise shape that any sail will assume under the varying conditions of wind and sea. This is why on racing boats where it is essential, despite the high stresses, that the sails should hold their designed shape with the minimum of distortion, woven cloths are replaced by various types of hard laminate. These sails are not only many times stronger, lighter (and more expensive), but are so stable and unyielding, with virtually no stretch at all, that the only way of varying their draft is to bend the spars that support them. They are also somewhat stiff and awkward to handle, and don't stand up well to repeated folding, flexing and flogging. For luxury cruising boats, the latest high-tech laminates combine strength and low weight with the ability to stretch, allowing the sails to be trimmed in the normal way. Being at the same time softer and more flexible, they are more convenient to handle and very much more durable than the hard laminates. But unfortunately they are even more costly.

BENDY SPARS

The usual preference for an offshore cruising boat, and others where performance is less important than ruggedness and simplicity, is a straightforward masthead rig (Fig 2.14), comprising a stiff large-diameter mast, with triangulated lower shrouds and its head held between the headstay and backstay, making it more or less bullet-proof. That is to say, if the aft lower chainplates are located behind the mast, with the forward lowers and/or a babystay (inner forestay) ahead of it, it is effectively prevented from moving around.

All masts, even those with the generous sections used on masthead rigs, are best set up with a slight amount of forwards pre-bend – say an inch in 20 ft, or 2 cm in 5 m on a stiff spar – because this will be pulled out when the mainsail is reefed with its head below the hounds where the spreaders or the lower shrouds meet the mast. This then leaves a virtually straight mast, which is what is wanted in heavy weather to resist 'pumping' and to avoid its being pulled out of column so that it bows aft, increasing the fullness of the sail just when it is least needed.

For all the merits of a stiff, masthead rig, when it comes to tuning, bendy spars provide a much greater degree of control over mainsail shape. They are fitted on the majority of fractionally rigged boats, in which the headstay is attached to the mast some three-quarters to seven-eighths of the way up, so

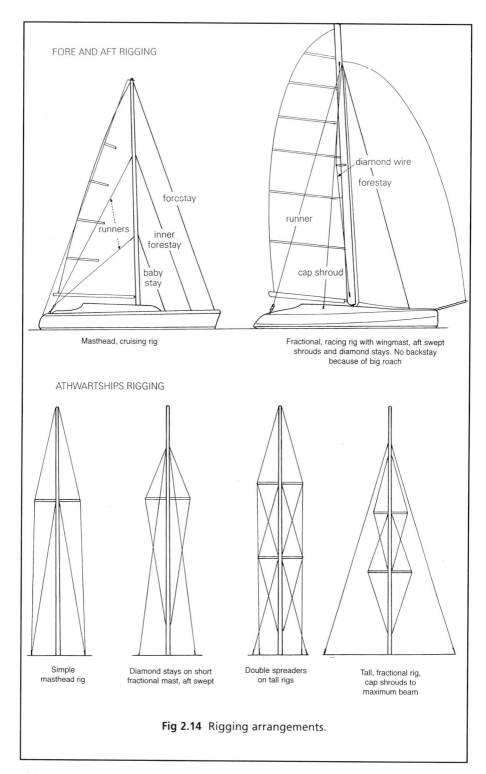

FORE AND AFT RIGGING

forestay

runners

inner
forestay

baby
stay

Masthead, cruising rig

diamond wire

forestay

runner

cap shroud

Fractional, racing rig with wingmast, aft swept
shrouds and diamond stays. No backstay
because of big roach

ATHWARTSHIPS RIGGING

Simple
masthead rig

Diamond stays on short
fractional mast, aft swept

Double spreaders
on tall rigs

Tall, fractional rig,
cap shrouds to
maximum beam

Fig 2.14 Rigging arrangements.

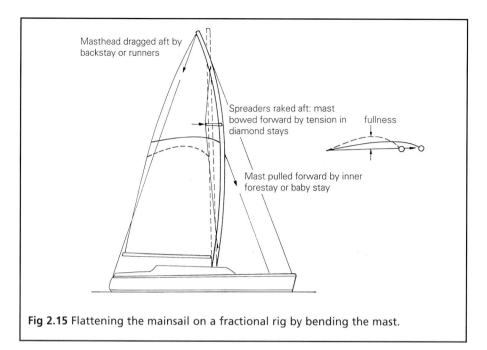

Fig 2.15 Flattening the mainsail on a fractional rig by bending the mast.

that its unsupported top can be sprung aft by an adjustable backstay (Fig 2.15). This makes it bow forwards in the middle, pulling the luff of the mainsail with it, absorbing the luff round and flattening the sail for heavy weather sailing. Drawing it away from the leech of the headsail also widens the slot between them, and allows more air to pass through it as the strength of the wind increases. In strong winds, however, avoiding excessive sag in a fractional headsail has to depend, to a considerable extent, on maintaining sufficient tension in the mainsail leech since this runs up to the masthead by appropriate use of the traveller. Dumping the traveller on a fractional rig also quickly depowers a larger proportion of the total sail area than it would on a masthead boat.

There are a number of other ways of bending a mast, some of them not so straightforward. For example, when the sail is considered too full or too flat for the anticipated weather and the mast is keel-stepped, the bending can be done at the dockside by blocking the mast backwards or forwards at deck level, or on a dinghy by using an adjustable chock. On some boats the babystay can be tensioned with an adjuster to pull the middle of the mast forward. Alternatively, angling the top spreaders forward reduces the bend at the top of the mast as it forces the shrouds out of line; angling them aft increases it. Some high-tech racers can even swing their spreaders fore-and-aft plane with hydraulic rams. On a rotating mast the diamond stays can be arranged to face slightly aft, so that they automatically bend the mast whenever it is turned either side of centre. The same principle can be applied to a rotating wing mast by giving it a curved trailing edge, which drags the draft out of the sail as it is swivelled.

The mainsail on a masthead rig can similarly be flattened by bending the mast, though not to the same extent. In this case, the luff is given rather more curvature than would be needed for a stiff mast, and bend is introduced either by tensioning the babystay, or by simultaneously tightening the backstay and easing the aft lower shrouds. On most taller masthead rigs, additional running (adjustable) backstays, known as 'runners', are needed to support the middle of the mast and prevent the jib luff from sagging as the mast is bowed by the standing backstay, being set up to windward and released on the lee side each time the boat is tacked or gybed, with the aid of tackles or Highfield (over-centre) levers. Masthead runners are of course essential to the security of the mast on any large, gaff-rigged boat, because the only alternative, a standing backstay, would foul the yard. On a fractional rig, runners (known in this case as checkstays) can be fitted to directly oppose the forestay loads and control mid-mast bend. Another way of flattening the mainsail is by bending the middle of the boom downwards with a powerful vang, but this needs to be used very judiciously, since it flattens only the lower part of the sail; it also tends to cock up the aft end of the boom and let the leech go slack.

Whatever the method of bending, the luff round should be cut to match the maximum mast curvature and the way this is distributed if the two are to work well together. Too much luff round and the mast won't be able to take in the slack to flatten the sail sufficiently; too little, and the amount of mast bend will be prematurely limited by the tension in the cloth. It has to be nicely judged, since mainsail shape can be altered by a mast bend of as little as 2 cm on a 9 m luff, and pro rata on taller ones.

Unless it is restrained by shrouds and spreaders, a mast will also bend sideways. This acts as an effective safety valve on a fractional rig, because as the top of the mast sags away to leeward in heavy weather, it spills wind from the head of the sail and reduces the heeling force. The tensioning of the shrouds and the length of the spreaders control the sideways bend lower down. Nevertheless a certain amount of lateral movement takes place whenever the mast is bent longitudinally, because this also forces it slightly to windward. In doing so, however, it quite fortuitously opens the slot still further as the wind freshens.

Despite the variety and scope of these various forms of control, it needs shrewd judgement by the sailmaker to ensure that he not only meets the basic design requirements in terms of static dimensions and draft, but correctly anticipates the shape that any particular sail may take under its specified range of operating conditions, and allows for any personal preferences the owner may have and the type of sailing he intends to do.

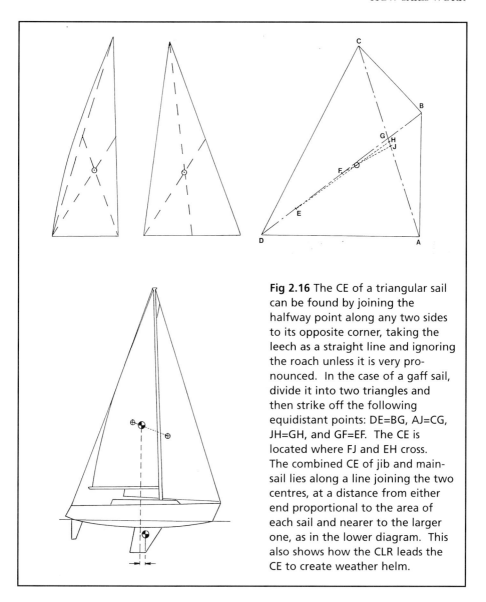

Fig 2.16 The CE of a triangular sail can be found by joining the halfway point along any two sides to its opposite corner, taking the leech as a straight line and ignoring the roach unless it is very pronounced. In the case of a gaff sail, divide it into two triangles and then strike off the following equidistant points: DE=BG, AJ=CG, JH=GH, and GF=EF. The CE is located where FJ and EH cross. The combined CE of jib and mainsail lies along a line joining the two centres, at a distance from either end proportional to the area of each sail and nearer to the larger one, as in the lower diagram. This also shows how the CLR leads the CE to create weather helm.

HELM BALANCE

Up to now, we have only been concerned with the forces generated by the rig. Before we leave the subject of how sails work, this is a good place to consider the effects of helm balance, since it is related to the way in which the sails should be trimmed, as well as to the design of the boat.

Balance is the ability to sail a steady course without having to apply helm. It is dependent on the delicate inter-relationship between the sideways force of the rig, and the lifting force and resistance to leeway generated by the keel and underbody of the hull. The mechanics of it may seem straightforward at first sight. But any imbalance has such a profound effect on a boat's behaviour and the quality of its handling, that it merits a clear understanding of how it is caused and why it can vary with the sailing conditions.

The centre of effort (CE) of a sail is the theoretical point at which the wind forces are assumed to be centred, and the CE of the complete rig is determined by proportioning its position according to the individual sail areas. Fig 2.16 explains the geometry, simple enough for triangular sails, but requiring a little more work on four-sided ones. Perfect balance occurs when the CE lies directly above the hull's centre of lateral resistance (CLR), which is the fore-and-aft centre of all its immersed parts, including the keel and rudder. This centre can be found by cutting out the underwater profile in cardboard and balancing it on a knife edge. If the CE falls behind the CLR, the resultant leverage would try to turn the boat to windward and would have to be trimmed out with the rudder. The boat would then be said to be carrying *weather helm*. Conversely, if the CLR lies ahead of the CE, which would force the bows away from wind, the boat would be carrying *lee helm*, and would have to be steered up to windward in order to maintain course. With the two centres aligned, the boat would be precisely balanced and would maintain course with the helm left free – provided that it remained upright, and with flat sails.

In practice, both the CE and the CLR are apt to wander about. The position of the CE varies constantly with the apparent windspeed, sail camber and angle of attack, while the CLR moves if the crew shifts its weight around, or if the centreboard is raised or lowered. It also occurs whenever the boat heels to the wind, causing the waterline shape to become asymmetric, with a bulge on its lee side which is almost always forward of amidships on a sailing hull. Consequently this side develops more lift than the other, upsetting the hydrodynamic balance, shifting the CLR forward and making the boat want to round up into the wind. This lopsidedness is worst on a beamy modern hull with a flattish bottom, hard bilges and a broad transom which levers the stern upwards and tries to bury the bows as the boat heels. A deep, traditionally shaped hull with slack bilges, and whose beam is distributed more evenly fore-and-aft, doesn't suffer to the same extent.

More importantly, heeling also displaces the CE to one side of the centreline, moving the rig's aerodynamic thrust out to leeward of the CLR and creating a powerful turning moment, proportional to the distance between the two centres, that magnifies any existing weather helm. The effect is therefore greatest when close-hauled, decreasing with the angle of heel as the boat is brought on to a reach, returning as the boom is squared off on a run, even while the boat is upright, and increasing still further as it rolls to leeward, until eventually it may broach on to its beam ends, slewing broadside to wind and sea.

The vang can play an important part in minimising weather helm. Holding down the boom as tightly as possible on a run stabilises the sail and reduces this tendency to roll. Similarly, tensioning the vang on a reach reduces weather helm by allowing the boom to be eased out, reducing twist and keeping the upper part of the sail drawing. Except in the case of a loose-footed mainsail, and assuming a powerful vang and even slightly bendy spars, the same effect can be achieved when beating by first bringing the boat head to wind and hardening the mainsheet as much as possible and then strapping down the vang. This flattens the sail by bending the mast and boom, straightening the leech and allowing the mainsheet traveller to be eased down the track to leeward.

Matters are somewhat different for a multihull. With such a small angle of heel and very narrow hulls, there is virtually no distortion of the waterline and much less leeward movement of the CE. But as the displacement transfers across from the weather float of a catamaran (or from the main hull of a trimaran) to the leeward float, so too does the CLR, with a resultant turning moment *away* from the wind.

Weather helm on any boat can be neutralised by positioning the static CE a certain distance ahead of the CLR, but a perfectly balanced helm has a nervous feel about it, because with constantly changing conditions it can seldom remain neutral for long, and the boat is unable to hold a steady course without continual helm corrections. Lee helm is equally undesirable, for although it is often unavoidable at very low speeds in light airs, when fortunately it is so slight as not to matter very much, it is potentially dangerous in a breeze because of the tendency to bear away the moment the helmsman takes his hand off the tiller and to end up in a spectacular gybe. Instead, the designer aims at a gentle touch of weather helm – ideally about four or five degrees when beating into a force 4 – by locating the static CE some 10–15% of the waterline length ahead of the CLR, so that it moves slightly aft of it while sailing. (The actual amount of 'lead' required varies with the hull configuration and the type of rig: rather more for a sloop, for example, much less for a schooner, less still for a multihull, depending on its overall beam.) The object is to give a light, responsive feel to the tiller, reassuringly firm without its becoming tiringly heavy, always a sure sign of excessive weather helm, with the boat hard-mouthed and forever trying to skew up into the wind.

Most boats feel pleasantly balanced with the rudder angled somewhere between two and five degrees to weather, steering away from the wind. This brings with it two further benefits that outweigh the small amount of drag it causes. It allows the rudder to develop some lift of its own, adding to that of the keel and helping to counteract leeway; and in the manner of a mainsail improving the flow on the lee side of a headsail, the angled rudder increases the upwash to the keel and the lift it develops. Both processes are, of course, reversed if lee helm is present. Imbalance, usually in the form of excessive weather helm, can sometimes be the fault of the designer or boatbuilder, or the sailmaker. It takes experience, shrewd judgement and a certain amount of luck – or the intelligent use of a CAD computer program – to strike the right balance first time. Getting it wrong can spoil a good boat. More often than not, however, the problem is caused by ill-advised modifications to the rig or the keel after the boat was built; carrying ballast or stowing heavy items of equipment in the wrong place; or because the mainsail leech is hooked with an over-tightened leechline, or has been badly cut.

The static lead of CE over CLR can be increased and weather helm reduced by plumbing the mast upright or raking it forward, or even moving it bodily; by lengthening the bowsprit if the boat has one; moving the centreboard or extending the keel aft; fitting a smaller or flatter mainsail, or a larger, more powerful headsail; shrinking the mizzen or possibly removing it altogether; or by moving the ballast and other heavy gear further aft. Such remedies would normally be carried out when the boat is ashore or docked, but the crew can correct weather helm at any time out on the water. They have the option of reefing the main or flattening it by tightening the luff; reducing its twist by moving the traveller to leeward and hardening the mainsheet, or by easing the mainsheet and pulling down the boom with the vang. Alternatively they can increase the area of the headsail by unrolling it or exchanging it for a larger one, or drag the headsail sheet slightly to weather with a barber hauler. Either forces the bow off the wind, until pressure on the mainsail starts to increase and push the bow upwind again. A big overlapping genoa which is bellying too much and trying to luff the boat because its leech is aft of the axis of rotation, can be tamed by moving its sheet lead aft so as to open the leech and spill wind without losing too much drive. A mizzen, being right at the end of the boat, provides the helmsman with an even more effective means of controlling it. If he wants to bear away, he can simply release the sheet and allow the boat to head off.

These and the many other variables we have been looking at determine the overall three-dimensional shape of the sails and the way a boat behaves. They are the true mechanisms that control its performance. Only by understanding the role played by each of them can the sailmaker, amateur or professional, be sure of producing good sails, and only by appreciating how those sails really work and the inter-relationship between their controls can a sailor ever hope to get the best out of them. The cruising skipper may be inclined to leave all that trimming and tweaking to the racing fraternity, but as well as giving him a more responsive and better balanced boat, the extra half knot can take an hour off a 60 mile passage and might enable him to catch a favourable tide, or reach port before the weather closes in. While there's enormous pleasure and satisfaction in simply sailing a boat, the real joy comes from being able to exploit its potential to the full.

CHAPTER 3

Rig Configurations and Features

One particularly fascinating aspect of sail is the variety of forms that it can take, and the ways in which these can affect the performance of a vessel. Visiting a boat show or looking around a crowded anchorage, the diversity of shapes and sizes of the sailing craft is plain to see, the scattering of ancients among the modern, a fascinating mix of venerable classics and contemporary reproductions with state-of-the-art masterpieces, the elegant and the ordinary. No two are quite the same. Even the production line look-alikes can reflect their owner's taste in rigs and gear.

The easiest way to describe a sailing boat, apart from size, is by her rig. This defines, in a word or two, the arrangement of her sails and spars – as distinct from the rigging, meaning the multiplicity of wires, ropes and fittings that support and control the rig, or her sailplan which describes the shape and precise dimensions of each sail.

Before setting out to buy or build a boat or to make sails for it, or simply to modify an existing sailplan, it is worth taking a look at the range of rigs that can be applied to small craft, many of them as well suited to dinghies and open dayboats as to full sized cruising and racing yachts. For on the choice of rig and some understanding of its characteristics will depend the behaviour of the boat and the amount of pleasure (or otherwise) that it can give its crew.

Generally speaking, a rig is best classified by the number and positioning of the masts. A boat with a single mast stepped near the bows and setting no headsail is said to be una-rigged (one mast/one sail/one halyard/one sheet), or is known in America as a *catboat* (not to be confused with a cat, as in catamaran). A *sloop* has its mast further from the bows, leaving room for a headsail; two or more working headsails turn the sloop into a *cutter* (in American terminology, a double-headed sloop, a cutter having a bowsprit and its mast stepped nearer amidships). With two masts, the after one (mizzen) shorter than the mainmast, the vessel is either a *ketch* or a *yawl*, depending on the relative proportions of her main and mizzen sails. A ketch's mizzen may be as much as half the size of the mainsail, sometimes almost equalling it in size, whereas the yawl's will usually amount to a quarter or less. A schooner – of the size we are concerned with – also has two masts, but her foremast is the shorter of the two, the taller one aft being the mainmast.

Each of these configurations has, as you can imagine, a considerable number of variants according to the type of spars and the sails they carry. The permutations are almost endless, so this review can only examine a selection of the best known combinations, and limit it to the size of boat that might concern the average family sailor – from dinghies up to, let's say, a maximum of around 40–45 ft (12–14 m), together with a few of the less orthodox layouts. It is also confined to triangular or four-sided sails set fore-and-aft, squaresails having for the most part become no more than a rare historic or eccentric oddity, despite their undisputed downwind pulling power. The rigs that follow have been chosen to illustrate as wide a range of features as possible, so that by interchanging these between one example and another, most configurations of small sailing craft can be represented.

While their leading characteristics are for the most part accepted as fact, every form of rig has its enthusiastic following, along with its critics and, as you might expect, opinion on the respective merits of each is often divided. There is no *best* rig. There is only the rig that any particular sailor likes best and can, if need be, handle under all conditions without assistance. Efficiency and performance are important design parameters, but they should to some extent be regarded as relative. Just how far their theoretical limits can be approached depends as much on what the sailor wants to get out of his boat and the way he uses her, as from his skill and experience with any particular rig, and his familiarity with its quirks and characteristics. 'Experience starts', someone once said, 'as soon as you begin.' Nevertheless there are nearly always 'horses for courses', with one rig proving consistently more successful than the others. The views expressed here are those of the author and the majority of the enthusiasts he has sailed with or spoken to, but it is in the nature of boating that such topics will always have their controversial aspects. On the other hand, how dull our life would be if there was nothing to choose between one form of rig and another.

DIPPING LUG

Sails for an open boat need a low centre of effort so as not to heel it unduly, and they should be capable of being lowered away and secured in a matter of seconds when a squall is approaching, whereas reefing on a larger craft can be a little more leisurely. Small lugsails are easily handled, their spars are short enough to stow in the boat, they can be made of cheap materials and they are not difficult for an amateur to cut and sew up. Despite their seeming simplicity, however, they can be made to set and perform surprisingly well, on account of their quadrilateral shape and scope for adjustment.

A lugsail is a fore-and-aft sail whose head is carried on an inclined yard, with a small part of it extending forward of the mast. In its various forms it pro-liferated throughout the 1800s in working vessels up and down the North Sea coasts of Britain and France. It continued to be widely used by fishermen and others such as lifeboatmen and pilots until engines became available during the 20th centu-ry and will long remain a popu-lar choice for dinghies and small

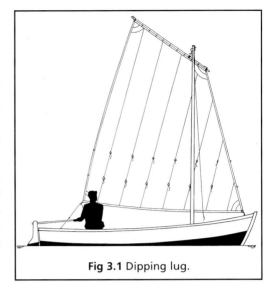

Fig 3.1 Dipping lug.

pleasure craft where low cost and simplicity are considered more important than performance. There are several types, including the dipping lug, stand-ing lug, balance lug, and their variants. One of these is the gunter rig, which is closely related to the balance lug and equally well suited to small boats, but its yard is tilted to such an angle that the sail is almost triangular; and there's the Chinese lug, arguably the ancestor of them all and better known as the junk. Both will be discussed later in the chapter.

The dipping lug, which is in effect a squaresail swung fore-and-aft and peaked up, is by far the most powerful of these, and arguably better than all others – certainly when compared with any based on such primitive technol-ogy – for driving to windward *in a straight line*, on account of its lee side being clean and uncluttered by a mast. The sail is boomless, with its upper edge laced to a yard extending ahead of an unstayed mast and its tack hooked down near the stemhead. Both yard and sail are set to leeward of the mast, held to it by a loose parrel and suspended by the halyard. As depicted here on a cat-rigged boat, the sail has been cut 'up-and-down' in the old fashioned way for the sake of appearance, with the cloths laid parallel to the leech, and hence with no roach and no need for battens to support it. It can present a corrugated or 'washboard' surface to the wind, to the detriment of flow, and is prone to stretch more than a conventional cross-cut, but on a naturally baggy rig such as this, neither matters much. It is certainly a most effective 'lifting' sail off the wind, especially when running, bellying upwards to heave the bows over the wavetops. It is also surprisingly efficient, not only because its luff is held well clear of the disturbed airflow from the mast, but because it is kept taut by the leverage of the after part of the yard. For this reason, the luff should not be too long in relation to the yard. Although the tension can be increased by moving the halyard attachment point forward, the strength and hence the weight of the yard normally limits the sail to a comparatively low, broad shape. (A high aspect ratio, with still greater efficiency, can be achieved by using carbon fibre spars, but their cost is at odds with the concept of a cheap and simple rig.)

A boomless sail must have a shorter foot than a boomed one, so that the sheet can roughly split the angle between foot and leech and tension the sail in the right direction. In common with other boomless rigs when running downwind, the clew cannot be held out to make the best of the available sail area, except with a whisker pole (or a boathook), but it has the advantage of having no spar to catch the waves to leeward, gybing is painless, and its lighter weight results in an easier motion in a seaway and less tendency to roll in a calm. Upwind, the optimum close-hauled sheeting angle is largely a matter of trial and error. The sheet needs to run via some form of traveller from a point well out from the centreline. This avoids excessive twist as well as a corresponding loss of tension on the luff; but too vertical a sheet lead only overtightens the leech and spoils the flow over the sail, to the detriment of pointing ability. In order to resolve the conflict between the tiller and the mainsheet, the latter is led through a block which travels on a rope 'horse' rigged athwartships above the tiller. Slackening the horse centres the sheet and tightening it lets the traveller run down to leeward.

Another feature of boomless sails is that they tend to carry considerable weather helm, much of their driving force being transmitted through the sheet which tries to drag the stern to leeward and skew the bows up into the wind. This can to some extent be mitigated on a dipping lug by hauling the tack out to the weather rail and bringing the clew inboard. Broad reaching or on a run, with the sheet run out and the tack brought back abreast of the mast, the rig becomes utterly docile, even when gybing.

It is when coming about that the one major disadvantage of the rig becomes apparent: the entire assembly has to be 'dipped', that is to say dropped to the deck, manhandled round the mast and rehoisted on the other side while the boat is in stays. This is hard and potentially hazardous work in heavy weather or in the dark, besides losing time on every tack to most other rigs that swing across by themselves. What's more the yard, perhaps carrying a load of wet sail, naturally capsizes and swings down with considerable force as soon as the halyard, which is attached well forward of its centre, is eased. The same happens when reefing. There is the further risk of being taken aback in a sudden squally windshift, when the pressure of the sail against the mast will make it almost impossible to lower and about the only way of avoiding certain capsize in an open boat is to change tacks, assuming there is sufficient sea room, by wearing ship. Although still a popular rig for small dayboats and replica fishing luggers, it demands some skilful seamanship.

STANDING LUG

The important difference between this and the dipping lug from which it evolved is that the tack of the sail has been brought back to the mast and remains hooked to the deck, using a lanyard or downhaul tackle to peak the yard and tension the luff for working to windward. It is not as powerful as the dipping lug, despite usually being cut with a higher peak to improve windward ability, because the sail stands closer to the mast which upsets the airflow. The high peak also narrows the spread of sail downwind, and doesn't lift the bows in the same way as the dipping lug, although it helps to rake the mast forward, supporting it against the pull of the sheet by running the halyard forward and through a block at the stemhead. But the standing lug is much simpler and safer to handle, especially with a small crew, because only the yard need be dipped around the mast when tacking, using a tripping line leading from the heel of the yard to the helmsman. Some versions project such a small area of sail ahead of their masts that there is hardly any need to dip at all, with only a slight loss of efficiency while the sail is on the 'wrong' side of the mast. Ideally suited to small pleasure boating, it's the rig that many of us met for the first time in Arthur Ransome's *Swallows and Amazons*.

The rig often includes a boom to hold out the clew, pivoted at its forward end on a gooseneck or jaws at the mast, which improves the downwind shape and performance of the sail. It also reduces a catboat's inherent weather helm, by transmitting the thrust of the sail through the mast instead of along the line of the sheet, and it makes it easier to get a good sheet lead. The boomless sail shown here needs to be sheeted more closely than one with a boom, with much less difference between the amount of sheet when close-hauled or sailing free. Its foot should be kept well inboard, even on a run, or the gaff will twist around and may end up ahead of the mast, resulting in a rhythmic rolling motion than can build up and lead to capsize. Nevertheless the boomless rig was always preferred by fishermen and for the majority of working boats, because it was easy to stow; and when coming alongside, or if the wind dropped, the deck could be kept clear for rowing by gathering the sail up against

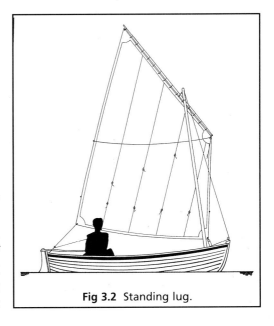

Fig 3.2 Standing lug.

the mast with a brailing line from the heel of the yard. It has the further advantage in a small boat of being easily manhandled and taking up less space; and it is certainly kinder to the heads of the crew.

Compared with a gaff sail, which the standing lug closely resembles, all-round performance is at least as good, its gear is simpler and can readily be detached from the mast, and its spars are short enough to be stowed inside the boat. But the long yard needed for a high peak tends to be top-heavy and can quickly get out of control while being set, reefed, or handed, because it swings over and the peak hangs down as soon as the halyard is released, and vice versa when starting to hoist, so an energetic and well judged procedure is needed, especially in heavy weather. For this reason, a standing lug is commonly fitted with an additional reefing halyard running on a wire span along the yard, so that it can be lowered to stand in line with the mast, the sail being made with a diagonal set of reef points. As a further safeguard, a parrel may be fitted to hold the heel of the yard loosely into the mast. It is clipped on with a snapshackle as soon as the rig is lifted off the deck and peaked up, and prevents the yard from thrashing around until the halyard is swigged up and secured.

BALANCE LUG

Working boatmen never favoured the balance lug because its long, low boom always seemed to get in the way of whatever they were doing, especially on the foredeck. But almost from its inception – it was developed from the Chinese lug (the junk rig) by a Thames boatbuilder round about 1870 – it became popular for small pleasure craft, and many people still rate it the best of all rigs for a simple, knockabout dinghy.

Like the junk, with which it shares many of its virtues, it is geometrically stable (though not in quite the same way) because of the all-important balance area of sail set forward of the mast, and amounting to some 15% of the total. With the yard hauled to the masthead, the sail is set by bowsing down the boom beside the mast with a tackle or lanyards. This keeps the luff tight and the yard well peaked up for windward working, with the leech and luff tensioned in balance against one another. The mast on a small boat rigged in this way, such as the dinghy in Fig 3.3, is sturdy enough to stand without shrouds. But you have to be careful not to pay the sheet out too far, because if you should get caught by a gust and let the sail gybe ahead of the mast, you can find yourself in real trouble which will be difficult to sort out if there is any weight in the wind and the gunwale dips under.

The sail, which is set flat regardless of weather conditions, needs no adjustment from one point of sailing to the next, and is conveniently docile when left to weathercock in the wind. On the other hand, its flat and rigid stance provides little or no lifting effect on the bows. When running before, it won't belly out; but the aft end of the boom cannot lift, reducing rolling and the risk of an accidental gybe, because the taut luff prevents the fore end from going down. (To do so, the entire rig would have to swing fore-and-aft, which it can't, being held at top and bottom to the mast.) It follows that no vang is necessary. And while gybing, even all-standing, the air cushion that forms behind the balance area slows the swing of the boom and absorbs the shock at the end of its travel. Another effect of this aerodynamic balancing act is to reduce the load on the sheet, which in a

Fig 3.3 Balance lug.

dinghy is so light that it is often run straight to the boom, with no block to flail about unpredictably when tacking or gybing. (It is shown here with a single whip tackle in order to provide a better lead, with its standing end running on a horse straddling the tiller.) Nor is the sail dipped when tacking, remaining on the same side of the mast – usually to port – with the fall of the halyard led down the starboard side. But should the luff be accidentally allowed to go slack and the boom to rise, the lifting characteristic can start to take over. The sail then kites up, windward heel develops, and you can easily lose control of the boat.

All in all, however, it is an effortless rig to handle. In good weather, and provided that the foot and head have been firmly laced to their respective spars, it presents a better driving shape than a standing lug, though neither rig can be said to be particularly close-winded. In light airs and for best performance off the wind, there's a lot to be said for setting the sail loose-footed so as to increase the draft in its lower regions.

In the event of missing stays while going about, the foot may be pushed out to leeward. This will stop the boat, but it usually gets the head round, the sheet then being eased to allow her to gather way on the new tack. In squally conditions, however, the rig is not so easy to handle. Its inherent balance can result in excessive rolling when running in strong winds, its rigidity throws undue strain on the mast, and in a heavy gust the long boom is apt to end up in the water and liable to trip the boat. When it becomes necessary to reduce sail, this one cannot be brailed up because of the boom, and reefing when it's rough is usually best done with the yard down on the deck. Then by bringing the reefed clew back to the after end of the boom and slipping the boom through the clove hitch which should be used to secure the downhaul, so that it leaves the other end projecting ahead of the tack, not only is the boom effectively shortened in the process, but unlike some rigs, the centre of effort of the sail stays close to where it was before it was reefed.

LATEEN

Generally considered the most graceful of all rigs, the lateen has been sailing the Mediterranean and Indian Ocean for a thousand years and more. In yachting form, it was a familiar sight on the Norfolk Broads during the 19th century, and there has been a recent revival of interest in the lateen for day-boats and dinghies.

Lightweight, at least in the smaller sizes, simple and efficiently shaped, the sail is traditionally boomless, its long luff laced to an equally lengthy and slender yard which runs right down to the tack. The yard is secured by a line through a block near the stemhead and is slung at about a third of its length from a short and stumpy, free-standing mast. This is usually raked forward to offset the thrust of the sail, and in heavy weather is stayed by setting up the halyard to windward.

It is easier with this rig to get the sheeting angle right than with any other boomless sail, using two sheets as with a jib, one through each quarter block. No adjustments are needed when tacking, but when coming off the wind, tack line and either one or both sheets are eased, enabling the heel of the yard to swing out and bring the clew forward and inboard. This process is continued as the wind draws further aft, with the heel of the yard being allowed to rise and the peak to drop until on a run, and depending on the proportions of the rig, it may be flown almost horizontally with the clew clipping the wavetops as the boat rolls.

The downwind driving power of the lateen is legendary, but its gigantic spar takes a lot of controlling under these conditions and is

Fig 3.4 Lateen.

only too easy to gybe, with immediate capsize almost inevitable. An additional line can be rigged to the peak to control the twist in the sail. Another worthwhile refinement, which most working boatmen don't bother with, is to rig a pair of moveable guys to the heel of the yard, so as to be able to adjust its vertical angle and position it more accurately athwartships to suit the different points of sailing. A good alternative is just to run a single guy back to the mast, so that the tack simply pivots round it without any adjustment being necessary.

A lateen will draw rather better on the lee side of the mast than to windward of it, as is the case with most standing lugs, but on a small boat the difference is usually fairly small and for a short tack it is seldom worth the trouble of dipping, which involves hauling the heel of the yard round the mast while the sail flogs furiously. This is impractical on larger vessels, such as the Arab trading dhows, which instead are tacked by 'wearing ship' – gybing round on to the new course.

The yard is sufficiently flexible to bend as the breeze freshens, effectively flattening the sail and reducing its power, and at the same time spilling wind off the peak and lessening the load on the rig. When it becomes necessary to reduce sail, it can either be partially brailed up to the yard, which unfortunately leaves a heavy bundle of cloth to catch the wind high up above the deck where it is least wanted. Alternatively, the sheet may be moved to a cringle further up the leech and the tack line eased to lower the yard proportionately, the reef points being tied in as indicated in the drawing; or the sail can be exchanged for a smaller one, which is what most fishermen do.

In a little known variant of the lateen, the yard terminates some distance above the tack, leaving a short length of free luff which considerably improves the airflow over the sail. Called a settee rig, it is an interesting cross between the lateen and a dipping lug, still needing the former's guys to best control the angle and swing of the yard, but as fast to windward as the latter, and with no need to dip when tacking.

SPRIT RIG

One of the best known examples is the tiny Optimist dinghy on which so many thousands of children have learned to sail. It is a versatile rig, cheap and easy to build, and a good choice for little boats, especially those too small to need reefing. In its various forms, the sprit rig survived on working craft in India and South East Asia until motors became widely available after World War II; but its origins go back to ancient times, and the Mediterranean lateen from which it is descended. Fishermen there must have discovered, by cutting off the forepart of the lateen's enormous yard and hanging the remainder of it from a point further down the mast (using a short rope strop, termed a 'snotter', running under its heel), the resulting quadrilateral sail was far easier to handle and could quickly be brailed up to its own head and into the

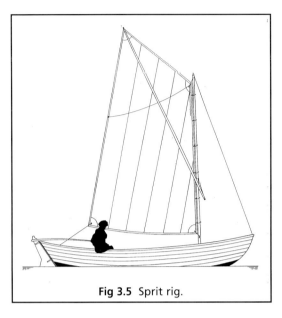

Fig 3.5 Sprit rig.

mast in a squall. The 16th century Dutch, finding it particularly suited to their boisterous North Sea waters, were the first to introduce it into Europe and Scandinavia, and some 100 years later to America, where it became the most widely used of all small boat rigs.

In shape the sail is similar to that of a gaff rig, but more efficient. With the 'sprit' that gives it its name running diagonally up to the peak, the top of the sail has no eddy-making spar ahead of it, none of its area is wasted in a narrow top triangle, and there is less tendency for it to heel the boat because its compact shape results in a lower centre of effort. On small open boats and dinghies it is a delightfully simple rig to work, with the further advantage of very short spars that can be stowed at the sides of the boat, out of the way of the oarsman. Bringing up or coming alongside, or to row the boat, you just let go the sheet and haul on the brailing line. To start sailing again, cast off the brail and sheet in. To run downwind on to a beach, free the sheet and let the sail stream ahead like a flag. As on the lateen, this boat's mainsheet is double-ended, spanning the tiller and running through a turning block at each quarter, enabling it to be handled from either side.

Most spritsails are boomless, so a wide stern is needed to offer sufficient base for a reasonable sheeting angle, and they tend to make a boat roll in a fresh following breeze. This is exaggerated by the swinging of the sprit, and because the boat is pulled along by the sheet instead of being driven by the thrust of the boom against the mast, boomless sails are also liable to generate considerable weather helm. Setting the sail – preferably loose-footed – on a boom not only improves these matters but holds the sail down when it is swung out downwind, and provides the means of adjusting its shape and reefing it. But the convenience of a simple brailing line to reduce sail or to stow it away is then lost, and if the boat is at all tender the boom may dip in the water, especially if it is a long one.

Scale works against the sprit rig too, because the yard itself starts to get unwieldy on any sail larger than 100 sq ft (9 sq m) or so, let alone on really big vessels such as the famous old 80 ft (25 m) Thames barges. On a boat of that size, the slender sprit has become an awesome great beast, so heavy that the snotter has to be made of wire or even chain in order to avoid stretching which would allow the peak of the sail to sag. Its centre needs the support of a lift to the masthead, with another to the peak, and a pair of vangs, one to either quarter. The windward one is set up to reduce twist in the sail as the sprit sags away to leeward, while both can be tensioned to steady the sprit when lying at anchor in a seaway. Since the set of the sail cannot be adjusted with the snotter, a peak outhaul is also needed, plus throat and topsail halyards, and multiple brailing lines to cope with the volume of canvas. Once furled, the heavy bundle stays up there, collecting rainwater in wet weather and adding to the weight and windage aloft at all times, but too heavy and cumbersome to be worth the effort of lowering and raising again. At least this keeps the decks clear, but far from being the beautifully simple little rig it is for small boats, big spritsails are among the most complicated, and handling them takes powerful tackles and plenty of muscle. As a general rule, a spritsail should be no larger than a man can handle on his own and without difficulty. In days gone by, a working boatman changing his boat for a bigger one would just add another mast to it with the same sized sail.

Although it means sacrificing the simplicity of a una rig still further, a jib is reckoned to be a worthwhile addition to it, even on a dinghy, because apart from being an efficient aerofoil in its own right, its forestay holds the mast up against the tension along the head of the spritsail and compensates for some of the twist that otherwise develops when the peak sags. Windward performance and pointing ability are also improved if the sail is cut with a fairly high peak, but as the angle of the sprit grows more acute, the less the head of the sail is able to support the peak, the greater becomes the loading on the snotter and the more it will stretch. For this reason a snotter should be kept short. But it must still be long enough to avoid binding the heel against the mast and leave the sprit free to swing through the best part of 360°. Even so, the tension of the snotter and hence the set of the sail will vary somewhat as the snotter winds itself round the mast. A rotating mast gets round this problem, although it's not always easy to arrange; and as with any other traditional type of sail, the luff hoops, lacings or robands (individual loops of rope tied around the mast) should be a slack enough fit to allow the sail to stand well clear of the mast and flop across to leeward on each tack, so as to reduce the turbulence in the wake of the mast by assuming a better leading edge shape.

CRAB CLAW

The Pacific lateen, to give it its formal title, was originated in ancient times by the Polynesian seafarers and is still favoured for small inshore boats by those who can't afford outboard motors, or prefer not to rely on them. But despite its primitive beauty and harmony of line, it is unlikely ever to become popular with yachtsmen, principally because it gives the impression of being

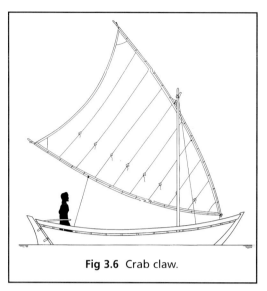

Fig 3.6 Crab claw.

too cumbersome, totally at odds with the slick, compact rigs that grace most of our pleasure craft. We are for the most part a fairly conservative bunch, which in this case is unfortunate, because wind tunnel tests* have shown that the crab claw can actually out-perform all of them on some aspects of sailing, notably on a reach, where its driving force was found to be almost double that of a Bermudan sail (of admittedly moderate aspect ratio).

It consists of a pair of long and slender curved spars, lashed together where they meet near the bows and carrying the luff and foot of the sail. This terminates in the sharply concave leech to which the rig owes its name. The upper (luff) yard is suspended about halfway along its length by a halyard from a short and usually unstayed mast, and the attitude of the sail – its sweepback angle and lateral swing – is controlled by playing the tack line, sheet and halyard, enabling it to be flown in the manner of a kite when the wind is well abaft the beam. In this mode, the rig can generate a considerable amount of lift as well as drive, which largely accounts for the high speeds achieved by the Pacific proas and double canoes.

The reason for this surprising performance lies in its ultra-low aspect ratio planform which is not unlike that of a delta winged aircraft. This type of foil, in addition to its normal lift, produces 'vortex lift' from the suction of the spiral coils of air rotating rapidly above its leeward edges. (Since the air in these helices is moving faster than the foil, its pressure is lower, hence the lift.)

For best speed to windward, the rig is angled at about 45°, and contrary to usual practice is flattened in light airs, because with the narrow side 'boundaries' that this particular shape presents to the wind, the flow is directed more along the trough of the sail than across it, and the normal effects of camber don't apply. The entire edifice has to be dipped round the mast when tacking or gybing, which takes time and would rule it out for racing, but at least the bamboo yards are fairly light and between them keep the sail tensioned so that it doesn't flog. It is then progressively lowered as the wind draws aft, and set almost horizontally for running. There are two methods of reefing. First, the lower yard is allowed to move up, producing power-

*C A Marchaj

reducing bulges in the sail close to the yards. Then in heavier winds, the upper yard is lowered and the reef points are tied off along the lower yard. The rig is stowed by collapsing it into a bundle on deck or in the bottom of the boat; or by lashing it vertically against the mast when it is necessary to keep the decks clear.

SAILBOARD

Surely the least expensive and the most personal form of watercraft, sailboards are among the fastest of all sailing vessels. They are also as demanding as any in terms of physical skill and concentration (and in strong winds of sheer strength and stamina, despite the use of a harness to relieve the strain on the sailor's arms). In case those readers more accustomed to conventional boats are not familiar with the anatomy and behaviour of these exciting little machines, the following notes give some basic detail about how they work, in addition to the more general sort of information provided on the other rigs in this chapter.

It was back in 1967 that two Americans, Hoyle Schweitzer and Jim Drake, one a surfer and the other an aerodynamicist and sailor, combined their activities by mounting a sail on a surfboard and calling their hybrid a Windsurfer. They promptly patented what they thought was their own invention, little realising that the concept was far from new, having been originated by an Englishman, Peter Chilvers, who had tried out a similar contraption in Chichester harbour ten years earlier. Nor could anyone have foreseen that windsurfing, as it was later to become known, would develop into a worldwide sport within five years and an Olympic one in less than twenty.

It is based on the principle of a 'free' sail which the sailor, standing on the board, holds up against the wind with the boom, which is clamped to the mast and which in turn supports him (or her). There is no rudder, and on most designs the only keel surface is a diminutive skeg (the *fin* in board parlance) near the stern, a daggerboard only being necessary upwind at comparatively low speeds. Instead, the heel of the mast is universally jointed, and the board is steered by raking the sail forwards or backwards to induce lee or weather helm, at the same time keeping it as upright as possible so as to develop maximum forward thrust. To tack, the sailor nips round ahead of the mast while head-to-wind and grabs the boom from the other side as he bears away; in gybing he allows the boom to swing across the bows while keeping his weight towards the stern (the *tail*). Race boards also feature a sliding mast track which is used to match the mastfoot position with the type of sail in use relative to the sailor's weight and position. There are only two pieces of rigging, the clew outhaul and the tack downhaul, which are used to adjust fullness and twist respectively, according to the weather conditions, plus a knotted line from the head of the boom for pulling the rig out of the water

Fig 3.7 Sailboard.

when starting, and a loop on either side of the boom to which the sailor can hook his harness.

Given the wind, speed is there for the asking. The ratio of sail area to displacement is so high and the wetted surface so small that even the most basic board will plane in any but the lightest airs. At the 35–45 knots that can be achieved by the fastest boards, the 'footprint' on the water is little larger than a pair of shoes.

Because of their speed, boards spend much of their time close-hauled, with the apparent wind well forward of the beam. They are not, however, particularly close-winded, due to their minimal keel surfaces, a long board with dagger tacking through about 90° at best, depending on the seastate. Short types can seldom do better than 110°, but they are travelling so fast – typically 20–25 knots hard on the wind in a force 4–5 – that their Vmg is still very competitive.

There are so many designs on today's market that it is difficult to categorise them, but they can be arbitrarily grouped according to length and buoyancy. The original types were all long boards of around 360–380 cm* and 200 litres volume and these are still used in updated form for instructing beginners and as low-cost family boards. Their construction consists of a blow-moulded polypropylene or polyethylene skin filled with polyurethane foam, a tough and durable combination, but rather heavy. Race boards are about the same length but have more buoyancy, with volumes as high as 280 litres. Like all other high performance boards they are of composite construction, with a skin built up of layers of glassfibre reinforced with carbon or Kevlar®, or a sandwich of hard foam laminated on to a soft foam core. They are lighter and stiffer than blow-moulded boards, but more easily damaged and much more expensive. With a very large sail and daggerboard they deliver good upwind performance in light airs, while low weight contributes to their high reaching speeds; but it needs quite a high level of technical ability to get the best out of them.

* In the USA, sailboard lengths are usually expressed in feet and inches, although metric measurements are used for volumes and sail areas.

Generally speaking, stronger winds require shorter boards for controllability, with correspondingly less buoyancy, the exception being a few of the exotic types such as the Olympic 370, which are competitive in any wind between one and forty knots. Some retain a dagger for non-planing conditions, but at high speed these develop too much sidways force, creating unnecessary drag liable to capsize the board. Most come with a choice of quick-change fins to match the sail size – the higher the speed, the smaller the fin needed – and alternative footstrap positions. Mid-length boards, giving a good mix of light wind and strong wind capability, fall in the 325–345 cm band, with volumes around 160 litres (although this can be a bit wobbly for a heavyweight). The most popular group on the market are the short boards for slalom, some more 'throwabout' than others, measuring 270–280 cm and 95–120 litres, and designed for blasting about at high speed in winds of force 4–5 and upwards.

Finally, there are the specialist (250–270 cm) machines for speed, wave riding and wave jumping. These are extremely fast in strong winds and surf conditions, but they are so manoeuvrable as to be positively twitchy, and so low in volume – as little as 75 litres – that they are strictly for the experts. Any boards of less than 90–100 litres are too wobbly and sinky to uphaul, so they require water starts. The sailor lies in the water, and as the sail fills with wind it pulls him up and straight into the sailing position; whereas he can stand on the higher volume boards – the 'floaters' – while he goes through the starting procedure.

Bridging these categories are a variety of compromise and multi-purpose boards, some more versatile than others, and there are various design features other than length and buoyancy that affect performance and handling. These include the amount of nose rocker (more needed for rough water operations); tail rocker (only on wave boards, to enable the sailor to make the board turn more tightly and to spring the nose up for take-off and landing); rounded, *tucked* (indented), or hard *rails* (the edges to the board) equivalent to the alternatives of road, competition or racing tyres on a car; the fore-and-aft volume distribution; and its profile (parallel railed or rounded – some are shaped like teardrops).

While boards can't be altered, sails can easily be changed and the choice nowadays is bewildering: someone has calculated that there are more different board sails on the market than there are models of car. But there are certain general types best suited to each size and shape of board, the choice depending on the weather and how the board is to be used on the day. Their wind range is limited compared with the average cruising boat's mainsail, for whereas this will cope with anything from a gale to a zephyr by reefing, it is impossible to reef a windsurfer sail. So instead they are made in a number of different sizes – from, say, 4 to around 10 sq m – to cover the same range. Aficionados keep a collection at their disposal, usually also carrying more than one style of board on the roof of the car, along with several different lengths of mast to suit the sail range. These are usually made, like the boards themselves, from a glassfibre/carbon-epoxy composite. For best performance, board sails need a mast of the correct length. Obviously it has to be long enough, but unnecessary length increases the 'swing weight' factor above the sailor's head. And if the top of the sail should come a long way below the mast tip, its larger diameter and consequently its stiffness will reduce the essential degree of twist in the sail which enables the leech to cope with the various gusts, lulls and speed variations by opening up or tightening so as to maintain a reasonably steady pull on the sailor's arms.

All board sails feature a sleeved luff surrounding the mast. Besides simplifying the process of rigging the board, this is essential on such a small, ultra-high performance sail in order to prevent the mast from interfering with its aerodynamics. As to materials, fabric is not much used in today's board sails, virtually all of them now being made from Monofilm, a lightweight, clear extruded polyester with extremely low stretch characteristics, with Mylar® for the sleeve. A stepped construction of varied thickness of Monofilm is normally employed, depending on the local loading, strengthened in the higher stress areas such as the sleeve, head, foot and clew with a scrim, or a lattice of polyester or Kevlar® thread, sandwiched between the Monofilm laminates.

The battens, between four and eight of them depending on the size of the sail, run full length, with screw tensioners or buckles and straps for camber adjustment. By protruding slightly forward of the sleeve line they automatically flip to the aerodynamically more efficient position to leeward of the mast each time the sail is tacked, hence the term used to describe it as a Rotating Asymmetrical Foil (RAF). Efficiency is further improved by the use of camber inducers (*cams*), in the form of little plastic A-frames on the batten ends, straddling the mast and sliding round it. These not only relieve the pressure on the ends of the sail pockets, but the larger sleeve needed to house them can make the entire luff area three-dimensional like the leading edge of a wing. Aerodynamic efficiency apart, however, oversized sleeves hold too much water, making the rig unnecessarily heavy to raise when starting, so they are usually made as small as possible. The cams themselves also add weight (and cost) and make the sail more difficult to rig. More importantly, by locking fullness into the sail they make it extremely difficult to de-power, so multi-cam rigs are normally reserved for racing and other speed-orientated boards. To improve controllability for more general use, most of the recreationally orientated sails have only a few of their lower battens fitted with these devices, leaving the others RAF-style.

The short, fat wave sails, usually with areas of 5.3 sq m or less and designed for use with very small throwabout boards, dispense with cams altogether, using a narrow, all-RAF luff for maximum manoeuvrability and so as to retain as little water as possible. They are constructed of heavy duty material to withstand the pounding of breaking surf, and feature a high clew to avoid catching the wavetops. At the other end of the size scale are the rare jumbos of 8 sq m and above, used for record breaking and light weather speed sailing, and the 7.5 sq m sails for international long board racing, with the emphasis on upwind performance in winds of up to 30 knots or more. Like the wave sails, they need a fairly low aspect ratio so as to obtain maximum power from the bottom area, and rely on twist to control the airflow near the top. But they use a rigid, multi-cam layout on a stiff mast, and a long, low foot, making it easy to close the slot above the board; but they are unforgiving and awkward to manoeuvre.

In between the full-on racing sail and the simple, comfortable all-rounder suitable for beginners, there are many different styles, for any given size, to suit the various disciplines (slalom, blasting, etc) and depending on whether maximum speed is needed upwind or down, and a range of what are in effect detuned racing sails, where performance is traded for stability and where flexibility and acceleration are more useful than top end power.

CATBOAT

The boat described here is the archetypal American catboat, shallow draughted, extremely beamy (almost half as broad as she is long) with full bows and broad quarters, a centreboard and a large gaff sail. Believed to have originated back in the 17th century on some of the small Dutch working boats, the rig later found favour in parts of Britain for inshore fishing and trading, and in the Solent, where the Victorians raced a fleet of una-rigged yachts. By the early 1900s they had become something of a rarity beyond the American lakes and north-east coast, where the current style of boat was developed and where large numbers have continued to be built and sailed. However, today's trend towards traditional boats has seen the comeback of catboats in Europe, where their simple rig and ease of handling (in light winds, at any rate) has made them popular for cruising and as hire boats in sheltered areas such as the Norfolk Broads and on the Swiss and German lakes.

Many are fitted with a Bermudan rig, which is lighter than the gaff equivalent and easier to hoist and lower from the confines of a narrow foredeck. This lack of width also precludes either mast from being effectively stayed by shrouds, but a free-standing spar has the advantage of bending in strong winds and de-powering the sail when beating or reaching. Which is just as well, for these are not the best of seaboats and problems are liable to arise when the weather worsens.

For one thing, having the entire weight of what is quite a heavy rig concentrated right up in the bows can cause violent, repetitive pitching, or 'hobbyhorsing', which shakes most of the wind out of the sail in light airs. But the main problem with nearly all catboats arises from having only the large single

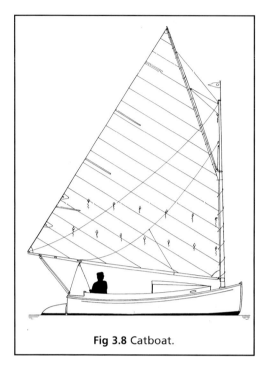

Fig 3.8 Catboat.

sail, set so far forward, to cope with the entire range of weather conditions and boatspeeds. Combined with the somewhat unpredictable behaviour of a shallow, beamy hull, this makes them very prone to helm imbalance. Some boats carry lee helm, arising from the forward location of the rig's CE, which makes them unable to perform well to windward and difficult, if not at times impossible, to tack. In others, lee helm has been avoided by giving the sail a long foot with an overhanging boom, like the one shown here; but this is liable to bring the CE so far aft as to generate excessive *weather* helm, a fault from which the majority of catboats seem to suffer. As well as causing unnecessary drag and a heavy tiller, it can make the bows reluctant to pay off while getting under way. Lowering the peak of the gaff – or with a Bermudan rig, backing the boom and reversing the helm – are often the only ways of setting off on the desired tack. Added to this, the long boom is liable to drag in the water whenever the boat heels sharply, dragging the bows to leeward and preventing the helmsman from luffing. This can usually be remedied by raking the mast forward so that it raises the boom as it swings forward, but there is then the risk of reintroducing lee helm in rough water, when speeds tend to be low.

One way and another, catboats can be quite a handful in boisterous weather, especially when running before a strong breeze, when they can be relied on to give their crews a wild, wet ride. They are hard-mouthed and heavy to steer, yawing and rolling as the boom swings up and the sail twists forward, with the helmsman's efforts to correct the yaw only making the roll worse. So it is essential that they are reefed at the first sign of worsening weather – although with a gaff rig, power can be reduced in a hurry by supporting the boom with the weather-side topping lift and dropping the gaff to the horizontal. This immediately relieves the boat of about half the pressure on the sail, shifts its weight and windage aft, and reduces any tendency to bury the nose.

In good conditions, however, catboats excel. Provided the designer has managed to draw a reasonable balance between the shapes of the hull and the sail, these chunky little craft are surprisingly close-winded. In light airs they are bound to be a bit slower than those with slimmer hulls, or sloops and others of similar length with more than one sail and thus able to set a larger spread of canvas. But with so few strings to pull, even a nervous novice can sit back and enjoy the scenery. The accent throughout the design is on simplicity. For example, on the boat shown here, the luff of the sail is attached to the mast by a lacing line. This allows the sail to feather behind the mast when beating or reaching, which helps clean up the airflow, and it goes slack as the sail is lowered. So although it might occasionally snarl up, it is easy enough to clear and there are no problems with jammed slides when furling. The cockpit is roomy and uncluttered, and the broad beam of a typical 25 ft (7.5 m) cruiser gives ample cabin space, despite the intrusion of the centreboard case and the somewhat limited headroom imposed by the shallow hull.

FRACTIONALLY RIGGED BERMUDAN SLOOP

No one can have counted them, but it's probably true to say that more than 90% of all pleasure sailing craft are Bermudan-rigged sloops of one kind or another, and it's easy to see why. From the point of view of performance, which was the original reason for its appearance on the yachting scene, the comparatively long luff of a Bermudan mainsail ensures good windward efficiency, and on average the total sail area is more or less equally and conveniently divided between main and headsail. Added to this the rig, in noncompetitive form, is economical to make and straightforward to handle, and on the majority of dinghies and cruising boats the rigging, both standing and running, is uncomplicated.

The mainsail, being so much lighter than a comparable gaff sail – the increasingly popular alternative in these days of a return to the traditional look – requires a lot less effort to hoist. Besides, there's no yard to thrash about in the process, or to come down on an unsuspecting head should the halyard be let go in a hurry. Neither does it need such a powerful mainsheet, because the boom is less heavily loaded in strong winds; and there is much less weight and windage aloft, despite the necessarily taller mast. On the other hand, unlike the gaff, the Bermudan main needs to be set or lowered while head to wind, or nearly so, otherwise it becomes difficult to handle as the upper part is blown against the rigging, with the headboard liable to jam under one of the lower shrouds while being hoisted.

A masthead rig, in which the top of the mast is supported against the pull of the jib and forestay by a standing backstay, or on some small boats only by the swept-back shrouds and spreaders, is the preferred option for the inexperienced and for the majority of cruising sailors. Leading the forestay to a point some three-quarters to seven-eighths of the way up a flexible mast, with an adjustable backstay to control the fullness of the sail, produces a fractional rig such as the one pictured here. (On the drawing, the backstay would appear to foul the mainsail leech, but in real life the wind in the sail draws the roach clear.) A mainsheet traveller, carried on a track across the cockpit and positioned by control lines at either end, provides a range of adjustment to the mainsail. In heavy weather, for example, with the wind forward of the beam, the mainsheet and vang can be left set to the desired leech tension

Fig 3.9 Three-quarter rigged Bermudan sloop.

while the traveller is played to adjust the angle of the boom relative to the centreline. In a gust, the main can quickly be 'dumped' with the traveller, while the sheet maintains headstay tension via the mainsail leech so as to avoid excessive sag in the luff of the jib. For broad reaching, the traveller is let down to leeward and the sheet used conventionally, with the vang tensioned on a run to prevent the boom from skying. On some small cruising boats where peak performance is not considered essential, the complication and cockpit clutter of the track and traveller are avoided by having a simple, central anchorage for the lower sheet block.

The boat shown here is carrying a radial head spinnaker on a conventional mast-mounted pole. A hassle-free but seldom seen alternative for leisurely downwind cruising is to set twin high-clewed staysails on a hinged pair of poles or 'twistleyards'. These are set flying from a spare halyard to the mast near the forestay, with a strop down to the stemhead and twin sheets, the sails being joined along their luffs. As well as extending the clews outwards, the poles push them downwards, minimising twist and maintaining a constant mean camber as the whole unit is rotated about the forestay by trimming the sheets, both jib and mainsail having been furled.

The small self-tacking and roller reefing jib is a useful option, its clew carried on a traveller running on a short track across the cabin top, with a single line for adjusting its fullness. In order to ensure that the angle of the clew relative to the centreline doesn't affect the tension on it – which might cause it to hang amidship while tacking in light airs – the sheet is taken back to the cockpit through a turning block on the deck near the tack (or alternatively at an equivalent distance up the mast). Its convenience has to be weighed against some loss of performance, due to the small size of the sail, and it cannot be backed. The alternative, an overlapping jib or genoa, is still moderately sized in comparison with its masthead equivalent and less of a struggle to handle; and in strong winds it is invariably faster for the same total sail area.

It is worth noting, however, that the overlapping area of a large jib is to some extent wasted. The specific thrust of a rig – that is to say, the amount of forward force generated per square metre of sail at any particular windspeed – is actually better if the same total area is split between the mainsail and a non-overlapping jib. (Come to that, it would theoretically be even better if all of the area were to be put into just one sail, main or jib, were it not for losing the slot effect.)

As well as the improved degree of control over mainsail shape, the fractional headsail is more efficient because there is less sag in the shorter forestay, provided it is kept tensioned by the mainsheet, and the smaller roller headsail reefs into a better shape. Besides this, the reduced vertical overlap allows the main to be eased out further without being backwinded or stalling, decreasing the heeling and leeway forces and reducing weather helm. However, the position of the swept-back spreaders and shrouds means that the boom can't be fully squared away on a run or broad reach. Over-sheeting only results in a heavy helm and loss of boatspeed, so the boom must instead be hove down with the vang. Conversely, if boat handling becomes difficult on a close reach, with the sail still full and plastered against the rigging, the vang needs to be let right off so as to open the leech and spill wind. Aside from these small problems, the main disadvantage of a fractional rig on a big boat – as distinct from a compact 25 footer like this one – lies in the reduced structural integrity of the mast in heavy weather. It also lacks some of the sheer, straight-line driving power of a large tall jib in more moderate conditions. But the smaller headsail is undoubtedly far easier to handle, the full-sized main is powerful enough to drive the boat on its own, and the majority of fractional-riggers can be made to tack under genoa alone.

Not that any Bermudan sail can be all things to all men. For one thing, it is far from being the most efficient of all shapes, as was discovered in the wind tunnel analysis referred to earlier, because its pointy top loses so much energy in the trailing vortex, causing induced drag. Indeed, it has been suggested that something like 10% of its head could actually be cut off without affecting the power output very much. Be that as it may, the best way to increase it is to introduce an elliptical shape to the leech, in the form of roach, like the one shown in Fig 3.9. Any more leech curvature than this requires the support of a larger headboard and full length battens which add to the weight and cost of the sail. Similarly, its aspect ratio is high enough to ensure an efficient windward performance without the enormous heeling moment, increased weather helm and leeway of the very tall rigs, and the consequent need for complex, highly tuned rigging and more beam or ballast, or both. Such rigs are really only appropriate for specialist racing boats and multihulls.

SWING RIG

This strange looking arrangement of spars and sails has been around for decades, just waiting for the right technology to make it commercially viable. There's no such thing as the perfect rig, however weatherly, efficient, or easy it may be to work, but this one goes a long way towards meeting such objectives.

Its origins, and the basic principle on which it depends, can be traced back to the earliest form of balance lug used on the Nile boats several thousand years ago and its Chinese counterpart, the junk. The *essence* of these lugs is the balance, which comes from having part of the sail ahead of the mast, with the entire sail and its supporting spar rotating as a single unit around it.

Pioneering experiments in Germany by Dr Manfred Curry during the 1920s had shown that in addition to the traditional virtues of the balance lug, keeping the jib and mainsail in line with one another *on all points of sailing* also resulted in greater overall efficiency. Thirty years later, an architect named

Fig 3.10 Swing rig.

Roger Stollery devised what he called a 'swing rig', in which the balance area was provided by a club-footed headsail carried, complete with its rigging, on a forward extension of the boom, instead of being tacked and sheeted to the deck. Radio-controlled models were followed by tests on the first full-sized craft, a Mirror dinghy, and the conversion of several small yachts, one of them a Bembridge Redwing which won so many races it was banned. A few of the rigs were subsequently built and sailed by amateurs, including a number of Punch dinghies designed by Stollery and still giving good service, and a handsome home-built centreboard cruiser in Holland. But despite the publicity that attended the later racing successes by a giant French swing wing catamaran, interest in the concept lapsed for a while. It was left to a noted British designer, Ian Howlett, working with the aptly named Carbospars Ltd (a company specialising in carbonfibre spars), to resurrect and develop it in its present high-tech form, known as the AeroRig.

The unstayed mast is rigidly attached to a deep box-section boom, which extends in one piece from the tack of the jib to the clew of a loose-footed mainsail, providing the basis for what looks, from a distance, like a normal Bermudan sailplan. The complete assembly, built in carbon/epoxy, is free to rotate on two bearings, one under the heel of the mast at the bottom of the boat, the other in the cabin top. The forestay, with its furling drum, a small transverse track for the self-tending jib, and the backstay are all directly attached to the boom, instead of to the stemhead and transom. The boom thus acts as a moving sail base, the mainsheet being the only connection between it and the deck, and *the only rig control* once the sails have been set.

AeroRigs have been installed on a variety of modern production hulls, ranging from a 13 ft (4 m) dinghy to a 90 ft (27 m) schooner. Figure 3.10 shows it on a mid-sized cruising catamaran, already a fast boat with a conventional rig but effortlessly outperformed by this one. Multihulls' high speed potential results primarily from their use of narrow, low resistance hulls, combined with shoal draft, and light weight due to the absence of any form of ballast. Multihulls are also able to resist the heeling force of the sails better than monohulls, standing up to their canvas and making more effective use of their sailpower, because of their wide-based 'straddle stability'. Given favourable sea conditions, a high performance multi can exceed the speed of the wind – even double it in light airs.

On the other hand, these craft are very sensitive to overloading with stores and equipment that would have little if any effect on a monohull, and which can turn a fast boat into a real clunker. And the prudent skipper will always reef early, because if severely overpressed a multihull is more prone ultimately to capsize than monohulls, which usually recover from a knockdown. One of the advantages of a free-standing mast is that it bends like a sapling in the breeze, acting as a safety valve and dissipating some of the overturning moment by spilling wind. To those unfamiliar with these masts, it can also be somewhat disconcerting to watch the tip deflecting in a gust.

The total installed weight of the new rig is virtually the same as that of a conventional Bermudan sloop of the same sail area, for although a normal mast, boom and standing rigging weighs rather less than the AeroRig's unstayed mast and massive boom, its deck hardware – winches, sheet tracks, etc – makes up the difference. The real benefit is a much better fatigue life, with no worries about corroded or cracked shroud fittings and a significant decrease in the overall form drag of the boat, amounting to as much as 10%, according to some estimates. Added to this, the centre of gravity is much lower, increasing the inherent stability and reducing the moment of inertia about the waterline by as much as 40%. Consequently there is less weight swinging around aloft and less strain on the hull – although this can be something of a mixed blessing, because there is also less damping on its rolling and pitching.

Sailing with the rig, it is best to forget the traditional wisdoms and think afresh. To begin with, the boat doesn't have to be brought head to wind when raising or lowering sail, or when reefing. The bows can point anywhere, even downwind, while the rig swivels freely, developing no forward drive. It is important, however, to hoist the mainsail first, because if the foretriangle loading were to exceed that of the main, the rig would suddenly and potentially dangerously invert. And if the rig is feathered across the deck, with the boom sticking out on both sides, spare a thought for neighbouring boats or pontoons.

Once hoisted, the setting of the sails can be left unchanged. The jib's transverse track keeps the chord line at a constant angle to the centreline of eight degrees. This has been found to provide the correct shape of slot between it and the mainsail, and the two are treated as one, regardless of the point of sailing. The sheet, which is only lightly loaded by virtue of the jib's balancing force, with correspondingly fewer blocks and less rope lying around the cockpit, is the power control. Haul it in to get under way, tighten it to accelerate, and ease it to slow down. Dump it and the rig weathercocks and stops driving, the sails lying quietly with no tendency to flog. This is as near as you can get to heaving-to, since like any other self-tending headsail the jib cannot be backed – the only real shortcoming of the rig. On the smaller boats, the jib is treated as an all-or-nothing sail, because with its combination of short foot and long luff it doesn't shape particularly well when partially rolled up, and anyway its sheet position can't be adjusted. So in strong winds it is usually rolled away and the boat sailed on the mainsail, reefed as necessary (*after* furling the jib, to avoid any possibility of the rig inverting). Finding yourself stuck with too much sail up when running in a rising gale is particularly dangerous on a fast multihull, and rounding up to reef or drop the main can be very uncomfortable on a conventional rig, to say the least. It

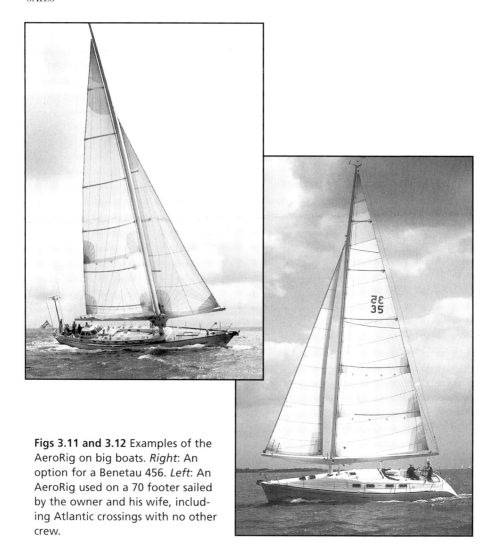

Figs 3.11 and 3.12 Examples of the AeroRig on big boats. *Right*: An option for a Benetau 456. *Left*: An AeroRig used on a 70 footer sailed by the owner and his wife, including Atlantic crossings with no other crew.

is easy to lower sail on a rotating mast, because side pressure on the slides is eliminated.

Larger boats – 35–40 ft (10.5–12 m) and upwards – are sometimes fitted with a secondary jib setting line, running from the clew to a point about halfway along the foreboom. This acts as a vertical barber hauler to help keep the leech tight when the sail is partially furled. In fact, AeroRigs balance well on the mainsail alone, even when heavily reefed in bad weather, unlike a conventional Bermudan which usually requires a storm jib to avoid excessive weather helm under these conditions. This is because the mast can be set rather further forward than normal (or the multihull's centreboard further aft), the location of the CE being more consistent throughout the reef variations and moving more or less vertically, so that the helm is not much affected.

Short-tacking, or dodging and weaving in close-quarters manoeuvring is simply a matter of putting the helm down, with the high boom providing excellent all-round visibility in tight traffic situations. For the performance-minded this compensates, to a considerable extent, for a slightly inferior windward ability compared to a conventional rig, once settled on a beat with an overlapping genoa and a more effective slot. As the wind comes on to the beam, the trick is to allow the rig to swing round so that the sailplan (not the boat) is still heading more or less directly into the apparent wind, at a constant angle of incidence of around 30°, in the manner of an aircraft wing. For broad reaching, the boom is eased out further so that the airflow remains *across* the sail, at the same 30° or so. An apparent wind direction indicator at the masthead, normally useless on rotating masts unless fitted with complex counter-rotating gearing, is handy for trimming the rig at night or in heavy weather.

It is not until the boat is brought on to a run is the boom squared off athwartships. There are of course no shrouds to get in the way – nor, for that matter, are there any to hold on to when moving forward! With the mainsail on one side, the jib is automatically 'poled out' on the other, instead of slatting and banging in the shadow of the main. Sailing by the lee is not a problem. It can be avoided simply by paying out more sheet to allow the boom to swing past 90°, but the rig will not gybe until the wind direction is almost parallel to the alignment of the rig, which means you can sail, if you want to, as much as 45° by the lee. Gybing, when it eventually occurs, is a thoroughly relaxed and tranquil affair, because by now the boat is effectively beam reaching on the opposite tack, so that after it has swung across, the rig feathers before it comes to the end of its travel on the mainsheet. Wind pressure on the jib acts as a damper throughout the swinging process, countering any potential shock loading that might otherwise occur when gybing through shallower angles, and it is reassuring to know that the boom can't lift. But crew should beware of it sweeping the foredeck while they are tending the anchor or handling mooring lines. Sailing for simpletons it may be, but there's no denying its attractions for the short-handed, nervous, infirm or just plain lazy sailor, while experienced racing helmsmen, relieved of many of their normal duties, seem to delight in driving these boats to the limit.

An alternative type of swing rig, the Freewing, is being built in Scotland by Richard Glanville. It features a wingmast, swivelling independently of the boom so as to smooth the airflow across the leading edge of the sail. But the gain in efficiency has to be offset against a necessarily more complex pivoting and control system. Not surprisingly, until development costs have been amortised and production output has grown, either type of swing rig is as yet comparatively expensive. There is, however, an economy of scale which improves with size; so that whereas the current cost of a dinghy AeroRig can be as much as double that of a conventional one, it adds probably no more than a quarter to the overall cost of a 30 foot cruiser, and makes very little difference at all on a 50 footer. Price apart, it is the unconventional appearance that is likely to deter potential customers, until people get more used to seeing these rigs around.

GAFF CUTTER

It is particularly true of boats that beauty brings its own rewards, and the gaff cutter is a case in point. In marked contrast to the stark simplicity of swing rigs, its multiplicity of sails provides plenty of strings to pull, along with a style that echoes the past and the long vanished fleets of working craft in which men once earned their livings. Properly managed, it ranks among the most versatile, safe and seaworthy of all rigs, but it is not one for the 'haul-it-up-and-go' sailor. With so much rope to handle and so many options in the setting of the rig, it takes time, skill and a certain amount of patience to sail one properly.

On a traditional cutter the mast tends to be set back towards the beamier middle part of the hull, where it can be better supported by the shrouds, and where it does less harm to the boat's behaviour in rough water by keeping the weight out of the bows. A bowsprit is also necessary on hulls with little or no forward overhang, in order to extend the foretriangle and provide space for the two-headsail arrangement, whose underlying purpose is to make lighter work of sail handling, despite there being two sets of sheets to attend. There is also the great merit of being able to adjust sail areas and balance the boat for a variety of wind conditions and points of sailing. It is easier to steer upwind in a blow and it is even possible, by trial and error, to make a boat with a long keel self-steering to windward; and if the staysail is made of sufficiently heavy cloth, it can double as a storm jib. She will also point up high to the seas when hove-to in a gale, thanks to her comparatively deep forefoot and because the CE of her rig doesn't move forward when reefed.

It has to be accepted that no amount of expertise can ever make a gaff-headed sail go as well to windward as a Bermudan. Admittedly the gaff's spar enables the boat to spread more canvas without the need for such a tall mast, but aerodynamic efficiency suffers from the comparatively short luff and a correspondingly low aspect ratio, and from excessive sail twist due to the gaff sagging off to leeward. Although this relieves some of the pressure on the rig in heavy weather, if, as sometimes happens, it is accompanied by a lifting boom, it can lead to a spectacular or even calamitous gybe. Performance is further hampered by the spar's considerable weight and windage aloft and the rig's veritable cobweb of drag-producing cordage. And because it is impossible to rig a standing backstay, all except the smallest boats require a pair of running backstays, to be alternately set up and slackened off each time the boat is tacked or gybed. Runners are an inconvenience at the best of times and a

Fig 3.13 Gaff cutter

potential risk to the integrity of the mast should they be mishandled in heavy weather. They do at least leave room for the boom to be extended well over the stern, so as to make up for the somewhat lacklustre behaviour to windward, but the whole mainsail assembly then becomes even heavier to handle.

The enemy of any rig is stretch in the wire of the standing rigging, which lets the mast go out of column and the headsail luffs to sag. On a boat like the one in Fig 3.13, which is no greyhound, it pays to rig her with oversize wire, despite the extra weight and windage. As in the other drawings depicting stayed masts, shroud tensioners have been omitted for the sake of clarity. Instead of the usual rigging screws, a boat such as this might be fitted with the traditional deadeyes and lanyards as being more in keeping with her general appearance. These need regular careful inspection, however, since despite the parts of the lashing being properly seized to one another, chafe through a single strand can still bring down the mast.

It is when downwind or reaching that the gaff rig really comes into its own. Aerodynamics now matter less than sail area, and a long boom and gaff can project a lot of area between them without having to resort to a spinnaker. Added to this, a triangular topsail can be set above the mainsail and sheeted to its peak, so as to fill the space between the gaff and the mast. Alternatively, it may be spread and extended with two light spars, one at the leading edge and the other, the jackyard, along its foot. By in effect lengthening the mainsail luff and catching the wind where it blows strongest, the advantages of a large sail area aloft are combined with the Bermudan's close-windedness. It has, however, to be treated as the first reef, and brought down when the breeze gets up, because of the considerable leverage it exerts.

The boom and gaff goosenecks are traditionally formed by leathered jaws bearing on the mast, with the sail luff held to it with lacing or wooden hoops, but for those who prefer an engineered alternative they can be replaced by ball-bearing cars and slides running in a mast track. Lazyjacks to gather up the bunt of the sail are another worthwhile piece of gear on any cruising boat, despite adding a little windage, and are particularly appreciated on gaff (or gunter) rigs, where the yard is liable to clout someone on the head while being lowered in a seaway. With the sail dropped on to the boom and nestling between the lazyjacks, it is also a simple matter to sail off a missed mooring just by peaking up the yard. Conversely, there is another handy old trick that was used by fishermen to shorten sail and slow down while they were trawling, or if the boat was hit by a squall: the topping lift is set up, the peak lowered to a near-horizontal position and the tack triced up towards the throat, effectively halving the heeling force of the rig in a matter of seconds.

A boomed mainsail, secured by lacing or a boltrope along its foot, puts less strain on the clew than the loose-footed one shown here. This is often chosen for its traditional appearance, as well as being able to carry its fullness right down into the bottom area, although a vang cannot then be used to shape this part of the sail, even if it were practicable to fit one, which on this boat it isn't, owing to the height of the cabin top. Since, however, the mainsheet runs on an iron horse across the transom, its tension is maintained until the boom is out over the quarter, preventing the leech from twisting off unduly while beating to windward, and a preventer is easily rigged for running. The alternative of a boomless sail is sometimes preferred for its sheer simplicity, despite its lack of leech control while running, and its tendency to induce weather helm when close-hauled. For a temporary stow in moderate weather, or as a makeshift reef, it can quickly be gathered in to the mast with brailing lines, and just as easily released, instead of having to lower and raise the entire sail and gaff; and of course there's no boom to clout the unwary head.

The angle of the gaff and the corresponding cut of the sail depends on the purpose for which the boat is designed. The old working craft used to have them slanted down to about 45° from the vertical for the sake of weatherliness; no one was particularly bothered about a few degrees of pointing ability. Racing rigs were peaked up as high as 15°, almost like a gunter, to minimise the amount of sag and make them work better upwind, but this precluded the setting of a topsail. So a good compromise for a cruising boat is somewhere around 35°.

A gaff rig is more versatile and provides greater scope for adjustment than any other. It benefits greatly from tuning, given the proper use of its controls, particularly the peak halyard, which merits constant attention while sailing. In light airs, this should be tensioned so that wrinkles begin to run from peak to tack, throwing more draft into the forepart of the sail, and in conjunction with the mainsheet, tightening the leech and reducing the gaff sag. For working to windward in a hard breeze, when a flat sail is needed, the peak halyard is eased slightly (but not so much that a wrinkle appears from throat to clew), the sail flattens out, the centre of effort comes down and the peak sags away and spills wind. The throat halyard is used in the normal way to adjust the amount and position of the mid-sail draft, and the clew outhaul to control the foot tension and lower sail fullness. Some boats are additionally fitted with a peak outhaul, not accessible under way without going aloft, to set the draft in the head of the sail. There is also the option of a gaff vang leading down from the peak as a supplementary means of controlling sag, but using it is largely a matter of suck-it-and-see, because any downward pull on it tends to be counter-productive by reopening the leech.

All this running rigging undoubtedly makes for more of a muddle on deck and a snakepit of sheets and control lines in the cockpit, but it offers the conscientious crew a tantalising selection of controls to play with, the majority of them essential for making the best of the gaff's somewhat unexciting performance to windward. Tweaking them adds interest to a voyage, and set against the rig's other virtues, the extra complication is generally considered to be well worthwhile. And anyway, the cruising sailor will usually take a fair wind as naturally as choosing the up or down escalator in a department store.

HIGH PERFORMANCE RIG FOR MULTIHULLS

Insofar as the trimaran in Fig 3.14 is 'single-masted, with a mainsail and two or more headsails', it satisfies the definition of a cutter, although the inner staysail is really the working jib and the forestaysail a gigantic genoa which is only used as a windward alternative to the spinnaker. The mainsail has much the same high aspect ratio as that on the monohull sloop pictured earlier, but it will be even more efficient, and size for size will develop considerably more power because of its square head. This not only reduces tip vortex losses, but the relatively large area high up in the sail makes the most of the increased windspeed aloft without the need for an excessively tall mast. However, compared with a conventional jib-headed sail of the same area, it also generates a greater heeling moment, making it unsuitable for monohulls, which are normally sailed as upright as possible. But it has much less effect on the broader beamed multihull – at least until this begins to approach its stability limit, by which time it should have been reefed anyway.

Since a vang cannot be used on a rotating mast, the boom is restrained when sailing off the wind by the traveller, running on a long track across the transoms of a cat, or spanning the even more widely spaced floats of a trimaran, some tracks being curved on a radius to the mast so that the sheet block can freely follow the swing of the boom, instead of tightening the sheet the further it moves away from the centreline. For the sake of compactness when berthed or on a trailer, and in order to minimise marina charges, the floats on some boats are arranged either to fold upwards as on this one or to swing inwards on their beams, parallelogram fashion. Since the track cannot then extend beyond the main hull, it has to be supplemented by a tackle rigged between the boom and the lee float, the tackle and traveller becoming the primary mainsail controls when sailing fast to windward or beam reaching. For maximum speed, a lightweight racing cat (as distinct from a family cruiser) is sailed, whenever possible, by playing the traveller so that the weather hull is kept flying clear of the water, resulting in a dramatic decrease in drag and at the same time enabling the boat to point rather higher. A tri is raced in similar fashion, but with its weather float clear and the main hull just kissing the surface, with virtually the entire weight of the vessel carried on the leeward float. For this purpose, and in the general interests of safety in heavy weather, each float will usually have a buoyancy of around double the total displacement of the boat.

Some are even larger, despite their extra weight and windage, each with its own centreboard and rudder instead of their being located in the main hull. With either hull configuration, great care and swift reactions are needed to avoid pitchpole capsize under these potentially dangerous conditions, the traveller control or sheet being hand-held and ready to be dumped the moment the lee bow shows any sign of burying.

On average, there is little to choose in all-round performance between a cat and a tri. If anything, the latter can be expected to point higher, especially in a seaway, because its headstay remains tight, fastened as it is directly to the stemhead instead of being carried on the crossbeam or wire bridle linking the bows of a cat and prone to flexing. The tri should also be faster on a dead run, since only its main hull will be immersed, instead of two with a combined wetted surface some 40% greater. Running is the slowest point of sailing on any boat, but a slippy multihull cannot be sailed to best advantage if the wind is allowed to go anywhere abaft the beam. So a helmsman looking for speed will tack downwind through an angle of about 110° so as to bring his boat on to a reach.

Nevertheless, even dead downwind, these boats are still very quick in a fresh breeze, and therein lies potential danger. Because of the high boatspeed, the apparent wind drops to a gentle and misleading zephyr, the sun feels

Fig 3.14 High performance rig for multihulls.

warm, the boat seems stable and secure. Suppose then, just as it tips down the face of a wave, a big gust were to come through from astern. The spinnaker can be let run (its sheet should never be cleated) but, by this time, the mainsail may be pinned against the shrouds. There would follow a sudden deceleration as the bows slam into the trough, the apparent wind would instantaneously flash up to full strength, and the boat would probably pitchpole.

So provided there is sea room, reaching in rough water is safer as well as faster. In fact, the big racers are so rapid – well over 30 knots with a big boat, 20 even on an 8 m (26 ft) 'micro' – that they spend more of their time close-hauled; and having added most of their own speed to that of the wind and drawn it so far forward, they find themselves in effect sailing into a permanent gale. Only a tiny jib is needed, as on the cruiser/racer we are looking at, because a larger one could not be sheeted in closely enough at top speed, neither could it be dumped quickly enough in an emergency. It is shown in Fig 3.14 as a self-tacker with roller reefing, with another roller for the enormous lightweight genoa, appropriately known as a 'screecher', on the outer forestay. Together with its furled sail, it can be lowered to the deck on a halyard to reduce wind resistance and leave the way clear for the asymmetric reaching spinnaker. This is tacked to the end of the bowsprit which in turn is guyed out to the floats, so that it can be hauled across to weather like a conventional pole, or hinged upwards for berthing. On boats without a bowsprit, the spinnaker can be tacked to the windward float instead of using a pole.

Because a multihull heels so little, there is considerable strain on its rig, especially in a gust (unless the mast is free-standing and designed to flex). However, giving the shrouds an extra wide base, by leading them to the outer edges of each hull or float, minimises the amount of pre-tensioning they require and hence the compression loading on the mast and its supporting structure. It follows that this benefit can only apply to fixed-geometry boats (there are 'collapsing' cats too, using various ingenious methods of articulation) so the rigging on a folding trimaran has to follow normal monohull practice, except that the shroud and forestay fittings on the mast are designed to accept radial movement.

Single line reefing is provided for the mainsail, which is loose-footed so as not to restrict the camber in its bottom area, and its heavy roach is supported by full-length battens. These hold the sail shape well, even in light airs and a choppy sea, maintaining a smooth and stable aerodynamic form and improving the windward performance, particularly at high speeds. With such good luff support, the sail is also less affected by backwinding from a tight jib, and less likely to flog when feathered or when motoring. Sailing becomes quieter and altogether more tranquil. When reefing or dropping the sail, it is easier to flake it down on the boom, especially with lazyjacks to gather in the folds and prevent them from flopping down on to the deck.

Sail shape is to a considerable extent predetermined by the long battens. The stiffer they are, the flatter the shape they induce, and the bendier the battens, the greater the fullness; and when light airs are expected, putting them under compression with buckle fasteners or screwjacks forces even more draft into the sail. On the other hand, they make the sail more difficult to 'read', because it is so stable, and they limit the amount of camber adjustment that can be made under way by varying the foot and luff tensions. Furthermore they need expensive, well-engineered luff hardware, in the form of swivelling pockets and ball-bearing cars, to avoid jamming under the compression loads, and their long pockets add to the overall cost of the sail, which – not counting the extra fittings – can amount to around 20% more than one with short battens. This particular problem can be overcome by terminating the battens a little way short of the luff and using conventional slides, but the resulting sail shape is not quite as good. The increased weight, even with three-quarter battens, makes raising sail harder work, and there is a greater likelihood of damaging it through chafe against the shrouds and topping lift. As in life, there is seldom something to be gained for nothing, and most good devices for sailboats have their disadvantages. Long battens are no exception; but on balance, they are generally considered to be well worth having, even on a relatively slow cruising boat, and are invariably fitted to high performance craft like this one.

MASTHEAD CUTTER

Cutters have earned an enviable reputation as snug cruising rigs – although in the absence of a bowsprit, the boat depicted in Fig 3.15 might be better termed a double-headed sloop. Masthead rigs are generally more robust and securely stayed than the more tuneable fractional rigs that are almost universal on racers and cruiser/racers. Added to this, two working foresails of moderate size are generally easier to handle than a single large one and require less effort by the crew. They also tend to set better when heavily roller reefed, need smaller winches, and offer more options in their setting, including a safer inboard position for a storm jib. A big overlapping genoa is a formidable handful in a boat of this size, not only in terms of roller reefing and sheeting between tacks, but also to handle when setting a pole for running downwind. It is nevertheless considered essential by many sailors on account of its immense driving power to windward and on a reach, despite more often than not having to be dragged forward and passed around the inner forestay when the boat is tacked; which makes life difficult for a short-handed or tired crew, especially in bad weather. Some prefer to roll up the sail sufficiently to allow the clew to blow across and then release the furling line and sheet in as quickly as possible – all very well on long legs, but hard work when short-tacking.

To avoid this hassle the vast majority of modern, mid-sized cruising yachts leave their builders' yards rigged as masthead sloops, relying on today's efficient and dependable roller furling gear to adjust the headsail area. But an increasing proportion of owners specify, or retrofit, a removable inner forestay, fitted with a combined hook and tensioner that allows it to be unclipped from a deck eye at a strong point in the centre of the foredeck and stowed to another eye near the shrouds. Since the loading on the attachment points can be considerable, it is essential that the mast is adequately supported, if necessary by running backstays and/or by additional shrouds and spreaders; and the deck may need to be prevented from lifting by a wire span in the forecabin, running down to the hull. By providing a third attachment for it just behind the roller drum at the stemhead, the stay can also be used with an extra-large genoa in light airs. Such a hybrid type of rig, sometimes referred to as a 'slutter', achieves the best of both worlds.

Although it is rather less efficient than a sloop in its windward pointing ability, the rig has a number of advantages over a sloop in heavy weather. As the wind builds through, say, 20 knots apparent, head canvas can quickly be reduced by taking in or rolling up the genoa, which relieves the strain on the upper part of the mast and helps the aerodynamics of the lower part of the mainsail which is the most likely to become stalled. Carrying on with the staysail and main, reefed as the wind increases further, the boat will perform much like a low foretriangle, fractionally rigged sloop, the small headsail, which may be heavily built to double as a storm jib, obviating much of the sheet track movement when reefing. On the other hand the mast, being fairly fat all the way up in order to support the long headstay, is inclined to spoil the flow across the upper part of the mainsail when only the staysail is set. Energetic sailors can rectify this by changing the genoa for a 'Yankee' jib topsail, which is a skinny little sail with a long luff, high clew and little if any overlap, but it has to be sheeted so far aft that there is seldom enough breadth to get a tight enough sheeting angle. With so many sail setting options and scope for adjustment on a rig like this, close attention must be paid to getting the sheet leads right. A small headsail close-hauled needs around 8° to make the slot work well, whereas those larger than the main, with a big overlap, are best kept as open as 15° – which is just as well, for the shrouds usually prevent a genoa being cranked in any closer. On this example, a permanent aft support is rigged for the staysail forestay, which consequently has no need for runners, and its lack of overlap (the genoa has to be walked round or rolled anyway) allow the shrouds to be taken almost to the rail, giving clear decks with wide, safe shroud angles and reduced rig loads.

Of the various methods of mainsail reefing, slab systems are the most efficient in maintaining a good sail shape and are the most trouble-free. Simplest of them is the conventional tack horn and reefing line, and for a well co-ordinated crew it is the quickest to use, but a single line system enables both luff and leech to be pulled down simultaneously, either at the mast or from the shelter of the cockpit. This is a blessing if you are short handed or with inexperienced crew members, although friction in the succession of blocks and sheaves can cause problems, particularly when hoisting the sail after shaking out a reef, when the mechanical advantage that makes it easier to take in a slab works the other way. By using twin lines led to a common point, one through the luff and the other through the leech cringles, the angles and the number of directional changes in the line are almost halved, but it is not quite so convenient to use. Spar makers offer various ingenious arrangements of balance blocks inside the boom in order to reduce the line friction, and also to encourage the luff to come down before

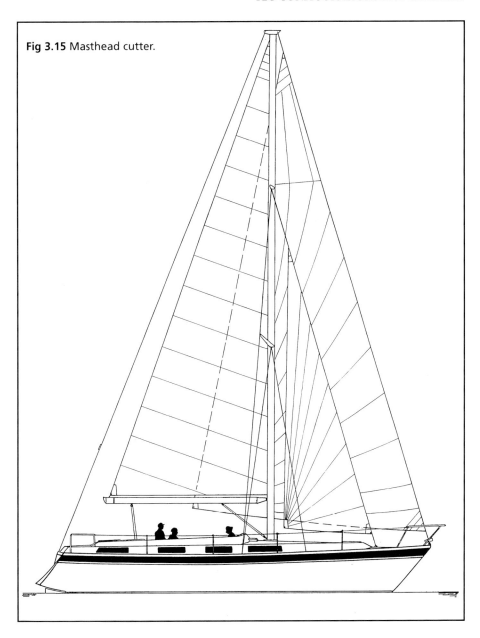

Fig 3.15 Masthead cutter.

the leech, so as to avoid any tendency for tension across the sail to jam the luff slides in the mast.

The traditional method of rolling the sail round the boom, using a handle at the gooseneck to rotate it, is dependable and even simpler to use, but it has its drawbacks. A vang can then only be used with a claw ring, restricting the downforce that it can apply to the boom, and it doesn't give such good control over the reefed sail as a slab system. The battens seldom roll down parallel with the boom and without careful co-ordination of halyard, topping lift and reefing handle, the fullness of the sail, combined with the angle of the leech, tends to roll the sail forwards into a creased bundle with insufficient foot tension.

The alternatives, of rolling up the sail on a furling spar, either inside the mast, as on this cutter (Fig 3.15), or the boom, provide arguably the two easiest of all the methods of reducing (and certainly of stowing) the mainsail. They enable small crews to handle big boats with large mainsails, and they have the added attraction of needing no sail covers. There are even press-button systems with built-in electric or hydraulic motors, as on some headsail installations. It must also be said of the earlier generation of these furlers, many of which are still around, that they encourage people who can afford them to depend on engineering that, should it fail – jam, for instance – could leave them in a dangerous situation. Modern equipment of either type is, for the most part, perfectly reliable, but they still involve considerable financial outlay and tend to compromise the efficiency of the rig in one way or another.

For luff reefing, the mast has to be oversized to accommodate the furled mainsail, causing increased drag and turbulence across it, while the extra weight aloft affects the motion of the boat. Added to this, the sail can have no battens and must be cut without any roach, with a corresponding loss of area and efficiency.

In-boom reefing has the advantage of keeping the weight nearer to the deck, and of using a fully battened, roached sail which can be dropped in an emergency independently of the reefing system. But the sail has to be cut with little or no luff curve, so its fullness cannot be adjusted very much by halyard tension or mast bend; and in order for it to roll evenly, without bagging, and to maintain proper foot tension, the boom must be supported while reefing by a rigid strut vang which can be locked at a precise angle of between 86° and 89° depending on the geometry of the particular sail. The use of 'rod' vangs is not, of course, confined to this type of boom. They are an effective labour saver on any fixed-mast, slab-reefing boat, because not only do they dispense with the need for a topping lift, but those that incorporate a steel or gas spring can also be used to push the boom up to the required working level; or to meet the next clew when reefing, so as to relieve tension on its reefing line. The angle of the boom is controlled in the usual way by a rope purchase which is neatly contained, in some models, inside the strut itself.

BERMUDAN CAT KETCH

The cat ketch is the simplest of all the double-masted rigs, along with its yawl and schooner cousins, by virtue of the location of its leading mast right up in the eyes of the boat and the absence of any headsail. It is also better balanced than a single-masted cat and more weatherly. For its area and height,

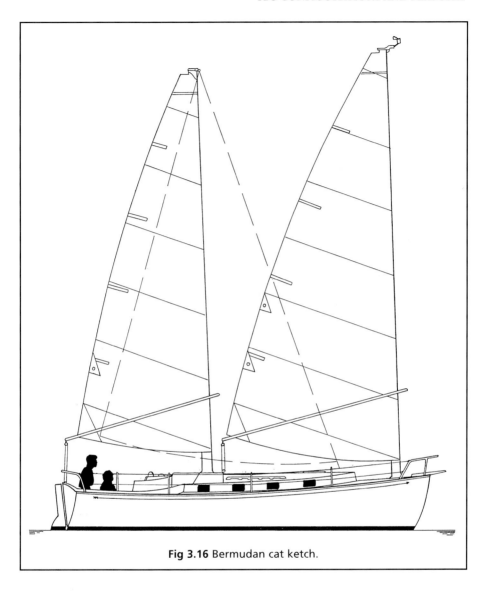

Fig 3.16 Bermudan cat ketch.

however, it is among the least powerful of all the common rigs for working to windward because the large mizzen standing in the airstream that has been diverted by the mainsail, tends to be backwinded or pinched when the boat is close-hauled. At the same time, its relative angle and distance from the main being such that it cannot provide an effective slot. With no help from a headsail either, the result is a noticeably sluggish performance and general lack of zip to windward, especially in light airs. But on a reach or running, these boats can really fly. Coupled with their ease of handling, this makes them very well suited to blue water cruising.

Among the best known is the Freedom shown here (Fig 3.16), a husky sort of a boat which was designed back in the 1960s by the American innovator Gary Hoyt and is distinguished for its unstayed masts, sprit booms and two-ply sails. Individually these features have been around for much longer than that, but Hoyt was the first to combine them in a single boat, providing us with a convenient opportunity to examine each in turn and its relationship to the others.

In normal rigging, the forces generated by the sails are resisted by the shrouds and stays, which in turn impose high compression loads on the mast. A free-standing mast is not subjected to these, but must instead be designed to withstand almost all of the boat's righting moment as it heels, and to spill wind in a gust by bending. In doing so, it also flattens and de-powers the sail, which in consequence can be cut very full for good drive in light airs. Many of these spars have been built in aluminium, but as in the case of the AeroRig, carbon-epoxy composite spars, though much more expensive, are many times stronger and weigh less than half as much. Their development can be likened to the evolution of aircraft wings. They too started off with stays and struts, but discarded them for the very practical reason that if one fitting failed the entire wing came off. One of the merits of carbon-epoxy is the way in which it enables fittings to be built into the spar. Instead of metal fittings for the shroud terminals, for example, a composite extension can be made to grow out of the main body, the stresses being distributed through a web of spreading strands of carbon, like the attachment of ligaments to a bone. Getting rid of the standing rigging and the multiplicity of components, such as bottle screws, spreaders, tangs and toggles, minimises the number of things that can compromise the security of the boat.

The theme of simplicity is continued, at least in theory, with the use of sprit booms, which are self-vanging. That is to say, when the pull of the sail tries to lift the after end of the boom, the foot comes taut and holds it down. Because no sheeting effort is devoted to this, mainsheet loads are that much lighter and there is no need for a traveller, the sheet only controlling the athwartships position of the boom and sail, while the leech tension, twist and fullness are adjusted by sprit angle and clew outhaul (or just a snotter on a dinghy). The simplest form of sprit boom is a straight spar and it is the most widely used, but it fouls the leeward side of the sail on one tack. The wishbone, which surrounds the sail and allows it to lie against alternate sides and take up its proper aerofoil shape as the boat is tacked, was a logical development. Its disadvantage on a conventional mast is that it can't be squared off as far as a straight boom before coming up against the shrouds, but it was a natural choice for unstayed boats such as the Freedom (and of course for sailboards).

Each wishbone is supported at the luff by a 'saddle' which is laced to eyelets in the sail and bears against the after side of the mast, with hoist and downhaul lines. Reefing – mizzen first – is by the normal slab process of setting up the topping lift, letting off a marked length of halyard and cranking down the new tack and clew ropes. The reefed area is then dragged down through the boom with another line and bridle between the two wings of the sail. The resulting arsenal of strings, seven to each mast, is funnelled back to the cockpit through a regiment of jammers. Sailing with wishbones may be simple enough, but reefing is rather less so – except that, as on any rotating mast, either free-standing or with the widely based shrouds of some multihulls, it can be carried out on any point of sailing, even on a dead run.

A two-ply sail is in effect two sails wrapped around the mast and laced together along the leech. The mast thus forms the leading edge of a very efficient rotating aerofoil which always stays in line with the wind, with its leeward surface always having a greater curvature to it than the windward one. Twice the area sounds like twice the weight and cost, but in practice a lighter weight of cloth can be used – around two-thirds that for a single-skinned sail. Nevertheless there is twice the area and a third more weight to be handled, and with a certain amount of friction on the mast, hoisting sail and shaking out reefs provides plenty of healthy exercise. When furled, the sails lie between cradles of shockcord stretched above and below them across their respective wishbones, which are not normally lowered.

For cat-sloops and bowsprit equipped cat-ketches, Freedom Yachts devised a highly original means of setting a jib from an unstayed mast. It consists of a curved aluminium batten like a half-wishbone, located in a wide pocket from the clew to the luff of the sail, with a form of thrust collar at either end, allowing it to roll over from side to side as the boat is tacked. This acts as a strut to tension the headstay (or the luff wire if the sail is set flying) as the halyard is hauled taut, holding the sail in an efficient aerofoil shape whatever the wind direction. It not only combines self-tacking with the automatic twist control that wishbone booms provide, but works as a poling out spar downwind.

Reaching and running performance can be considerably boosted by means of a mizzen staysail, the largest being a ghoster like the one shown here, which virtually doubles the area and power of the rig. It is set flying, tacked on a short strop from the coachroof, with either its halyard or a separate running backstay taken round the windward side of the rig and hooked to the toerail to give the mast some support. Like all staysails, it is outstandingly powerful and effective because there is no spar immediately ahead of it to spoil the airflow and the sheet can hold it at the optimum angle and curvature over its entire surface. So it is generally considered a worthwhile addition to the wardrobe, despite the inconvenience of having to lower and rehoist it whenever the boat is put about.

Without it, tacking is merely a matter of putting the helm down. These boats will sail tolerably well under mainsail alone, which is handy when manoeuvring or coming alongside, or in heavy weather with mizzen furled and double-reefed main. On a broad reach, the boat is usually sailed goosewinged, with the main boom eased out over the weather bow where the sail can work without interference from the mizzen. Sheeted in this fashion, the boat also has a high angle of tolerance downwind and can be allowed to swing widely either side of the course without any danger of gybing. With no shrouds or kicker, you can also sail up to a mooring with the wind aft of the beam by letting off both sheets until the sails are pointing forwards and flapping (and the same thing in reverse when leaving the mooring).

But for all the merits of wishbones and two-ply sails, they can be hard work at times. Small wonder, then, that many owners opt for fully battened single-ply sails running in mast tracks with conventional booms, because they are undoubtedly easier to handle. Whichever form of rig is chosen, one thing all are agreed on: how strangely quiet these boats are, with no howling in the rigging, no drumming down below in the hull from taut stays and shrouds. Only the sounds of the sea.

GUNTER YAWL

Combining the handiness of a ketch with the weatherliness of a sloop, the yawl – Bermudan, gaff or gunter – has established an excellent reputation as a pleasant, easy-going rig for fishing and cruising craft of all sizes, even dinghies, whereas the ketch is better suited to boats of, say, nine metres and above. Not that it's always easy to distinguish between the two. Back in the grand period of yachting, a ketch was recognised as having her mizzenmast stepped forward of the rudder post, while the yawl's was abaft it. The latter layout was much favoured at the time for racing, because its mizzen wasn't measured and consequently gave the boat a favourable rating. Not surprisingly, some cruising men were inclined to dismiss the rig as no more than a good cutter spoiled. Others swore by it, and many still do.

Measurement rules have long since changed, and anyway you nowadays seldom see a rudder post projecting below an overhanging counter. The difference between the two rigs has become more a matter of purpose than of proportion. A yawl still has a much smaller mizzen than a ketch – about one-quarter the size of the mainsail compared to a half or more, and is stepped about a tenth of the deck length from the stern instead of around a quarter. But in practical terms it means that the ketch's mizzen contributes an important part of the drive, unlike a yawl's which is primarily for balance and as a handling and manoeuvring device, with the benefit of being set so far aft that it is clear of a fisherman's working area and doesn't intrude on a yachtsman's cockpit. Nor does its boom have to be carried high enough to clear heads, which on a small ketch tends to look ungainly, and the downdraft from the sail doesn't give the helmsman a stiff neck, which it sometimes can on a ketch. On this example (Fig 3.17), the boom is a wishbone in order to reduce the

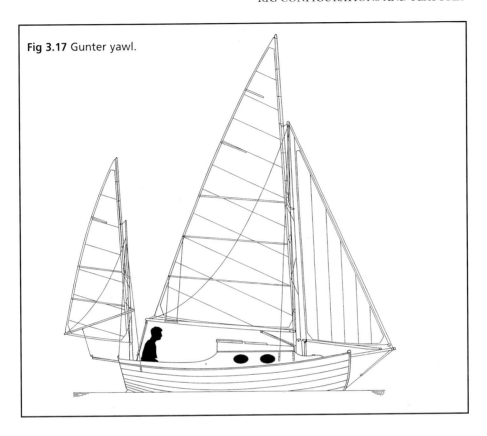

Fig 3.17 Gunter yawl.

sheeting load and hence the upward pull on the bumpkin, which is unstayed for ease of shipment.

There are, however, a couple of potential snags with a yawl's mizzenmast. It has either to be offset to one side so that the tiller can swing through 45° without hitting it, or the tiller must be sickle-shaped, or split and bowed either side of it, or mechanically linked to it with crossheads and cables. There is also the problem of its staying, which is usually restricted by the breadth of the stern and has to rely on sheeting tension to resist the forward thrust of the sail.

Nevertheless, with a bowsprit to carry the headsails well forward, the yawl's well spread-out sailplan also offers good directional steadiness in a sea-way, which is valuable for comfort and for progress to weather, plus a low centre of effort and a very much smaller heeling movement compared to a tall Bermudan rig of the same area. All mizzens need to be cut fairly flat, because they stand in the downwash of the main, and the yawl's must at least be large enough – say 10% of the total working area, not just a toy sail tacked on the tail of a sloop – to pay its way and compensate for the drag of its mast and rigging. Even so, it cannot contribute much to the windward performance, which is not exactly sparkling at the best of times, but the wide spread between mizzen and jib means that, provided she is headed a few points off the wind or brought on to a reach, a yawl will sail steadily – albeit somewhat slowly – under these two sails alone, and without the heeling effect of the main. This makes for a snug, happy rig in heavy weather, and with all sails being moderately sized, particularly well suited to a single-handed helmsman. Alternatively, unlike many ketches, a yawl can potter along quite nicely under main and jib, with the mizzen only being used to adjust the helm balance when the other sails are shortened, or when heaving-to with the jib backed.

Most modern yachts have a considerable amount of windage forward, especially with a rolled up genoa, so that in a crosswind their heads tend to pay off too readily at slow speeds, such as when approaching a mooring or quayside. This can effectively be countered by windage aft, in the form of a flattened, hard-sheeted mizzen, which will also hold her head up while drifting astern after picking up or dropping a mooring in a crowded anchorage, and will improve the riding behaviour when lying head to wind in rough weather. The little mizzen is equally handy for heaving-to with the jib aback, and as a steadying sail when motoring; and its masthead provides a point from which a staysail can be set. On this example (Fig 3.17), the jib is self-tacking on a club boom. This is pivoted on the bowsprit a short distance behind the tack, the resulting geometry allowing the sail automatically to take up increased camber when running downwind. As well as having no sheets to handle when tacking, it behaves better than a boomless jib, tacking itself when necessary instead of repeatedly collapsing and filling with a thump. For the purpose of furling, the clew is carried by a sliding ring on the boom, using an outhaul to adjust the fullness of the sail when partly rolled away.

So much for the yawl; now for the gunter. This evolved from the gaff rig as a means of setting a tall sail on a short mast, working on the principle of a sliding topmast. Its yard is peaked up so high as to extend more or less vertically above the masthead, making the sail virtually triangular, like a Bermudan. As a result it is markedly superior to a gaff sail in its performance to windward. It has the further important advantage that as reefs are taken in, the yard is lowered along with the sail, reducing the weight and windage aloft; and its spars are compact enough to stow inside the boat, which is a blessing for those left on exposed moorings or trailed on the road. The masts on this 7 m (23 ft) trailer-sailer, for example, are small enough to be lowered single-handed, which is useful on waterways with low bridges, and short enough for a man to reach halfway up and put a tie round the sail as a quick furl. Both are mounted in tabernacles which are skewed in opposite directions a few degrees off the centreline, to enable the masts to hinge down beside one another.

On the early types – and some of today's replicas – the yard was held to the mast by two leather-covered metal hoops, or sometimes by a pair of parrels, which kept it more or less vertical as it rode up and down. The problem with this arrangement, known as a sliding gunter, was that it chewed up the mast and was prone to jam, despite liberal applications of grease, so the current variation was devised. It comprises a span shackle travelling on a wire bridle, stretched along the forward face of the yard and hauled to the mast-head by the peak halyard, and a second halyard running to the bottom of the yard to set the luff taut. The throat halyard is simply eased for reefing, while the peak halyard stays put, but this can itself be eased in order to exercise a certain amount of control over the shape of the sail, or to drop the peak in a gust. There is nothing to jam, but inevitably there is some slop between the mast and the yard which tends to sag away to leeward.

The simplest solution, adopted on a number of small boats such as the Mirror dinghy, is to tie a single halyard directly to the yard so that this ends up as close to the masthead as possible. However, this involves moving the halyard up the yard when reefing, which is difficult under way. Instead, the halyard can be fastened to the yard at about the point of balance, and its angle adjusted with a parrel line round the mast and leading down to the deck via a sheave on the yard above the halyard attachment. One of the neatest alter-natives is to run the heel of the yard in a track on the mast, with a second slide intercepting the peak halyard en route from the masthead sheave. This enables the yard to move downwards for reefing, but holds it close to the mast and stretches the luff as soon as the halyard is re-tensioned. It does not, however, allow the angle of the peak to be adjusted.

All things considered, the gunter is a thoroughly practical and versatile rig, but it is generally restricted to small boats with sails of up to 15–16 sq m (161–172 sq ft) or so. Larger than that, the yard starts to become unwieldy; and since the peak halyard must be attached above the yard's point of balance, the mast can become almost as long as a Bermudan's.

GAFF KETCH

A gaff sail is usually proportioned more like that of the cutter on page 100. But since traditionally styled Dutch yachts will long continue to lend grace and character to the sailing scene in Northern Europe, no rig round-up would be complete without including at least one of the many types in which there has been such a revival of interest in recent years. Although the major-ity of them are in fact single-masted, ketch rigs are to be seen on the larger 'klipper yachts', such as the *tjalk* shown here (Fig 3.18).

The gaff is believed to have originated in 16th century Holland as a devel-opment of the sprit. It had been customary to leave a sprit standing with its sail brailed up to the mast. But over the years, as the sprit grew shorter in order to make it less cumbersome to handle in a seaway, it assumed the form of a short gaff that could be lowered, together with the sail, which became shaped like a shoulder of mutton – hence the name by which it was known –

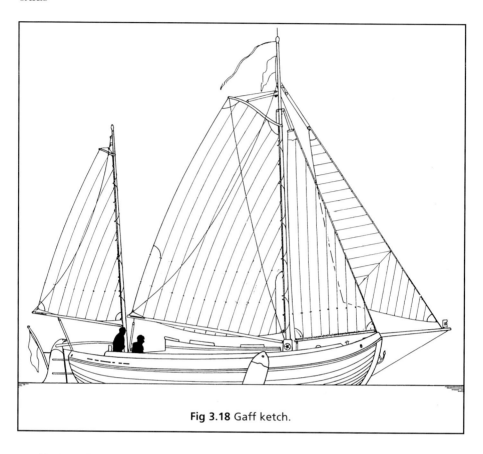

Fig 3.18 Gaff ketch.

as distinct from the squat 'leg-o-mutton' triangle of the early jib-headed mainsails. A problem with these was that their headboards were always pulling out, whereas the little Dutch gaff spread the stress of the halyards over a wider area, like a coat hanger. Likely as not, it was curved so that if it became necessary to tack with the mainsail scandalised during a squall, its tack triced up and the peak lowered (a quick alternative to reefing), the tip of the gaff would pass more easily under the topping lift set up to support the boom. Or it may have been argued that since a straight gaff bent under load, why not make it curved to begin with?

For whatever reason, these short, curved gaffs*, along with their loose-footed sails and leeboards, have remained a distinctive feature of many traditional Dutch boats. So too have their massive, free-standing wooden masts. These have been replaced on a few of the 'modernised' boats by tapered aluminium alloy extrusions which need less maintenance, but they are outlawed by sailing clubs specialising in historic vessels. And anyway, wooden masts

---

* Most *tjalks* have straight gaffs, but the opportunity has been taken on the one in Fig 3.18 to show what curved gaffs look like.

have the flexibility needed in heavy weather, allied to a virtually infinite fatigue life. Extended periods of working in light winds also called for generous sail areas, but the relatively poor stability due to the shoal draft required the rig to be kept low to reduce weight and windage aloft. This in turn enabled the lines and sailcloth to be stout enough to endure years of chafe and abuse with the minimum of maintenance, and the spars were similarly heavy. A loose-footed sail needs a stiff boom anyway, because with all the stress concentrated at the ends, and the boom tending to sag under its own weight, compression from the outhaul and sheet acts to increase the bend. No vang can be used to hold the boom down off the wind, because this would only bend it even more. With no support between tack and clew, there is a similar concentration of loading on the lower corners of the sail, and any end-plate effect there may be from the average laced or bolt-roped boom is lost. On the other hand, freed of the restriction of a boom, the sail can assume a natural curve and develop more drive low down where it is most needed, its reef points are easier to tie in, and quite a lot of extra area can be worked into it with a big foot roach.

Some of these boats even have a buntline under the foot of the mainsail, if it is set particularly low, to flip it over the coachroof when tacking and to let the helmsman see if there's anything under its lee that he ought to know about. There is also a certain amount of downdraft off the sail, sometimes visible as a fine spray drifting in over the lee rail when the boat heels steeply, which must help to dampen the gyrations of the boom when running before a strong wind.

Instead of having a large foot roach, a 'watersail' is sometimes set beneath the boom for running in very light winds, almost clipping the surface of the sea. Another effective but ungainly looking extra sail, peculiar to Dutch sloops, is the *aap*, a triangular sail which is poked out over the stern by a sprit, its luff stretched between the ends of the gaff and the boom – or sometimes tacked down to the deck.

Except for the jib, which nowadays is usually mitred, the sails are cut 'up-and-down' in the traditional manner, as if they were made of flax, whose cloth is stronger lengthways than across. In fact they are more likely to be made of one of the modern warp-orientated synthetic fabrics whose introduction has brought the vertical cut back into fashion. Without battens to prevent the leech from curling, the sails cannot have anything like the amount of roach shown in Fig 3.18, if any at all. But they are cut for maximum drive in light airs, with such wide broadseaming at the top and bottom of their panels that when full of wind, they appear from most angles to be carrying generous amounts of roach.

The staysail on this boat has been laced to a boom, with a single sheet running on an iron horse across the deck, making the sail self-tending (except when the shackle which acts as a traveller hangs up and needs a kick). When short-handed, supplementary control lines can be rigged on either side to haul the sail up to weather when heaving-to, or to help the bows across when tacking; or to harden in the sail when close-hauled. Where a large overlapping and consequently loose-footed headsail is set, an old Dutch method of controlling it when close-tacking is by means of a pendant, bent to the foot of the sail just ahead of the mast and travelling on the horse. This constrains the greater part of the sail, with the sheet needed only to flatten the leech area.

No one can pretend that these vessels are as easy to handle or as close-winded as a canoe-bodied, fin-keeled lightweight, powered by long-luffed Bermudan sails with little twist, set behind an efficient mast. But for the sailor in no particular hurry, who rates rugged, slug-it-out dependability and spacious accommodation above sheer performance, they are an attractive alternative to a more modern boat.

SCHOONER

The modern sloop rig is so effective and simple to use that it would be difficult to justify some of the more complex arrangements were it not for their sheer beauty – and the satisfaction to be had from playing with a multiplicity of sails. Of all these configurations, there is something especially attractive and romantic about a schooner, qualities that are often overlooked in today's pursuit of efficiency at all costs. Nostalgia apart, however, the rig has three great traditional virtues: power, seaworthiness, and the ability to ride out storms.

By definition, schooners are fore-and-aft rigged on two masts, the taller one aft, and the majority still set gaff sails on both, in keeping with the time honoured nature of these handsome craft. Some set square topsails or various combinations of gaff main and square foresails, and a few have three or more masts, but these are mostly on larger vessels that are too far outside our notional 45 ft limit to concern us here.

In contrast to the sails of ketches and yawls, those of a schooner are progressively larger and further apart as you look aft. This results in the flow off each of them, when they are all set and sheeted properly, smoothing the airstream along the lee side of the following one more effectively than it can on the other two-masted rigs. The small forestaysail forms a slot for the foresail which in turn, without interfering too much with the action of the mainsail, directs the airflow on to its luff. Nevertheless, a schooner's mainsail is not as powerful as that of a sloop, and the vessel can never be as close-winded, because the foresail is not as well shaped or located to help it, compared with the sloop's jib. In fact, the foresail is usually the rig's weak link because if, with its unavoidably short boom, the head is allowed to sag off through insufficient sheet or vang tension, a schooner won't point.

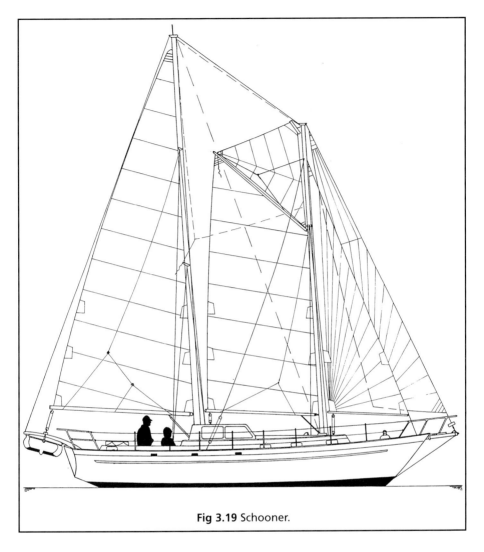

Fig 3.19 Schooner.

The jib adds useful area and lifts the flow on to the forestaysail, extending the overall circulation area, but it is normally treated as a moderate weather sail, to be furled when the wind pipes up. Its staying is seldom rigid enough to keep the long luff tight in heavy weather, even with the tension transferred along a springstay to the mainmast and down to the deck via the standing backstay. (This is needed anyway to set up a main staysail, the shrouds having insufficient drift to prevent the mast from bending forward.) With the fore-staysail on a boom, this boat can be tacked with only the jib sheets to be handled. Furling the jib brings the whole rig inboard, snug and well balanced, but still effective for manoeuvring, with sails at each end of the hull imposing the minimum strain on it. As the wind freshens, the heavily reefed mainsail becomes a useful steering sail with plenty of power low down, while the foresail provides the main driving force and the staysail does the rest. In a gale, a schooner will lie steadily under reefed foresail, sheeted flat, with helm lashed down and the furled mainsail providing sufficient windage to act as a riding sail

Another advantage of having the largest sail aft is that it can be hoisted first and lowered last without causing the boat to charge around her anchor, and can even be left standing in light weather during, for example, a trip ashore in the dinghy. On the other hand, schooners are notoriously hard to handle on a dead run because the big main, set so far back in the boat, has a tendency to make her round up into the wind. Goosewinging, besides reducing the inevitable rolling, prevents the foresail being entirely blanketed by the main, but ketches and yawls invariably win downwind, where their mizzens throw less of a shadow ahead of them. Upwind, the behaviour of most schooners can only be described as indifferent, so it is not surprising that some of the more modern-minded owners opt for a straightforward Bermudan sailplan which, besides being simpler to handle, provides rather better windward performance, though at the expense of being considerably less attractive aesthetically. The mixed rig shown here (Fig 3.19) has proved to be a good compromise in these respects.

It is on a reach that schooners really excel, because with a long main boom and a bowsprit they can spread such a broad expanse of low-level working canvas, and can augment it with a variety of light weather reaching sails to fill the unoccupied spaces between the masts. The main staysail, which is tall and triangular, has the best aerofoil shape. It is set flying from the mainmast head, tacked down beside the foremast or shifted to windward of it to clear the foresail and improve the flow on to the mainsail, and sheeted just inside the main shrouds. As with a genoa, it can sometimes restrict or completely block forward vision, becoming an awkward liability in crowded waters; and since it has to be lowered and rehoisted every time the boat is put about, it is only worth flying on long tacks. Nor does it work well in strong winds, because the luff sags. But as long as it can be made to hold its shape, it is an immensely powerful driving sail. So good is it aerodynamically that on a staysail schooner, which also carries a Bermudan mainsail, it is set standing as an integral part of the rig, replacing the foresail altogether and worked like a sloop's jib. This is arguably the simplest and most weatherly of all schooner rigs if you don't count the Luna, which consists solely of two tall, slender roller-reefing staysails, both of them loose-footed and self-tacking, one to each masthead. Though highly efficient to weather, its unboomed sails put it at a disadvantage downwind, when it is best close-tacked, and its shorn appearance is not to everyone's taste.

A schooner's reaching sail area is commonly augmented by a four-sided lightweight known as a 'fisherman', on account of its working boat origins. The head is set flying above the main staysail between the two mastheads, its short luff tacked with a pendant to leeward of the foremast, and sheeted back to the rail near the stern. In order to keep the head taut and prevent the sail from falling into a useless bag shape, with the consequent heeling effect and loss of drive, the main backstay has to be hardened up as much as possible without bending the mast. A fisherman can be set to either side of the foresail, but with standing rigging more often than not being in the way, it cannot be tacked without lowering and re-hoisting it, and it is easily lost overboard in the process, with four control lines – the peak and throat halyards, tack pendant and sheet – needing some smart handling while going about.

For reaching in the very lightest of airs, the foresail can be furled away and both of these staysails replaced by a single gigantic queen staysail, or 'gollywobbler', which almost doubles the working sail area. Like the fisherman it is four-sided, with its head stretched between the mainmast head and the foremast partner, its long luff tacked down vertically beside the foremast, and the sheet running right back to the quarter or to the after end of the main boom. It can be tacked by walking the clew round the mainmast, but because of its awe-inspiring size and featherweight construction, such a sail is vulnerable to damage if it gets out of hand, and the crew must be ready to take it in at the first signs of a freshening breeze. One way and another, staysails can be hard work at times. But they utterly transform a schooner's offwind performance, especially that of heavy displacement boats.

JUNK RIGGED SCHOONER

The term *junk* is an English invention, probably derived from *chaun*, the Chinese word for a ship, or the Javanese *djong*, meaning a Chinese sailing vessel. The bamboo battened sail, in the form of a balanced lug shaped 'like an ear listening for the wind', was in use in the Far East more than two thousand years ago, long before the English language existed, on the single-masted riverine craft we know as sampans, with their flat bottoms, free-standing masts, leeboards and rudders, as well as on multi-masted ocean-going ships. The rig was not seen in the West until near the turn of the 19th century, after old Joshua Slocum adopted the Chinese lug for his beach-built *Liberdade*, pronouncing it 'the most convenient rig in the whole world'. Another 60 years were to elapse before Blondie Haslar brought it to the attention of the yachting fraternity on the famous little Folkboat *Jester* with which he initiated single-handed trans-Atlantic racing, prompting several British and American yachtbuilders to feature the rig on their cruising craft. To the majority of untutored occidental eyes, however, it looked outlandish, crude and complicated, and although the boats sailed well enough and are still regularly built in small numbers, they have never really caught on and seem destined to remain something of a rarity.

More's the pity, for the design of the junk sail and its gear has a lot going

Fig 3.20 Junk rigged schooner.

for it, embodying as it does, in an extraordinarily subtle way, the first two essentials for relaxed, economic cruising: simplicity and fail-safe durability. It is fundamentally a low stress rig, in which the shape of the sail is created by its spars and battens, instead of by tension at the corners. The Chinese considered the entire rig – the sail, with its spars, battens, running rigging and controls – as a single entity which they supported on an unstayed wooden mast and usually set to port of it. The latest interpretation of the rig's aerodynamics is at variance with accepted theory, the sail having been found to operate most efficiently in a *turbulent* airstream. Consequently it works best on port tack, with the sail plastered against the mast, whereas on starboard tack, with a smoother leeward airflow, the sail is slightly less powerful. This seemingly strange behaviour is the subject of an ongoing research programme. On schooners ('periaguas' to the purist; schooners are supposed to have headsails) the discrepancy can be countered by setting the sails on opposite sides of their respective masts. Any helm imbalance on a single-masted rig can be corrected by moving the entire sail slightly fore or aft with the tack downhaul or kicker, or by hauling or slackening the luff lacings or parrels. This helps to make junks particularly fast on a reach. Not that they are all that slow to windward. They cannot point as high as a Bermudan rigged boat, but some of the latest yachting versions can rival them in terms of Vmg, the effective speed made good to windward. They have to sail a greater distance through the water, but under these conditions they are often faster and likely to arrive at an upwind destination at much the same time as the other boat, despite its narrower tacking angle.

Each sail is made up of multiple panels with full-chord battens between them, each batten acting as a boom, with its own rope parrel round the mast. At the after ends, spans connect adjoining pairs of battens to intermediate 'sheetlets' which on the majority of Western yachts such as the schooner pictured here (Fig 3.20), converge through a series of blocks at a single control, the mainsheet. Its action is thus distributed all the way up the leech, with – in theory – no tendency for the sail to twist. In practice it does, to a certain extent, because the upper parts of the system are working at a less advantageous angle than the lower parts, and the topmost batten is usually left free altogether, or extended beyond the leech, because its sheet would otherwise catch on the other spans when tacking.

On the original rigs the Chinese, well aware that excessive twist was the limiting factor in windward sailing, evolved various highly efficient but more complex sheeting patterns (Fig 3.21) to allow for different numbers of battens and to give more or less mechanical advantage, with some of the blocks being replaced by simple pieces of wood with holes through them. These cunning devices, called *euphroes*, act as friction blocks, and are controlled from a master block. The system has the advantage of being able to gather the spans into groups, whose trim can be adjusted individually with multiple mainsheets to provide a comprehensive control over the leech. Some yachts are rigged in this way, but a single long-running sheet is usually preferred for the sake of simplicity, despite needing a lot of overhauling when lowering the sail completely. On a typical installation, this would make a total of nine lines to each sail: upper and lower luff parrels, yard parrel, halyard, tack downhaul for luff tensioning, vang, port and starboard topping lifts, and the sheet. All can be led through turning blocks to a central position in the cockpit or in the wheelhouse, so there is never any need to go on deck to fight flogging canvas. Admittedly it all looks rather complicated at first sight, but in practice it is surprisingly simple to use, and few other rigs are able to provide such a wealth of sail adjustments, with such accurate, independent control of both sail shape and incidence.

The battens themselves contribute considerably to the performance of the sail. Instead of the usual thin flat strips, they are quite sizeable wooden poles or alloy or GRP tubes, either contained in pockets, or alternatively mounted externally, with a control batten on one side, laced through to a retaining 'keep' on the other. Either way, the sail becomes a series of wind channels as each panel is blown into a concave shape, with the battens creating vortices and hence the turbulent airflow on which the rig is now thought to operate. In the West it was generally assumed that junk sails were always set flat as a wall, resulting in good aerodynamics in high winds, reducing heeling moment while maintaining plenty of drive, but with correspondingly indifferent performance to windward in light airs. Recent studies of Chinese sails have revealed, however, that they are in fact slightly cambered, using bamboos of suitable diameter to provide the required elliptical shape. The problem with bendy battens that Western experimenters have found is that if they are made to flex sufficiently in a light breeze, they are apt to bend too much before reefing in stronger winds. Striking the right balance seems to be more of an ancient art than any sort of science, but an effective compromise can be achieved by using GRP for the battens and making the lower ones, which operate in slower windspeeds, more flexible than those above. One alternative, where batten pockets are used as on the majority of Westernised rigs, is to cut them with a rounding along their length, the sloppy fit near the middle allowing the sail to sag to leeward and take up an appropriate camber – typically 8–10% in the lower panels, rather less higher up. A better though more complex way of doing this is to fit two or three hinged joints in each of the battens.

In addition to a number of highly developed versions of the rig, with high-peaked yards and rounded leeches, there are a couple of interesting variants that depart from all accepted practices in their quest for improved aerodynamics. The first is the Swingwing, with a hinged trailing edge that allows the sail automatically to take up the correct camber in light airs, locking up so that it bends no further as the wind increases, and reversing its camber from tack to tack. The other is the Gallant, which has rigid two-ply sails shaped like an aircraft wing and supported by internal wishbone battens in the form of self-stacking aluminium girders. All have proved to compare well with a Bermudan in their windward performance, besides being simpler to handle, but their building costs, notably those of the winged Gallant, are inevitably somewhat higher. (Details are available from the Junk Rig Association, 373 Hunts Pond Road, Titchfield, Fareham, Hants PO14 4PB, England.)

With a junk, as with a swing rig, it is best to forget conventional sailing principles. The most obvious aspects to strike a newcomer are the uncanny quietness, with no flogging sails even when head to wind; the easy motion,

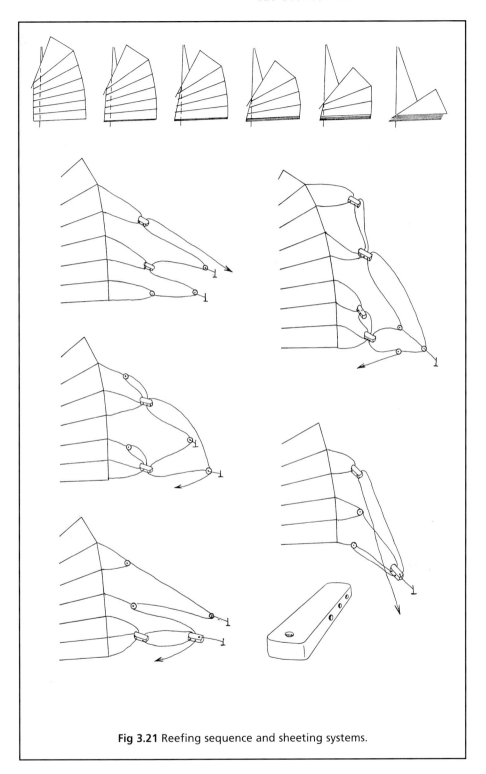

Fig 3.21 Reefing sequence and sheeting systems.

because an unstayed mast sheds many of the stresses from the system by bending in the puffs instead of heeling the boat; and the unobstructed visibility, the entire rig being above the line of sight, with no boom to bang heads. In these respects it has a number of similarities to the swing rig. Both have a unitary aerofoil surface that pivots round the mast, so that as the after part sweeps down to leeward, the forepart moves up to windward – Haslar likened it to a great barn door swinging silently on its hinges – maintaining a degree of aerodynamic balance and acting as an airbrake when gybing. There is no need to gather in the sheet prior to doing so because the whole process is so steady and controlled and the boom itself is virtually just another batten – although anyone in the cockpit should beware of being scooped up in the loose cradle of cordage as the boom comes across. As for tacking, with no headsails to be tended, a junk can wriggle through a line of moorings like an eel by simply a matter of putting the helm down and letting the sails look after themselves.

There are really only two basic rules to follow on the junk rig: (1) due to its long chord and small amount of overall camber, the sail needs to be set at a relatively small angle of incidence compared with a Bermudan sail – somewhere around 25° to the apparent wind – so as to allow the air to flow from luff to leech; and (2) the booms should never be allowed to go much forward of 90° to the centreline when running. This is because not only will they be difficult to pull back without having first to alter course, but there is also the risk of battens being broken whenever they are put in compression against the pull of the sheets. On a beam reach, with the sails again trimmed more or less athwartships to maintain the fine angle of incidence, the resultant force is still mostly along the centreline, with correspondingly little tendency to heel the boat. But sailing nearly upright, with so little load on the sheet and no flow indication or stall warning from the sails (because their stalled lift is not much less than their maximum) it is often difficult to know whether they are set to best advantage. On most points of sailing, best performance calls for a sensitive helmsman with a light touch, for even a small amount of over-sheeting is liable to stall the rig and kill its drive; but with good judgement most modern versions of the rig can be made to tack through 90°, and some of the most highly developed can better 80°.

The junk's ease of reefing, on the other hand, can hardly be bettered. Due to the weight of the battens (and to some extent the friction in pulling out the multi-part halyard and sheet runs), hoisting the rig is a bit of an effort if there is any wind in it. Getting under way, one can if necessary take a breather and move off sedately through an anchorage with just one or two panels up, completing the hoisting later. But release the halyard, and even without luffing, the sail comes rattling down until the required number of panels have stacked themselves neatly one above the other like a venetian blind, nestling securely between the lazyjacks. A further benefit is that should a sail tear through old age or in prolonged heavy weather, the damage is confined to a small rectangle bounded by the battens and the seams of the cloths, which are laid vertically, parallel to the leech. As a temporary measure, the torn area can always be 'reefed out' by tying two adjacent battens together, although in China, junks are often to be seen sailing around quite unconcernedly with holes in their sails. There are no heavy stresses anywhere in the rig. For blue-water voyagers without access to a loft, even making a complete new sail is quite straightforward, because having no three-dimensional form it is just a flat sheet without edge curves, broadseaming or pleats, and stresses are so low that at a pinch almost any locally available material such as acrylic or poly-thene sheeting can be used, instead of polyester. Old flour sacks have been known to last thousands of miles and to have sailed through gales without damage – scarcely recommended practice, but it's hard to think of any other form of sail that would let you get away with it.

Because the rig is so docile and quick to reef or dump, and so easy to adjust without stopping the boat or changing course, it can safely be given an oversize sail, and consequently can be driven hard and can make good passages despite some inefficiency to windward, when progress can best be described as resolute rather than racy. Sailors who like to keep busy might miss the excitement and tensions of a Bermudan boat with a big genoa to be tamed, and would doubtless find the junk rather boring. But it has great appeal to families and single-handers with limited amounts of crew energy, and to the elderly who have begun to find conventional rigs a liability – indeed to anyone with a philosophical turn of mind who doesn't mind others sailing past him to windward, knowing that the tables will probably be turned if the weather changes, and meanwhile enjoying a quieter and invariably more comfortable ride.

CHAPTER 4

Sailmaking

The hallmark of the small-boat sailor is self-sufficiency. Most of us try our hand at cabinet work or other interior 'improvements', install instruments and repair rigging. Some even find the time and energy to build their own boats. Yet we are usually content to leave sailmaking to the professionals, regarding it as some sort of a cross between a black art, with hidden secrets handed down from one generation of craftsmen to the next, and a high-tech industry requiring specialist skills and precision equipment. This is to some extent true. Sailmaking is engineering with cloth, and it takes an experienced commercial loft to produce a good suit of racing or high performance sails, or large ones of any sort; and generally speaking only the professionals have the necessary floor space and facilities for handling large areas of cloth, and machines that can work with heavy materials. But there's nothing particularly difficult about making sails for a dinghy or a small cruising boat, and more often than not it proves to be a very interesting and satisfying enterprise for the amateur. Besides saving money, it helps him to appreciate more fully the functioning of the rig as he watches his own handiwork drive the boat.

SAILCLOTH

There are two vital ingredients in a successful sail: what it's made of, and how it's made. The sailmaker's contribution is to transform lifeless rolls of flat cloth into living, responsive sails, designed for maximum performance and reliable service. But even the most skilled craftsman can't make good sails from poor cloth or material of the wrong type. That may sound obvious, but the current pace of technological development, not to mention a certain amount of advertising hype, has led to some confusion over just what material is the most suitable, and bargains of uncertain origin have all too often led to disappointment and wasted time. It pays to play safe by selecting a brand-named cloth from one of the leading manufacturers, and making certain that its specifications are suited to the shape, cut and duties of the sail it will become, and the conditions under which it will be used. Cost, though important, should be a secondary consideration.

The number of different cloths on the market runs into hundreds, but they can be grouped under three main categories: polyesters, nylon, and the various laminates. Each has a different form of construction and physical properties that govern its performance and may affect its suitability for any particular type of panel arrangement or working conditions. The first two are woven fabrics, and as such are by far the most widely used in yachting and best suited to amateur sailmaking, while the highly specialised and much more expensive laminates are generally reserved for racing boats, large cruising craft and board sails.

Woven cloth is constructed of warp and fill (or weft) yarns, interlaced at right angles to each other along the length and width of the fabric respectively. (Think of warp as a rope and it's easier to remember which is which.) Loads that are parallel to the warp or to the fill cause only slight elongation of the yarns, but those that are not produce considerable bias distortion at 45° – diagonal stretch – which increases with the strength of the load. This spoils the original optimum shape of the sail, with a corresponding loss of efficiency. On the other hand, a certain amount of stretch can be more of a help than a hindrance for cruising. When used intentionally, for example in tensioning the luff to draw cloth from other parts of the sail and pull the draft forward (and provided that other areas such as the clew are reinforced against unwanted distortion and wrinkles), a cruising sail becomes more versatile.

Besides being heavy, unwieldy and prone to rot, sails made from natural fibres such as flax and cotton used to stretch permanently out of shape in a hard blow. This didn't matter very much on a square-rigged ship, but fore-and-aft sails needed recutting every so often to regain any semblance of their original performance. These materials are only used nowadays in preference to synthetic fabrics where authenticity is the prime consideration.

POLYESTER

Polyester yarn, on which much of today's sailcloth is based, was developed in the 1940s and 1950s by ICI Fibres in Britain, where it is known as Terylene®, and by DuPont in America, under the tradename Dacron®. There are half a dozen other manufacturers of polyester cloth in other parts of the world, each with their own name for it.

The choice of characteristics in a cloth starts with the yarn, which is formed from bundles of continuous extruded filaments of a plastic polymer. First its thickness and hence its weight (a figure expressed in 'decitex', the metric equivalent of denier) is selected for the warp and fill, which are usually different from one another. Each thread is made up of a specific number of filaments – typically 6000 to 8000 – twisted together, and whose count will affect the fabric's performance. In addition, the yarns themselves may be twisted, and two or more can be plied together, further affecting the properties of the finished fabric. Stretch along the cloth also depends on the degree

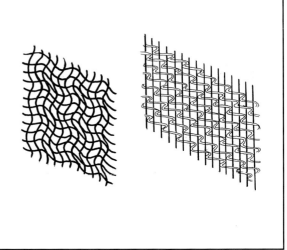

Fig 4.1 Crimp, the corrugated shape which the warp and fill yarns are forced to adopt as they go over and under one another in the loom. The relative amounts of crimp directly affect the bias characteristics of the cloth. *Left:* Balanced weave, warp fill yarns have equal amounts of crimp. *Right:* Vertical yarns are straight for minimum stretch in this direction, with crimp restricted to the crossing yarns.

to which the fill yarn distorts the warp as it goes over and under it in the loom, and vice versa. The resulting corrugated shape which the warp and to a lesser extent the fill yarns are forced to adopt is known as the 'crimp' (Fig 4.1). Their tensioning has to be precisely controlled during the weaving, since the relative amounts of crimp directly affect the all-important bias stretch.

In high aspect ratio sails, such as tall and narrow blade jibs and mainsails with long luffs and short feet, most of the stress is imposed down the leech, so its fabric needs to resist this with low-stretch, high-decitex fill yarns with the minimum of crimp. Such a sail will usually be cross-cut, so as to align the fill from head to foot. Bias stretch is less important, because the central area of the sail is comparatively small and not under high stress, and the fullness here can be controlled by using mast bend and Cunningham controls. In low aspect ratio sails, however, such as overlapping genoas, the large central area is under more stress than the leech, so bias stretch is reduced by using a more balanced construction with heavier decitex warps and crimping the fill yarns, making the fabric more suitable for vertical or radial panel layouts.

Newly woven material, known at this stage as 'greige' cloth (a term derived from the old French word for raw silk), is then scoured to remove the size that was applied to the warp yarn to lubricate it during the weaving. If dying is required, this is when it is done. Next the greige is impregnated with melamine and other resins chemically similar to it to act as a filler, together with an ultra-violet inhibitor to help protect it from the degrading effect of sunlight. When heated, the yarns shrink and bulk up, the filler becoming as one with them, reducing the movement between them and producing an altogether stronger, tighter and more stable weave. Some cloths are further stabilised by depositing a thin film of resin on the surface of the fabric to produce a particularly firm finish. The more resin that is added, the stiffer and more stable the cloth becomes – and the more prone to damage, as the resin can break down with hard use. Intricate control of the yarn tensions is again essential at this stage, for it continues to affect the characteristics of the cloth until, once the heating process has locked up the crimp, they become permanent. This is important for stretch recovery, because it gives the fabric a 'memory', so that it always wants to regain the precise shape of the weave.

Heat setting is also the key to its ultimate durability, since in chemically bonding the filler to the polyester it becomes part of the fibre structure. A sail made from a firmly finished, stable cloth, will set well and hold its shape, but tends to be stiff and crackly, and doesn't suit every application. For example una-rigged dinghies, such as the Finn and Laser, need greater bias stretch for the wide range of mast bend over which the same sail has to operate. Cruising yachtsmen generally prefer a soft finish because it also furls well and is easier to stow. Finally the cloth is 'calendered', being pressed through heated rollers under tons of pressure to flatten the weave and consolidate its structure by sealing the interstices between the yarns. This reduces the porosity of the fabric, glazes its surface and makes it feel smoother to the touch – the 'hand', as it's known. The selvedges are then trimmed to conform to the standardised 36 in (92 cm) or 54 in (137 cm) widths, and heat sealed.

NYLON

Originally a DuPont tradename, nylon has long since become a generic term. It is a thermoplastic polymer similar to polyester, extruded and drawn in the same manner, but woven into a cloth with very different characteristics. It is no accident that nylon is universally used for spinnakers, whose requirements are totally different from those of fore-and-aft sails. Weight is of prime importance, because as well as the problem of carrying it so high up above the deck, a spinnaker depends on the wind to keep it full and maintain its shape, being fixed only at head and tack. The lighter the sail, the less wind is needed to fill it and the more efficient it will be; and the lower its porosity, the more it will remain pressurised at low windspeeds, especially when the pole is squared off and the apparent wind angle increases. So light airs and general purpose spinnakers are specially coated to reduce their porosity to zero. (The heavier yarns and tighter construction used for racing reachers and heavy weather runners, or for very large spinnakers, make such a coating unnecessary.)

Since the dimensions of a spinnaker are not determined by a mast and boom, stretch has to be accepted and controlled, rather than minimised or eliminated as in the case of fore-and-aft sails. Most sail nylon is warp orientated, but because it stretches so much more than polyester it is better able to absorb the energy from the frequent shock loads as a spinnaker collapses and refills. It also has good tear strength and resistance to abrasion, but is weakened by exposure to sunlight to a much greater degree than polyester.

Polyester laminates

Laminated fabrics have very little in common with their woven counterparts. The problems of crimp and bias stretch have been solved by laying straight yarns in the required direction and not weaving them at all. Instead they are held in tension and bonded to one or two thin plies of polyester film (usually DuPont Mylar®) which has the same strength in all directions. This forms a composite warp- or weft-strong sandwich, its resistance to stretch without any crimping being entirely due to the stretch resistance of the particular yarn used and the orientation of the fibres.

Another fundamental difference between laminates and woven cloths is that the former are able to operate much closer to their tensile strength limits, because of their low stretch right up to almost the point of failure, whereas for safety reasons woven cloths have to be used well down their tensile strength curves to give a suitable stretch performance. Laminates therefore offer clear advantages in weight savings, particularly aloft. On the other hand they have lower safety margins and leave less room for error, with an increased chance of catastrophic failure if the sail is used outside its recommended operational limit, besides being more susceptible to wear and tear.

Polyester was the first of these reinforcement materials and is still the most widely used on account of its good all-round performance and comparatively low cost, although all laminates are more expensive than woven fabrics. Moreover, the Mylar® itself is not so highly resistant to bending and flexing as polyester yarn, and therefore needs protection and careful handling, with loosely woven taffetas (uncalendered cloth) often being included in the sandwich to provide extra strength and longevity. And because of the inert nature of the film surface, complex chemical systems are needed to bond it. Overall, because of the high cost of laminates and with certain exceptions their shorter working life, their share of the sailcloth market remains limited.

Kevlar®

The search for materials with less stretch and greater strength than polyester led to the development of a range of so-called exotic yarns and their laminates. Best known of these is Kevlar®, DuPont's tradename for their golden coloured aramid. Not only is it 2½ times stronger for the same weight as polyester, so that sails made from it can be much lighter, but more importantly its resistance to stretch is some five times greater, and its high dimensional stability means that it will not 'creep' and permanently deform during extended periods of high load. Small wonder, then, that Kevlar® was considered revolutionary when it was introduced by Hood in 1972, first as a woven cloth and later as a Mylar® laminate.

Unfortunately, however, Kevlar® is also considerably less durable than polyester, due to its poor flex-and-bend performance – the ability to retain its strength after repeated folding or flogging – which makes it unreliable and totally unpredictable in terms of fatigue failure. Added to this is its high cost, poor resistance to abrasion, and an exceptionally high rate of UV degradation, losing around three-quarters of its strength after only four months of exposure to sunlight. Technora®, a similar aramid sailcloth made by the Japanese company Teijin, is dyed black to improve its UV resistance, and has a slightly better abrasion resistance, but it costs more than Kevlar® and is inclined to 'creep' (stretch permanently).

Spectra®

Much more durable (and even more expensive) are two recently developed polyethylene yarns, Spectra® from Allied Signal and Dyneema® from the Dutch company DSM. They withstand abrasion, stress flexing and UV exposure better than Kevlar®, and result in a fabric that is 40% stronger, one-third lighter and three times more stretch resistant than Kevlar®. Size for size, a Spectra® rope is as strong as steel – and floats. Unfortunately, however, these yarns are unsuitable for racing because of excessive creep, with sails quickly losing their designed shapes. But they are capable of handling the massive loads found in the sails of large cruising yachts where cloth strength, durability and weight aloft are more important than either cost or the last fraction of performance. They cannot be tightly woven in the way that polyester can, due to their slippery nature, nor can they be heated to shrink and tighten the weave, because of their low melting point. So they are used in the form of structural scrims and laminated to Mylar®. (A scrim is an open-weave fabric with measurable spaces between the yarns. Two Mylar® films encasing a scrim actually touch each other in these spaces, bonding the yarns very securely.)

Alternatively, in order to avoid Mylar's® shortcomings, they are inserted as minimally twisted yarns between two layers of woven polyester. One side is a heavy decitex, tight weave for the low-stretch property that Mylar® would have provided, the other a taffeta scrim of polyester as a backing to hold the polyethylene yarns in place. The process, termed warp insertion, gives substantial weight savings with great strength and stretch resistance, yet the cloth remains pliable for easy handling and roller reefing, and has the potential to last as long as conventional polyester fabric.

Carbon

Carbon fibres have been used, with varying degrees of success, in top level racing such as the 12 metre campaigns for the America's Cup. They have an extremely high ability to resist stretch, which is why they are used to reinforce epoxy composite spars and hulls, but they are so brittle that if you try to fold one in your fingers it will snap almost immediately. So sails incorporating carbon are fragile, to say the least, and require such careful handling as to make them totally impractical for everyday use.

Vectran®

This is the latest super-yarn to arrive on the sailing scene, produced by Hoechst-Celanese. Spun from a liquid crystal polymer, it has the low-stretch performance of Kevlar®, better flex and abrasion resistance, UV properties similar to those of polyester, but the highest cost of all the performance fibres. Unlike polyester, however, it doesn't creep. For racing sails, it is applied in the form of a stabilising diagonal grid across a Kevlar® warp and fill, sandwiched between Mylar® film and a base fabric of woven polyester. In a further technological advance, Hood Textiles have succeeded in interweaving Vectran® yarn with a high-tenacity polyester to produce a much softer and more durable material than the laminate, and one that can be used for roller furling sails. Although costing considerably more than straight polyester, sails made from woven Vectran® hold their shape better, besides being lighter and stronger. It may well prove to be the ultimate cruising sailcloth – for the time being, at any rate.

CHOOSING THE CLOTH

The amateur sailmaker would be well advised to steer clear of laminates and exotic fabrics. Most of them are not only unsuitable for the small cruising boats and knockabout dinghies whose sails he would be capable of making, but they are difficult if not impossible to buy in short lengths and awkward to sew. Besides this, their high cost can make mistakes very expensive. Better to choose an ordinary woven polyester with a reasonably close, tight weave that won't distort badly under load. Try pulling the cloth at 45° to the threadline. It should have a certain amount of give, but feel stable and secure, and the resulting crease should largely disappear after the tension is released. If it doesn't, or if the weave feels coarse and tends to open up, give it an extra tug to see what happens. If you're not sure what finish you are looking for, it's a good idea to compare the cloths used on one or two boats similar to yours. (This doesn't, of course, apply to nylon. There are seldom any problems with spinnaker cloth, provided you select the right weight, but it might be worth blowing or sucking through it to check its porosity. A lightweight nylon shouldn't be porous at all.)

Another test is to repeatedly twist and crumple it in your hand and see whether it crazes. (Lowell North used to tie a sample to his car radio aerial and observe the results of violent fluttering after some fast journeys between home and office.) The cloth may appear to be well enough finished, but if it was poorly woven in the first place, its initial stability may only be temporary, performing well at first but deteriorating rapidly with use. With too firm and

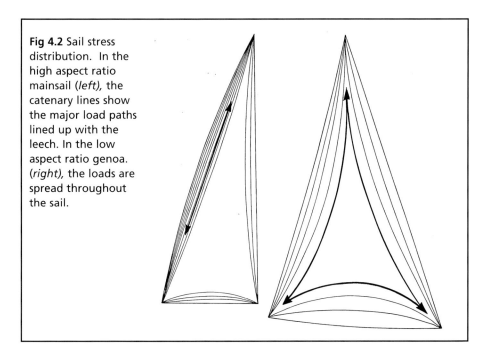

Fig 4.2 Sail stress distribution. In the high aspect ratio mainsail (*left),* the catenary lines show the major load paths lined up with the leech. In the low aspect ratio genoa. (*right),* the loads are spread throughout the sail.

harsh a finish, a sail will be difficult to fold and prone to damage. Too soft, and despite being aesthetically pleasant to handle and easy to fold and stow, it will be unlikely to last more than a season or two of hard sailing without becoming baggy.

The dimensions of a sail largely determine the distribution of the stresses within it, and hence the most suitable form of construction and finish for the cloth. Using computerised stress mapping to determine the direction of the loads, weaves can be tailored to suit the way in which the cloth will be used by varying the relative size, spacing and crimp of the warp and fill yarns, and by orienting them in the appropriate direction when the sail panels are cut.

The key factor is aspect ratio, as we saw earlier. In the high aspect ratio mainsail we looked at, or a No 3 jib, short on the foot and long on the luff, the primary loads are lined up head to clew along the leech, with comparatively moderate forces acting on the bias in the middle of the sail (Fig 4.2). This calls for an *un*balanced cloth construction, with low-stretch high-strength yarns tightly woven with little or no crimp, into a high density, low-decitex warp. Tight separation, further stabilised by heavy resination, means that as the fabric ages its stretch properties will change very little, allowing the sail to maintain its designed shape over a wide range of working conditions.

At the other end of the scale is our low aspect ratio genoa, whose sheet lead virtually bisects the angle of the clew. The loads are more evenly distributed, fanning out radially from clew and tack towards the head and requiring good stretch resistance in both fill and bias directions. This is achieved by using a balanced construction, with warp and fill yarns of similar decitex and count, and only light resination. Peak directional performance is deliberately compromised by crimping so as to increase bias stability, the shared crimp creating more contact surface between the yarns, which in turn mechanically reduces bias movement. These balanced cloths, with their even stress response, are also well suited to gaff and other four-sided sails, and in the lighter weights make good jibs for dinghies with short, wide foretriangles.

In between the two, there are a number of general purpose fabrics using high tenacity yarns in a moderately unbalanced construction, with the fill tending to be slightly the stronger threadline. Tightness of weave and the amount of resination is varied according to the bias stability required in terms of stretch and the ability to return to normal after repeated elongations. The more unbalanced the construction, the greater is the tendency for the sail to develop a tight leech after some use, whereas with the more evenly balanced 'blade' cloths, the draft tends to stay forward with an open leech. These are excellent for mainsails with modest aspect ratios, particularly those with short battens; in the lighter weights for dinghy mainsails; and on cat-rigged boats and those with fractional sailplans featuring a long-boomed main and a small non-overlapping jib.

If the budget allows, it is always worth paying a bit extra for material from a well known company such as Bainbridge or Hayward, with the dependability that such names ensure. Hayward*, incidentally, are one of the few manufacturers from whom you can directly obtain small lengths, the majority supplying only their account customers, the professional lofts and wholesalers. You would be unlikely to find any of the big lofts willing to sell you a bolt end of cloth, since they can hardly be expected to encourage amateur competition. But if Hayward don't happen to have what you want, or a small length proves too expensive, it would be worth approaching one of the smaller sailmakers who might have some leftovers on his hands, or asking around the general chandlery firms.

ESTIMATING THE YARDAGE

The most common widths of polyester are 36 in and 54 in, with 54 in for virtually all the laminates, and 41 in or 54 in for spinnaker nylon. There is no need to allow for stretch in polyester when estimating the quantity you will need for each sail. But to be on the safe side, it is as well to make the luff in particular an inch or two shorter than the plans show, for there's nothing more frustrating than hoisting your new sail hard up to the halyard sheave, only to find that the luff is still slack.

To determine the area of a sail based on an approximately right-angled

* Richard Hayward & Co, Tiverton, Devon EX16 5LL, England.

triangle, such as a Bermudan mainsail, assume that the sides are straight and multiply the height (luff) by half the base (foot) length. For a sail with no right-angle, such as a typical headsail, again assume its sides to be straight and draw a line from the clew to join the luff at 90°. The area will be the length of this line, times half the luff. For a four-sided sail, cut the outline shape into two triangles and add their areas together. It is difficult to determine the areas of the curved surfaces of a spinnaker, but fortunately nylon is reasonably inexpensive and you won't be wasting much cloth if you multiply the luff by the foot and take three-quarters of the result.

Dividing an area in square feet by nine gives the number in square yards and hence the length needed in a 36 in width; pro rata for 54 in cloth. To this figure must be added a substantial allowance for seam overlaps, tablings, reinforcement patches and reef points, and for roach. In America, where most of the cloth comes from, a yard run – on which the weight is based – has long been counted as $28\frac{1}{2}$ in, the reason being that the cotton cloth for sailing ships was woven $28\frac{1}{2}$ in wide, while its weight was measured per running yard. Using this figure, known as a 'sailmaker's yard', results in an apparent discrepancy of about 28%. To arrive at the length of cloth needed in this measure, you should add 50% for an averagely reinforced sail with a reasonable amount of roach, and anything up to 100% for a heavy weather sail with extra-strong reinforcements and multiple reef points. Use half these percentages if you want the answer in the ordinary English yards used by most British sailmakers. Just to complicate the matter of American weights still further, particularly as they apply to spinnaker cloth, the weight is quoted – for the benefit of owners demanding the lightest possible fabric – for the cloth as woven, before it is shrunk and finished. So although described as $\frac{1}{2}$ oz, it may weigh as much as $\frac{3}{4}$ oz American or 1 oz per English yard. Cloth is also sold in metric lengths but English widths; in which case multiply the length by 1.3 to arrive at square yards and proceed as before.

CLOTH WEIGHT

From one standpoint, the lighter the cloth the better, for not only is it easier to sew, but the sail will be easier to handle, set and stow, and will fill in light airs that would scarcely pull the creases out of a heavier one. Another factor to consider is weight aloft. A sail may not feel heavy to lift off the deck, but it can exert considerable leverage when set on a tall mast. A boat needs to be sailed as upright as possible, and minimising the weight of the rig helps reduce the overall heeling and pitching forces acting on it. Just as this is necessary on a high performance, highly tuned racer to enable the sails to work efficiently, so it is on a cruising boat in the interests of safety and comfort aboard.

However, by far the most important consideration in choosing the weight of the cloth is its resistance to stretch. Since for any given type of cloth, the lighter it is the more readily it will stretch, the weight determines the effective range of winds in which the sail can be used. The minimum windspeed is that which is just sufficient to fill it to the designed shape; below this, it will simply sag under its own weight. The upper limit is reached when the sail, already reefed, needs to be taken down to avoid permanent distortion. Other factors relating to stretch are the area and profile of the sail, since this affects the wind pressure acting on it, and the size and type of boat. Clearly a heavy, beamy cruiser with a powerful righting moment will require stouter sails than a slim round-the-buoys racer of similar length.

Some boats carry more or less sail than the average, so it can be misleading to use sail area as a parameter in deciding on the optimum weight of cloth. Instead, waterline length, being a fair indication of the size of a yacht, is a better and more convenient yardstick to use for the working sails. The figure can be varied up or down if the boat is particularly light or heavy for her size, if possible making some allowance for the weather conditions she can be expected to meet and the way she is likely to be handled.

The mainsail cloth for a ketch or a yawl can in theory be a little lighter than a sloop's, being a bit smaller; but it's usually best to play safe and use the same weight, because it probably won't be reefed quite as often. Similarly, it makes sense for a mizzen, despite being even smaller, to be made of the same cloth, because except on boats with particularly broad and buoyant sterns, the chances are that it will be used in a gale long after the main has been taken down. Headsails are a different case, for although boat length again exerts an overall influence on their size and weight, there are obvious differences between masthead and fractional rigs, sloops and cutters. Generally speaking, the larger the headsail, the lighter its cloth can be, because the sooner it will be changed for a smaller one in freshening winds. The exception is a genoa, especially one with a large overlap. Since this is often left on to drive the boat after the main has been reefed right down, or in the case of a roller furling genoa, used part-rolled as the wind increases, it needs to be as heavy as a working headsail, or for the leech area of the roller sail to be made of heavier material than the luff.

WEIGHT MEASUREMENTS

Although the American sailmaker's yard is currently the most commonly used measure of sailcloth weights, you are increasingly likely to find them expressed in grams per square metre as metrication becomes more widely adopted.

- To convert oz per sailmaker's yd into oz per English yard, multiply by 1.29 (divide for vice versa).

- To convert oz per sailmaker's yd to metric (gm per sq m), multiply by 43.74 (divide for vice versa).
- To convert oz per English yd to metric (gm per sq m), multiply by 33.91 (divide for vice versa).

Alternatively you may use this ready reckoner, whose figures are accurate enough for most purposes:

American	English	Metric	American	English	Metric
oz/sail-maker's yd	oz/sq yd	gm/sq m	oz/sail-maker's yd	oz/sq yd	gm/sq m
$\frac{1}{2}$	$\frac{3}{4}$	22	6	$7\frac{3}{4}$	263
1	$1\frac{1}{4}$	44	$6\frac{1}{2}$	$8\frac{1}{2}$	285
$1\frac{1}{2}$	2	66	7	9	306
2	$2\frac{1}{2}$	88	$7\frac{1}{2}$	$9\frac{1}{2}$	328
$2\frac{1}{2}$	3	110	8	$10\frac{1}{4}$	350
3	4	131	$8\frac{1}{2}$	11	372
$3\frac{1}{2}$	$4\frac{1}{2}$	153	9	$11\frac{1}{2}$	396
4	5	175	$9\frac{1}{2}$	$12\frac{1}{2}$	416
$4\frac{1}{2}$	$5\frac{3}{4}$	197	10	13	438
5	$6\frac{1}{2}$	219	$10\frac{1}{2}$	$13\frac{1}{2}$	460

No set of figures can serve as more than a rough guide to selecting the optimum cloth weight for any particular duty, because of the wide variety of qualities, types of construction and characteristics. It takes an expert to select the right cloths for a big boat or for serious racing, just as it does to make them. But fortunately it is far from being an exact science when it comes to the sort of sailmaking that can be undertaken by an amateur. The table on page 40 gives some typical figures, based on a general purpose single-ply polyester of moderately balanced construction. (A handy formula for determining the approximate weight of cloth needed for a working sail, expressed in ounces per sailmaker's yard, is to take the waterline length of the boat in feet and divide by five.) The choice is much simpler when it comes to spinnaker nylons: $\frac{3}{4}$ oz is sufficient for dinghies and small dayboats, while 1 oz is suitable for almost any other size of boat. Only on large offshore cruisers or for bullet-proof heavy weather spinnakers is it necessary to move up to the $1\frac{1}{2}$ or $2\frac{1}{4}$ oz cloths.

Suggested Polyester cloth weights in oz/sailmaker's yd					
They should be varied up or down if the boat is particularly heavy or light, or frequently sailed in strong winds or light airs.					
	Average dinghy	Small keel-boats and daysailers up to 20 ft	21–25 ft	26–30 ft	31–35 ft
Mainsail and working jib	$3^1/_2$–4	$4^1/_2$–5	5–6	$5^1/_2$–7	7–$7^1/_2$
Light genoa		3–4	3–4	3–4	$3^1/_2$–$4^1/_2$
General purpose genoa		4–$4^1/_2$	4–$4^1/_2$	$4^1/_2$–5	5–6
Furling genoa		$4^1/_2$	5	6	7
Storm sails		6	$6^1/_2$	8	$9^1/_2$

SAIL DESIGN

Nowadays many of us either have a computer in the household or have ready access to one, and even if we don't know how to work it, our children usually do. With so many sophisticated and skilful games that can be played on these magic boxes of tricks, it is easy to imagine that using one to help design a simple sail might be child's play too. In some ways it is. However, the software needed for three-dimensional computer aided design is so complex and expensive, and requires so much expertise to be used effectively, that the use of CAD is mostly confined to the major lofts.

The much simplified 2D programs and instructions available with this book have been specially written for the amateur sailmaker or small loft interested in taking a look at this branch of technology. Nevertheless it is important, before setting out on any such course, to understand the basic principles of sail design and the methods of lofting that served sailmakers long before the computer age – and in many cases still do. Familiarity with the manual process not only helps us to appreciate just how much the computer can do to help, but total commitment to electronics without this background knowledge can sometimes lead to misinterpretation of the computer's instructions, and also – as in navigation – might one day leave us high and dry if it should malfunction.

Details of the rig, showing the profile and dimensions of each sail, will have been drawn by the boat designer. Besides aiming for an aesthetically pleasing appearance, and observing any class or international measurement rules that might apply, he will have integrated the underwater shape of the hull with the sail area needed for a fair performance in light airs, adequate stability in heavier weather without the need for inconveniently early reefing, and a comfortably balanced helm. His sailplan is certainly useful for estimating the quantities of cloth required, but it is only a two-dimensional diagram and doesn't pretend to represent the flying shapes of the sails, least of all the spinnaker. The sailmaker has to make a construction plan for each of them, indicating how the individual panels are to be cut to give the right amount of built-in shape where it is needed, taking account not only of the type and weight of cloth to be used, but of its likely stretch under freshening winds, the effects of mast bend and forestay sag, and of the tensions applied to the edge curves along the luff and foot. Factors such as these are fed into a computer to form an integral part of the CAD program, but the manual design process relies entirely on rule of thumb methods that have been derived from decades of practice.

Spinnakers are the exception. They are extremely sophisticated sails, as difficult to design as they are to set and control, compared with other forms of headsail. For much of the time the wind blows across them from luff to leech, but they lack the jib's straight luff and flat leech, and both the tack and the clew have to be continuously adjustable. Only when the wind is blowing from 10–15° either side of dead astern can the spinnaker act as a simple wind-blocker to drag the boat downwind – and then only when either it is badly set and stalled, or when the mainsail is lowered. To remain stable under those conditions it needs lift from a full head, but this makes the luff all the more likely to curl in and collapse the sail as soon as the boat is brought on to a reach. Properly set, with the mainsail drawing, the two sails together act as an aerofoil, the spinnaker deflecting most of its airflow sideways into the lee of the main. Very little of it spills out under the foot, so flying a spinnaker high for the sake of lift is just giving away power.

The amateur can make a basic old-fashioned parachute spinnaker by unpicking an old sail and copying its panels, bearing in mind that it will probably have stretched out of shape, or by guessing at the curvature of its centre seam; but even if he gets it right, the result will be disappointing compared to any of the modern cuts. It's not as if the eventual spherical shape can be marked out on the loft floor. Spinnaker design nowadays involves so many variables and complex mathematical calculations that it requires a computer to process them, so we will confine this section on manual design to fore-and-aft sails.

If you want to make a replacement for a worn-out mainsail and don't have a drawing of it, a straightforward method of obtaining the outline measurements, assuming you have access to the boat and the mast is stepped, is to top up the boom to its working position and send a tape aloft on a halyard, or a length of rope which you measure afterwards. Ease it a little way down from the headsheaves to allow for stretch – say 250 mm on a 500–750 mm in luff. It's even worth hoisting the mainsail, if you can, to check whether it can still be set without the tack and clew being pulled past the black band markings on the mast and boom that apply when racing, and if the sail is particularly old and dilapidated, making sure there is still a safe margin of travel before neither the headboard nor the clew become chock-a-blocked at their sheave. You can do the same sort of thing with a headsail, but if it overlaps the mast, remember to lead the tape outside the shrouds.

Alternatively, you can measure the old sail. Lay it out flat, spike the head and pull the other corners out with a tackle until the edge reinforcements appear to be stretched out to their working tensions, balancing these as best you can to ensure that the sail isn't distorted in one direction or another. You will need to take the diagonal as well as the peripheral lengths. Using a piece of string pulled taut between the corners, you can then measure off the edge curves, allowing for a small degree of deformation that will have occurred over the years, notably along the luff and leech. Needless to say, if you are lucky enough to have a large enough clean wooden floor to work on, you can loft the new sail right there simply by tracing the old one and making the necessary allowances including the hems, known as 'tablings'.

Should you decide, in the interests of performance, to increase the sail area, it would be worth taking the precaution of checking the centre of effort of the rig before and after your proposed modifications, using the procedure shown in Fig 2.16. Giving the mainsail a larger roach, for example, without some corresponding alteration in headsail area or mast rake, might result in excessive weather helm. Conversely, if the boat has always been a bit hard-mouthed, even with the mainsail flattened as much as possible, straightening the leech or taking a few centimetres off the foot would probably move the CE forward enough to put matters right.

More difficult to guess at, lacking the experienced eye of a professional sailmaker or unless you know the boat particularly well, is how much too full a sail may have become due to permanent stretch in the cloth, even if it isn't obviously baggy. The following procedures take out a lot of the guesswork in deciding on how much fullness should be built into the new sail, whereabouts to position it, and how to draw the curves that produce it.

As we saw in Chapter 2 there are two methods, usually combined with one another, for introducing draft into what would otherwise be a flat area of cloth (Fig 2.12). The first is to give the luff or the foot a convex curvature, so that by tensioning it along a straight spar, or gathering it up a headstay, surplus material is forced into the body of the sail. (The converse principle is used to compensate for forestay sag by giving the upper part of a headsail a hollowed luff which straightens under tension and drags the adjacent cloth with it.) The other is the technique of broadseaming, in which one or sometimes both edges of the panels are cut in a convex curve for part of their

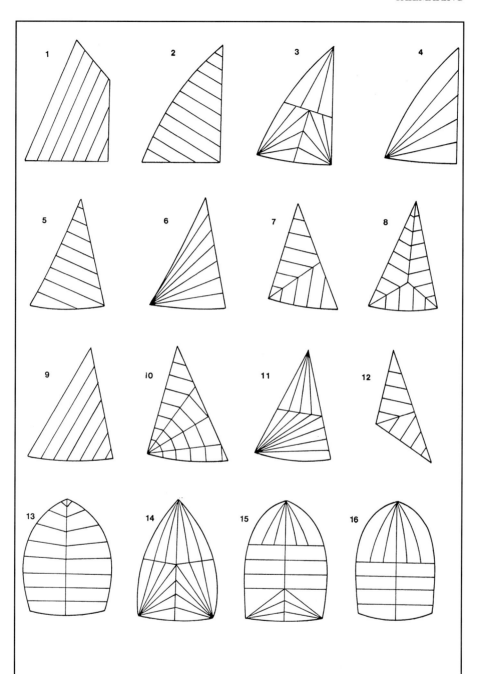

Fig 4.3 Typical cloth layouts. *Mainsails:* 1 Vertical cut. 2 Cross-cut. 3 Starcut. 4 Radial cut. *Headsails*: 5 Cross-cut. 6 Radial cut. 7 Mitred. 8 Triple mitred. 9 Vertical cut. 10 Spider web. 11 Bi-radial. 12 Yankee. *Spinnakers:* 13 Horizontal. 14 Starcut. 15 Tri-radial. 16 Radial head.

length, so that when they are sewn to adjacent panels, the sail assumes a moulded three-dimensional shape. How much of either method to use depends on the specifications of the cloth, the depth of camber required and its positioning, and the cut – the manner in which the panels are to be laid out (Fig 4.3).

The vertical cut, with the seams running up-and-down parallel with the leech, was the accepted pattern in former times when sails were made without any roach, and is still used for the sake of authenticity on many traditional boats, whose sails are usually made of a soft cloth, and where the panels and their warp threads were lined up with the leech in order to minimise stretch on its unsupported edge. The mitre cut, with the upper section having its cloths perpendicular to the leech, and joined along a diagonal seam to a lower section with its cloths square to the foot, was developed for headsails in an attempt to control and limit stretch in either direction. However it is seldom seen nowadays except on stormsails, where it has the advantage of having no seams striking an edge. A third alternative was the Scotch cut, which was the same as the mitre except that its cloths lay parallel to the leech and foot.

With the development of more stable fabrics, bias problems on the foot and leech have largely disappeared. The horizontal or cross-cut is currently by far the most widely used for cruising sails, with seams running roughly parallel with the airflow and the fill yarns bearing the brunt of the luff and leech loads. Lastly there are the various radial and multi-radial cuts for high-performance sails, in which the warp yarns are aligned with the stresses that fan out from each corner. The problem that these complex patterns pose for the amateur is how to shape the panels so as to put the requisite amount of draft in the right place. A computer, fed with a sophisticated program, is about the only alternative to a lot of inspired guesswork.

Draft is readily induced in a loosely woven fabric by bias elongation and needs little or no help from broadseaming, whose purpose in that case is to position the draft and to shape the entry profile, whereas a stiff and stable cloth, designed to resist bias stretch, can make good use of broadseaming to give it belly, especially on cross-cut sails where seams run more or less parallel with the chord, and on vertically cut gaff, lug or sprit mainsails. It is rather less effective on some other cuts whose seams strike an edge at too shallow an angle.

In this instance, we are going to make a suit of sails for a typical 23 ft Bermudan rigged dayboat or small cruiser, compromising between a softly finished cloth that furls well, and a hard finish that sets well, by using a medium-finished 5 oz polyester for main and jib, both of them cross-cut. The length of the seam tapers will define the draft points, each seam starting to widen at the point where maximum fullness is required, and opening out further as it approaches the luff. Excessive tapering near the after end would hook it to windward like an over-tweaked leechline, so less broadseaming is used in this area so as to produce a flattish exit from which the airstream can run off cleanly. Too flat, and the leech will become structurally unstable and flutter, unless it is supported by long or full battens.

There are no hard and fast numerical rules governing a sail's camber – the maximum depth in relation to its straight-line chord length between luff and leech – or whereabouts this should be placed. But there are some useful guidelines that can serve as substitutes for experience. A camber ratio of 15–16% can be considered to be very full and so powerful that it is only suitable for light weather and reaching, while at the other end of the scale 5–6% will give very little drive until the wind really pipes up. So a good compromise that is generally adopted for cruising sails is to make them moderately flat at around 12% and to rely on edge tensioning or mast bend to reduce power in strong winds. On a mainsail the point of maximum designed draft halfway up the sail is best positioned no more than 35–40% back from the luff, because in a fresh breeze it will blow aft to around 50% as it assumes its flying shape, and around a third of the way up from the foot. For high pointing, a jib needs a finer entry, with the airflow at the exit from the slot streaming off parallel to the lee side of the mainsail, so the designed draft point can safely be brought back as far as 40–45% from the luff. For the sake of simplicity in cutting the sail panels, and especially in amateur sailmaking, the depth of the sail is best kept to a constant proportion of the chord length near the foot. This results in there being very little actual draft towards the head, but it doesn't matter very much in cruising, because the top part of the sail does comparatively little work, tending to heel the boat almost as much as it drives it. Professional sailmakers looking for the last ounce of competitive power will increase the draft in the upper regions of the sail. But it will flap if there is too much shape in it, with any sag in the headstay only adding to the fullness.

In order to put some actual values on seam tapers and edge curves, let us assume that the boat looks something like the one on page 90, a fractionally rigged 23 footer with a small self-tacking jib (but cross-cut for our purposes, leaving the complexity of radial panelling to the professionals).

We will take the mainsail as having a foot length of 3.3 m, a roach projecting 300 mm beyond the straight line between head and clew and about halfway up it, and an 8.7 m luff*. Incidentally, when you come to draw a sail full size, always allow for some stretch in the luff when the halyard is swigged up, amounting to 25 mm per 2 m of length – that would make it about 100 mm on this one. To end up with the 12% camber we are aiming for, we will need a minimum of 20 mm of luff round per metre of length, say 170 mm in this case. Its widest part should be located about 3 m above the tack, taper-

---

* Although cloth weights and lengths are mostly expressed in imperial units, metric measurements are invariably used in sailmaking, for convenience in percentaging and proportioning.

ing off in a convex curve towards the bottom of the sail, and upwards to a point about two-thirds of the way to the head. From here the luff can be made *slightly* hollow to help keep this part of the sail flat, but it should run straight up if the mast is designed to be bent In action (by about 180 mm in this case) and the luff round doubled to compensate for the draft that will then be absorbed. Foot round should amount to some 25 mm per metre of length, so call it 100 mm at its widest point, positioned about 1.25 m back from the tack and curving off smoothly in both directions, but not hollowed.

SEAM TAPERS

The roundings are combined with a series of broadseams at the luff, starting with the one striking nearest the tack, and which in this case are parallel-sided until they reach a point about two-thirds of the way forward from the leech. They then widen progressively towards the luff, their angle of taper depending on the type of cloth. A ratio of 1:60 will be about right for this sail, using a medium-firm cloth. So a 1 mm increase in seam width will be needed for every 60 mm of length, giving a nominal 12 mm seam that opens to about 18 mm at the luff, except for the tack seam, or the lowest luff seam, whose taper angle should be doubled to 1:30. Proceeding up the luff, taper every seam for the initial one-third of the way towards the head – their width will be decreasing anyway as they become shorter – then start reducing the draft by tapering every other seam for the next third, before reverting to all-normal seams on the upper part of the sail which is to be kept flat.

EDGE CURVES

Broadseam (Fig 4.4) can if necessary be put into headsails, but generally speaking they are best cut fairly flat, extensive broadseaming being mostly reserved for large jibs and overlapping genoas. All headsail shapes are, however, affected by forestay sag, which by itself will induce a certain amount of camber and has to be allowed for in the edge curvatures. The jib we are to make has a luff of 8.2 m, so aiming at a 12% camber, the lower part of the luff need only be given a convex rounding of about 20 mm at its maximum, changing to 25 mm of concavity in the upper half where the effects of sag will be most pronounced. These are in fact such shallow curves that taking the easy option, and cutting a small short-chorded jib such as this with a straight luff, will not greatly affect its draft. It is advisable, on the other hand, to give the leech some hollow, amounting to around 15 mm per metre at the mid-point, or about 120 mm in this case. Not only will it ensure a clean exit, but the hollow leech will stand better than a straight one. The allowance for foot rounding can be taken as 25 mm per metre, the same as for the mainsail, which works out at 70 mm on this jib, although without a boom it won't have the

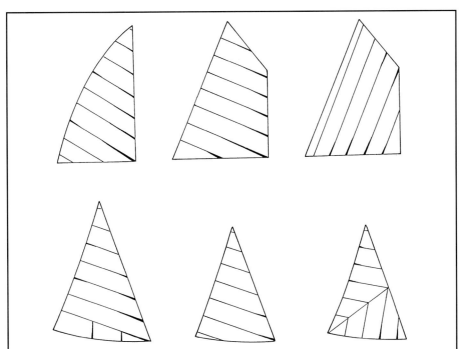

Fig 4.4 Broadseaming. Like dressmakers' darts, tapered seams introduce draft into what would otherwise be a flat sail until its curved edges are tensioned. Tapers can also be used to support the foot round in boomless sails such as a cross-cut genoa, and to produce additional draft in fixed-footed gaff sails.

same effect, just adding some area and matching the profile of the deck.

Similar principles are applied in different ways to other shapes and cuts of sail. There are so many variations that it takes a specialist book to describe them all in detail. A gunter mainsail, for instance, is usually treated in the same way as a Bermudan, ignoring the kink where the yard joins the mast, whereas on another frequently encountered example, a four-sided sail such as a gaff, lug or sprit mainsail having its cloths laid parallel to the leech, the seams are broadened in the region of both the head and the foot. They should start at around 7.5% down from the gaff, with a nominal 12 mm seam opening out to 18 mm at the head. Nearing the bottom of a boomed sail, a rather larger taper runs from a point some 15% up from the foot, broadening from 12 mm to about 25 mm. If the sail is boomless and doesn't have a boltrope to help support its foot, the requisite draft in the lower areas is provided by doubling the degree of bottom broadseaming, with the tapers originating a quarter of the way up from the foot, and opening out to about 50 mm. Head rounding should amount to 25 mm per metre, with the apex halfway along it; luff round 25 mm per 1300 mm one-third up from the tack; boomed foot round 25 mm per metre and one-third aft of the tack; and

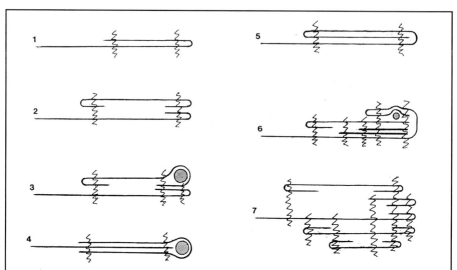

Fig 4.5 1 Sail edge hotknifed and folded over. 2 Traditional cut tabling. 3 Cut tabling carrying luff rope. 4 Luff rope in tape. 5 Rolled tabling. 6 Rolled tabling with internal patches and leech cord. 7 Cut tabling with one upper and two lower patches.

anything up to three times that depth of curvature if the sail is loose-footed without a boltrope.

Returning to our design for the 23 footer, the accessory items can now be pencilled in, starting with the reinforcement patches at the corners of each sail (see page 170). These form an essential part of the sail structure, dispersing the high corner stresses into the body panels and along the hems, known as tablings, that are used to finish the edges (see Fig 4.5). It is very important that these tablings are made correctly, because they affect the way a sail sets. Too flimsy and it will flap; too stiff and it won't stretch with the body of the sail which will be liable to end up with a loose belly. On the leeches, allow an extra 30 mm of cloth which will be folded over and sewn down to form their tablings, with the leech lines inside. This simple process can only be used where the cloths meet the edge at right angles, allowing the threadlines on the sail and the tabling to run in the same direction and both to stretch in the same way. At other angles the weaves won't match and wrinkles would form under tension, so either the tabling must be cut off and resewn, or replaced by 30–40 mm wide polyester webbing tape folded and sewn round the edges of the sail. But to avoid a hooked leech, its a good idea to stretch the cloth and fit the tabling untensioned, so that the stretch in the leech will match that of the adjacent cloth when there's wind in the sail. The same tape in wider form can be used to form a tough pocket or channel for the mainsail footrope and for both the luff ropes when these are fitted.

Batten pockets are also subject to high loadings and need to be carefully fitted. On this particular mainsail, four battens divide the leech into five roughly equal sections. Battens must be long enough to avoid any risk of a hinged leech, so the general rule is for each one to be three times as long as the depth of roach it is supporting. On a cross-cut sail they are laid parallel to the cloths, except for the bottom one, which has to be in line with the foot, so that it can be taken in with the reef.

Finally there are the two rows of reef points to be positioned, in the form of eyelets on diamond-shaped patches, spaced at 50 cm intervals (30 cm on a small dayboat) and running in straight lines parallel to the foot. The rings or cringles at either end, sewn on to heavily reinforced patches, should be raised about 10 cm above the line of points (15 cm on larger boats) to ensure that they, and not the reef points, take most of the strain, which can be considerable, because a reefed sail is effectively loose-footed. The height of the first reef above the boom should be calculated to reduce the sail area by roughly one-third, and the second reef then placed about the same distance above it.

These and all the other design calculations can be done for you automatically by a computer.

COMPUTER AIDED DESIGN (CAD)

This section is a short one, since it has only to serve as an introduction to the Sailmaster CAD programs that are available with this book. These are contained, along with a step-by-step tutorial, on a $3\frac{1}{2}$ in floppy disk which you can obtain free of charge by sending off the form at the back of the book. The disk will automatically install the software in the computer, allowing you to view or to print out the full documentation, or any part of it, simply by pressing the appropriate keys.

The function of the programs is to design mainsails, genoas and spinnakers, guided by your input figures and using traditional 2D techniques. The end product will be a set of co-ordinates from which the sail panels can be drawn and cut out on the loft floor. The values quoted in the tutorial are those for the 23 footer we are using as an example, but the programs can be used for virtually any size or shape of sail, and whatever design curves you produce can be stored on disk and recalled whenever you need them.

The limitations of these simple programs are that they don't include radially cut mainsails and jibs, which require more complex detailing, nor can they drive a plotter or a cutter such as are used by all the big commercial lofts; and they do not try to predict the 3D flying shape of the sail. It takes a suite of far more sophisticated (and hence expensive) programs to model the many combinations of mast bend, forestay sag and the sail deformation from wind pressure and tensioning of the rig controls, and to produce competitive high-performance sails. Even then, the resulting panel shapes are not always developable – that is to say, they cannot always be laid out on a flat roll of sailcloth.

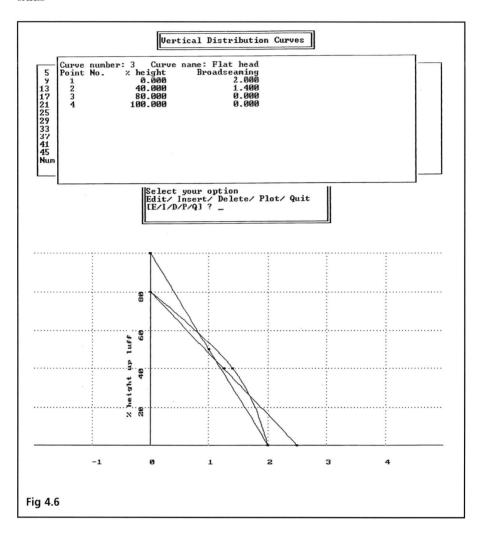

Fig 4.6

(Try wrapping a sheet of paper round a football without getting any creases in it.) It takes experience, expertise and the right equipment to make proper use of a professional 3D program, but the 2D versions we are looking at here will help an amateur, even a novice, to design a perfectly satisfactory suit of cruising sails for his boat.

Vertical distribution curves

The first part concerns the amount of broadseaming to be used and where to place it. A set of vertical distribution curves are drawn on the computer screen (Fig 4.6), starting with a straight line from the foot to the head of the sail. This would give it the same draft all the way up and would make the head too full for most purposes. So in order to have no broadseaming above a certain height, say 70%, the top of the line is moved down to that point. Then

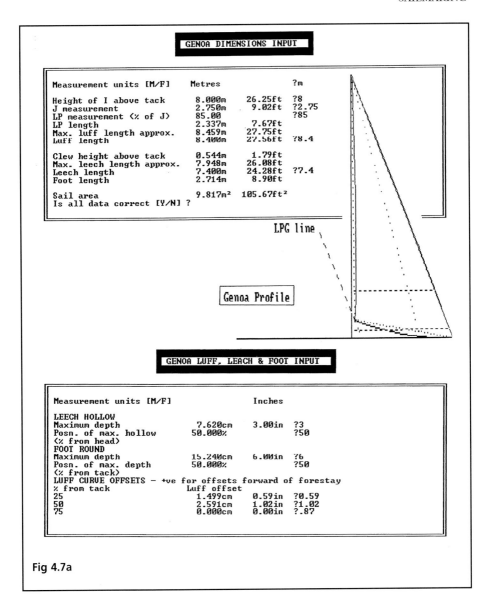

```
                    ┌─────────────────────────────┐
                    │   GENOA DIMENSIONS INPUT     │
                    └─────────────────────────────┘

  Measurement units [M/F]    Metres               ?m

  Height of I above tack     8.000m      26.25ft   ?8
  J measurement              2.750m       9.02ft  ?2.75
  LP measurement (% of J)    85.00                 ?85
  LP length                  2.337m       7.67ft
  Max. luff length approx.   8.459m      27.75ft
  Luff length                8.400m      27.56ft  ?8.4

  Clew height above tack     0.544m       1.79ft
  Max. leech length approx.  7.948m      26.08ft
  Leech length               7.400m      24.28ft  ?7.4
  Foot length                2.714m       8.90ft

  Sail area                  9.817m²    105.67ft²
  Is all data correct [Y/N] ?
```

LPG line

Genoa Profile

```
          ┌────────────────────────────────────────┐
          │  GENOA LUFF, LEACH & FOOT INPUT          │
          └────────────────────────────────────────┘

  Measurement units [M/F]                Inches

  LEECH HOLLOW
  Maximum depth               7.620cm      3.00in   ?3
  Posn. of max. hollow       50.000%                ?50
  (% from head)
  FOOT ROUND
  Maximum depth              15.240cm      6.00in   ?6
  Posn. of max. depth        50.000%                ?50
  (% from tack)
  LUFF CURVE OFFSETS - +ve for offsets forward of forestay
  % from tack                Luff offset
  25                          1.499cm      0.59in  ?0.59
  50                          2.591cm      1.02in  ?1.02
  75                          0.000cm      0.00in  ?.87
```

Fig 4.7a

suppose, for example, that the boat has rather a wide jib-sheeting angle, due to the spread of the shrouds, but you want to flatten the middle of the foot to improve windward ability. All you do is insert an extra point on the curve and move it around to give the necessary fullness. As you do so, all the other points on the curve automatically change position to maintain a fair shape. Half a dozen of these VDC curves will usually cover all your sail designs, and a table of figures showing the amounts of broadseaming, either as offsets or as percentages of each seam, can then be called up on to the screen.

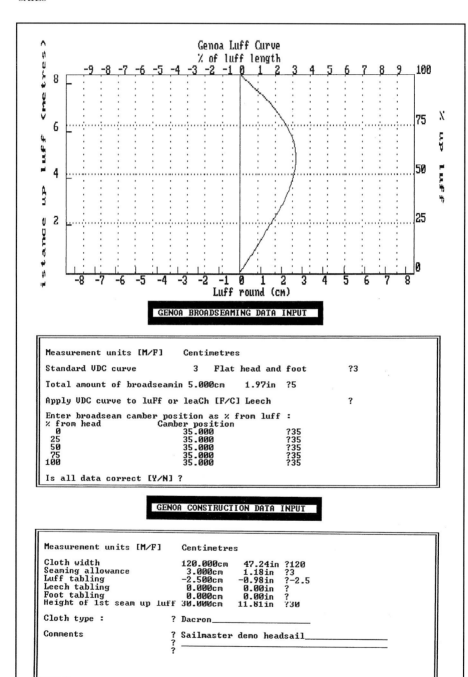

Fig 4.7b

Designing the jib

The next step is to design the jib. Start by typing in the outline dimensions (Fig 4.7a). You can set up the basic foretriangle shape by entering the length of the forestay above the tack fitting, known as the 'I' measurement, and the distance 'J' from the tack to the fore side of the mast, followed by the jib overlap. This is the 'LP' (longest perpendicular of headsail, in other words the distance from the clew to the luff) expressed as a percentage of 'J'. On our self-tacker we will set this at 85%, so that the leech is sure to clear the mast, provided the clew is not located too high off the deck. (It is not yet positioned, so it can still slide along the LP line.) Follow this with the actual luff length of the sail and the screen will display the area of the sail, calculated on the assumption that its edges are straight. Finally, the clew needs to be fixed along the LP line, either by entering its height above the tack fitting, or its leech length. This completes the first page of data entry.

Next come the leech hollow, foot round and luff curves (Fig 4.7b). The leech hollow is entered first, expressed in terms of its maximum depth and its position as a percentage of leech length, followed by the greatest depth of foot round and its position measured from the tack. The luff curve is then defined by entering the offsets at several positions along the luff, using a positive value for an offset forward of the forestay and a negative one aft of it, remembering that the greater the luff round the less the necessary broadseaming, as both increase the draft of the sail.

The computer will then ask you which of the VDC curves is to be used to locate the broadseaming and the size of it; whether it is to be applied to the luff or the leech (as in this case), and the point where the maximum value occurs, as a percentage of chord length at various heights. (It is constant on this sail.)

Having so far designed the sail without regard for panel width, this must now be entered so that the program can lay out the seams so as to make the best possible use of the cloth and minimise wastage. The computer will therefore request the allowances for seaming and for the tablings, taking account of whether the cloth is to be folded or taped (or both), and whether a boltrope will be fitted internally. Finally you will be asked for the height of the first seam, since this will act as the reference point for positioning all the others, and is also the lowest one to which broadseaming can be applied. The computer can now perform all the necessary design calculations, print out a summary of the input data for you to check before it files them, and produce a drawing of the sail, together with the dimensions of each panel to be marked out on the cutting table.

Designing the mainsail

The procedure for designing the mainsail is similar. As with the jib, the first screen defines the basic dimensions: 'P', the mainsail luff length; 'E', the foot length; 'HB', the width of the headboard; and the boom droop, in degrees (none in our case). The computer then wants to know the length and the amount of 'poke' of the battens – the amount by which each extends beyond the straight leech line, measured as a percentage of 'E', to support the roach. This is followed by the foot round, as before, and then the luff curve. This has to take account of mast bend, which is designated as occurring at 50% of 'P', so that by altering the bend at half height, you change the amount of bend along the entire mast. It is an arbitrary figure which the spar maker can usually advise on. For this boat we are estimating a bend of 180 mm, entering 75% of this at 25% and again at 75% of 'P'.

The section on broadseaming works in exactly the same way as it did in the jib program, and so does the section on cloth width and tablings, except that an additional page asks you for details of the finishing, such as the positions of the Cunningham hole, reef points and the ends of the batten pockets, all of which will be shown on the cutting sheet for the appropriate panel.

Shaping spinnakers

The last of the three programs is a particularly versatile tool that enables you to design star-cut, tri-radial, radial-clew and cross-cut spinnakers (Figs 4.8 and 4.9a and b), and is therefore rather more complex than the others, as you might expect. The example we are using here is a good general-purpose sail for a cruising boat, with a radial head to absorb the loadings in that region, and horizontal panels in the lower half that allow it to develop a moderately deep belly for running, but to be kept flat enough to remain reasonably stable, and to reach with the apparent wind on the beam in light conditions. Being symmetrical (unlike a single luffed cruising chute or genniker, which is more of a lightweight genoa than a spinnaker), this sail is designed as if it were folded in half, so that the two leeches coincide. When the edges are pulled taut, the only remaining fullness is due to the shaping of the seams.

To begin with, you enter the basic 'I' and 'J' dimensions, as with the jib. From these, the maximum recommended luff and width and minimum girth values are calculated and displayed. You then enter the sizes you want, as a percentage of those limits. We will accept the full luff and width dimensions, and 85% of the maximum foot. As soon as you input these figures, the computer works out the resulting area and shows it on the screen.

The critical curve in the design is the one running down the adjoining centrelines of the two halves – the mitre curve – as the more pronounced this is, the fuller the sail will be. It is defined at 20, 40, 60 and 80% distances from the head down an imaginary straight centre seam to the foot, the offsets at those points being themselves expressed as percentages of the length of that head-to-foot line. Traditionally the offset at the 40% level is the one used to specify the overall fullness of the curve, leaving the other three, *expressed as percentages of the first one*, to describe the shape of the curve. (Sounds rather

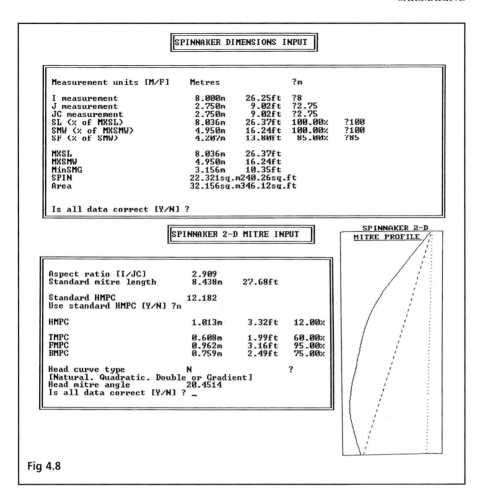

Fig 4.8

complicated, but that's the way it's always been done, and it works well.) Since you need a moderately flat sail for a good, all-round spinnaker, you should select a 12% offset at the 40% level, 60% *of that value* (ie 24%) at the top point, with 95% and 57% at the lower ones respectively. When all this data has been typed in, the profile of the sail appears, as if by magic, on the screen.

By defining the all-important mitre curve and the width of the spinnaker, you have already done most of the design work on its radial head panels. The only information the computer still lacks is how far down the sail the radials are to extend, so this is now entered as a percentage of the luff length – 40% in this case – measured along the mitre curve. Next, input the cloth width (60 in) and seaming allowance (20 mm) – such a mixture of metric and Imperial units is commonplace in sailmaking. This is followed by the number of panels you wish to fit across each width of cloth, whether you want an odd or even number of head gores and how wide you want those adjacent to the leech – the wing gores – to be as a percentage of the main gores. If you have

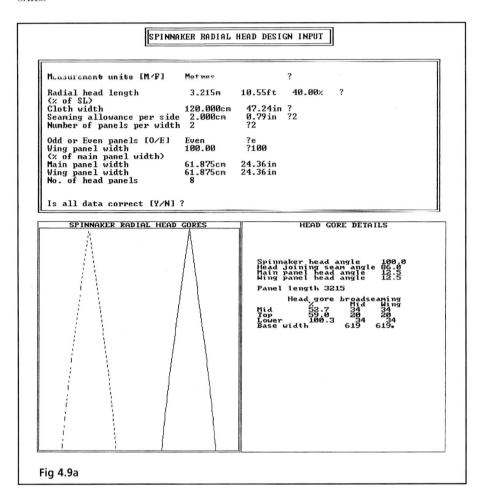

Fig 4.9a

no particular figure in mind, you can simply ask for 'Large', to make best use of the cloth, or 'Small' if you are more concerned with appearance. The main gores are all identical, resulting in circular arc sections in the head of the sail, although this may be modified by broadseaming at their bottoms. In response to your input, the screen now displays a drawing of a head panel beside a wing panel, accompanied by a set of data indicating the head angle of the complete sail and of the main and wing panels; the head seam angle between the base and side of a main panel; the panel length; and the extent of the broadseaming, tabulated as horizontal offsets.

Moving down the sail, a similar procedure is followed for the cross panels, which are then automatically added to the screen picture, together with a note of the foot aspect ratio. The computer assumes that you intend these panels to lie square to the mitre curve, but if you want to change the angle, for example to ensure that the threadline follows the leech more closely, or to alter the amount or shape of the broadseaming on the bottom of any

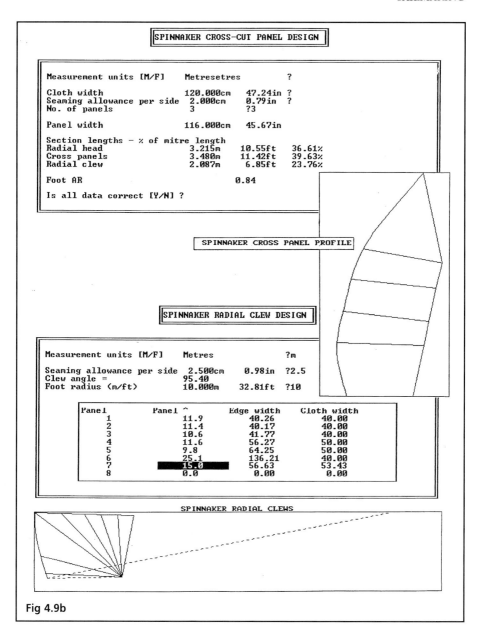

Fig 4.9b

particular panel, you can modify each seam individually. The further away from the centreline that the cross panel remains parallel-sided, and the tighter the curve that is applied to the broadseaming, the more elliptical the sail will be. You also have the option of altering the shape of the leech if you don't like the look of it, by entering plus or minus offsets at 20, 40, 60 and 80% of its height. The program then draws a fair curve through the new points, if necessary modifying the clew height to match the required luff length, and

157

then displays both the old and the new leeches side by side, noting the change in sail area. The cross panels on our sail continue on down to the foot, but there is a further section of the program for the design of the radial clew panels that feature on some styles of spinnaker.

The computer has infinite patience! If at any stage you have second thoughts about the panel shapes or dimensions, or the seaming allowances, you can go back and alter your figures until you are satisfied with the final result. An output menu will then display or print out all the input data and the intermediate calculations, followed by the sheets detailing the offsets for the radial main head and wing panels, the number of panels required and the seaming allowance, together with a set of figures for the broadseaming on each panel. Similar tables of offsets are produced for the cross panels, and for the radial clew panels too, when these form part of the design.

These and far more detailed explanations and instructions are given in the tutorial that accompanies the programs. And all this on one small floppy disk.

TURNING DESIGNS INTO SAILS

The first thing you will need, in addition to a generous measure of determination, is plenty of space in which to work on the sails and around them. This means finding a covered, flat area that will accommodate the largest sail, preferably with a wooden floor, so that the cloths can be laid out and held in place with awls or 'prickers'. It is sometimes possible to borrow a room in the village hall or other local amenity for the purpose, but if it comes down to commandeering your living room and there is some objection to leaving holes in the floor, thumb tacks or map pins make smaller marks and 4–5 lb (1.8–2.3 kg) weights, if you can get hold of some, leave none at all. These alternatives are fine for marking the edge curves, but prickers are better at taking the strain at the corners of the sail. If space is limited, the sail can be folded and worked on a bit at a time, but to begin with the full area of floor will be required for lofting, since this consists of drawing out the design life size on the floor, working from the scale drawings, tables of offsets, or cut sheets. It won't become essential again until the sail has been sewn together, although the more space you have the better.

Part of it can be used to house a bench. Except when he is on hands and knees lofting and laying out, a sailmaker mostly sits and sews. An ordinary kitchen chair will do if you intend only to make the occasional small sail, but a proper sailmaker's bench is a lot more comfortable and does wonders for the ergonomics of the operation. For unlike a workbench that you stand at, a sailmaker's bench is for sitting on. It needs to be just high enough to allow your lap to be level with the floor, and about 6 ft (1.8 m) long, with all the tools and spools of twine grouped within easy reach to your right (for right-handers). It should have a raised back to prevent things from falling off, with a loose seat pad so that you can slide to and fro on it. Such a bench has to be stout and stable, but basically it's a simple piece of furniture that is easily made and soon pays for itself many times over. A small portable workbench and vice will also come in handy.

THE TOOLS

For the lofting process you will need the following:

- Half a dozen prickers for designating the end points.
- Cheap screwdrivers, with their blades sharpened to a point, are an economical substitute for traditional sail prickers.
- A piece of chalk and a reel of twine. This is stretched tightly between the prickers, and the peripheries of the sail are established by chalking the twine, pulling it up and letting it snap back, leaving a fine white line on the floor.
- A 5 m locking steel tape and a 12 in rule.
- A 15 m linen tape, or a roll of $^3/_4$ in polyester webbing, which is laid curved on the floor as a guide for drawing the luff, foot and leech roundings, a process known traditionally as 'throwing the tape'. The long, flexible wooden or grp splines used by boatbuilders, sprung into curves against aluminium pushpins, are a better alternative to tape, because they make it easier to draw a fair curve. A few lengths of plastic curtain rail make a good substitute.

Now for the sailmaker's tools. The one crucial piece of equipment is a sewing machine. An ordinary domestic model can be used on fairly lightweight synthetic materials, provided it can do the zig-zag stitching which is necessary to distribute the stress in each seam over a reasonably wide area. Such a machine can cope satisfactorily with up to four layers of the 4–5 oz cloth we will be using. But for more layers or heavier cloth, a second-hand industrial machine with a wider throat and more power, or one of the portable semi-industrial types, such as the Reed Sailmaker or the Necchi 512, designed to be carried aboard large cruising boats, would be a wise investment.

The rest are hand tools, foremost among which is a leather sewing palm (Fig 4.10), an indispensable item for any sailmaker ashore or afloat and a particularly personal piece of kit, because after it has been wetted and worked for a bit, it moulds itself to the hand and becomes comfortable to wear for long periods. It is used for pushing the needle through the cloth, in the manner of a dressmaker's thimble, except that this has a metal eye set in the palm, with indentations to take the head of the needle. It comes in two types. A seaming palm, as its name implies, is for all the day-to-day sewing of seams, tablings and patches and is in constant use during sailmaking. The other is a roping palm, used primarily for sewing on boltropes. This is heavy work

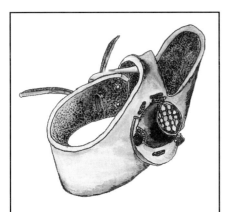

Fig 4.10 The leather seaming palm used for most hand-sewing work.

requiring stout needles, so it has larger indentations in a deeper set needle guard, and a protective piece built up around the thumb hole to allow the thread to be wrapped round it and pulled tight. However, the amateur may find it somewhat clumsy compared with a sewing palm, and if boltropes or very heavy cloth do not figure largely in the work, he can invariably manage without one. Both types are made in left- as well as right-handed versions.

Next, some sailmaker's needles. These are triangular in section, with their corners rounded so that the needle separates the yarns as it is passed through the cloth, instead of cutting them. They are graded by numbers conforming to the standard wire gauge, the size to be used depending on the weight of cloth being sewn and hence the weight of thread. They are not expensive, so it pays to have a good range, with some spares. For small yacht sails such as ours, with cloth in the 4–6 oz range, you will need No 17 and 18 needles – three or four of each in case of breakage or bending – some 19s (the smallest made) and a packet of household darning needles for nylon and other light cloth or for detail finishing, and a couple of 16s for multiple thicknesses and heavy cloths. The larger the needle the easier it is to thread and to hold, but the bigger the hole it makes in the cloth, so resist the temptation to use a 16 when an 18 is heavy enough and will make a neater job.

The corresponding sizes of hand seaming twine, which is made of spun polyester, are a 5-strand No 40 for most of the work and a 3-strand No 20 for the spinnaker and any other light cloth. It comes on small spools, ready waxed. (There are equivalent machine threads, which are identified by a variety of numbering systems. Choose the thread to suit the needle(s) on your machine.) It's a good idea to blunt the point of one of your 17s to use for roping, so that it will pass more easily between the strands of the rope without penetrating them and getting stuck. The other needles should be kept sharp with a fine stone, all of them oiled regularly or smeared with Vaseline and stored in an airtight container to prevent them from rusting.

Finally there are the various tools for cutting, stretching and flattening the cloth (see Figs 4.11a and 4.11b):

- A really sharp knife. The type doesn't matter – it can be a sheath or clasp knife, or one from the kitchen – but it should have a vee-ground blade, kept razor sharp, clean and oiled.

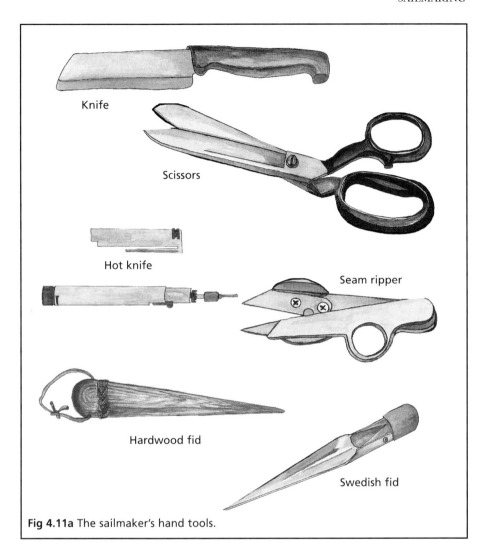

Fig 4.11a The sailmaker's hand tools.

- A good pair of large dressmaking scissors.
- A bevel-edged soldering iron or hotknife for cutting and sealing the raw edges of synthetic cloth, and preventing twine and rope ends from fraying. (The process produces acrid fumes, so make certain there is adequate ventilation.) You will also need a piece of aluminium, plastics laminate or stainless steel as a backing plate against which to do the cutting.
- A dressmaker's seam ripper; it is much faster and surer than a knife for removing stitching.
- Two or three fids of different sizes. A fid is a tapered hardwood spike, used for opening the lay of a rope when making a splice, stretching cringles before setting in the metal rings, opening up holes in cloth, and with a few turns of thread wrapped round it, for heaving up on stitches. There is also

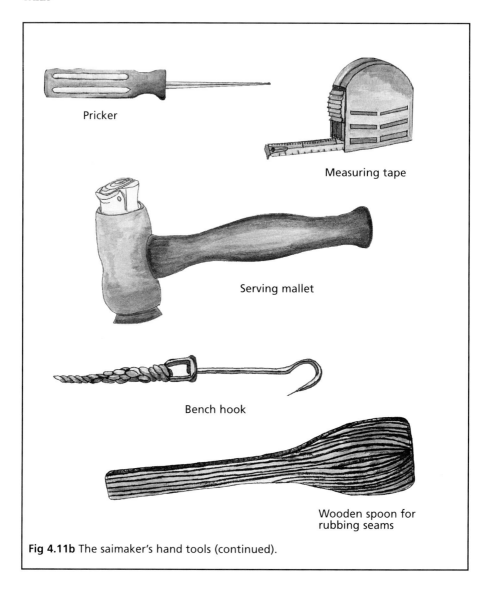

Pricker

Measuring tape

Serving mallet

Bench hook

Wooden spoon for rubbing seams

Fig 4.11b The saimaker's hand tools (continued).

a useful variant called a Swedish fid, which is made of steel and shaped like a gardener's trowel. This makes it easier to tuck in the strands of a laid rope when splicing it.

- A selection of eyelet punches and dies for two or three sizes of rings and turnovers.
- A light ballpeen hammer and a rawhide or wooden serving mallet.
- Pliers, for pulling needles through stubborn cloth and heaving tight on seizings.
- A bench hook. This is a steel hook with a swivel spliced to a lanyard. The sharp point is stuck into the cloth and the lanyard is tied away to one side

to tension the work against the pull of the needle. It effectively provides the sailmaker with an extra hand and makes sewing easier and neater.

- A seam rubber for creasing the cloth and smoothing the stitches. A short-handled wooden spoon will do both jobs nicely, but you can use the rounded back of a knife or the blunt edge of a pair of scissors for creasing.

LOFTING, LAYING OUT AND CUTTING

Working from the measurements on the design plan, begin by spiking out the corners of each sail full size on the floor (Fig 4.12). Start at the tack by driving in the first pricker, followed by another to locate the head (assume for the moment that it is pointy – the headboard can be drawn in later) allowing for the stretch we can expect in the luff. From there, using a piece of twine as a trammel, scribe an arc in pencil on the floor roughly where you expect the clew will be. Repeat the procedure with the twine tied to the tack pricker. Where the arcs intersect, push in the definitive clew pricker, and stretch the twine tightly round all three, half-hitching it at each corner. Then simply chalk it and twang it to produce the basic outline of the sail.

The next step is to draw in the true line of the sail edges, with their respective roundings. Scaling the amounts of curvature off the design drawing, or working from the tables of offsets, transfer these measurements to the floor at the mid- and quarter-points, or at closer intervals if possible. Then sketch in the profiles, following the line of the tape arranged in a fair curve, or use thumb tacks and string to give a rough indication of the shape before free-handing it. A more surefire alternative is to draw along a spline, sprung

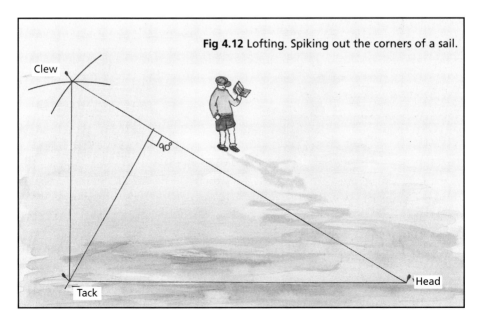

Fig 4.12 Lofting. Spiking out the corners of a sail.

Clew

90°

Head

Tack

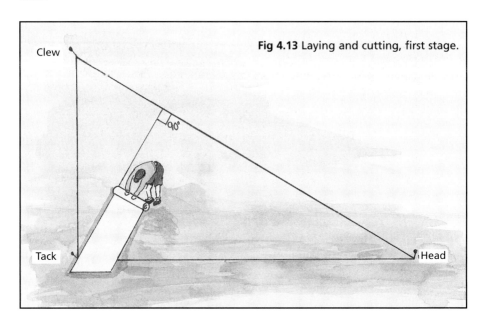

Clew

90°

Tack

Head

Fig 4.13 Laying and cutting, first stage.

against pushpins at the key points or held down with weights. Whichever method you use, check the fairness of the curve for any bumps or flatspots by lying down on the floor and eyeballing it. Finally, draw a dotted line round the outside of the sail where tablings are to be formed, and at a distance out according to their depth and type. This will only apply to the leeches in our case, since we propose using webbing tape on the other edges.

Now for the actual laying and cutting. Draw a seam line perpendicular to the leech – or to the straight-line edge of it, to be precise – down to the tack. Unroll the cloth so that its lower edge lies along the tack seam line and slightly overlaps the dotted line at either end (Fig 4.13). This is to allow for the subsequent broadseaming at the luff, which may shorten it a little, and in case one cloth should creep over another during the sewing. Then pin it down to the floor and cut it with the hotknife, using a backing plate to reflect the heat and save tattooing the floor.

Next, draw a sewing guide line parallel to its upper selvedge and about 15 mm down to allow for the seam overlap (the rule-of-thumb is 1 mm for every 10 gm/sq m of cloth weight). Even though the edges are heat sealed, they can still fray in time, so the professionals usually allow an additional 5 mm and turn them under, so that the needle will pass through three thicknesses of cloth. It is sound practice, albeit somewhat fiddly and by no means essential. Where broadseaming is to be introduced, allow the line to fall away in a smooth curve as it approaches the luff so as to produce the appropriate taper (see page 146) and draw a new sewing guide parallel to it. Then lay another cloth, starting at the luff, with the bolt turned round so that the slanting edge lies neatly along it. Number each panel on its forward end as you go along,

Fig 4.14 Overlapping the cloths.

and put strike-up marks – short pencil lines – at intervals across the real seams. When these come to be sewn, the two halves of each mark can then be lined up to ensure that the seam is sewn exactly as laid. Continue the procedure up the sail to the head, followed by the area under the tack seam – but with the upper edges of these panels and their sewing guides placed *under* the preceding cloth, so that all the seams overlap in the same direction (Fig 4.14). Finally, starting with the top panel, lift it and, without turning it over or around, lay it on the next one below. Lift both of these and lay them on the next panel and so on until they are all piled on one another, the top one being the first to be sewn. This may all sound a bit pernickety, but it saves getting into a muddle later.

JOINING UP AND RUBBING DOWN

The novice sailmaker will do well to stick the cloths together with double-sided tape, to make sure they are correctly positioned before being sewn. Take the top pair of cloths off the pile; tape up the whole length of the first seam, leaving the paper backing on the upper side of the tape; roll away the upper panel and working from the leech towards the luff, unroll it along the sew-to line, including the broadseaming, aligning the strike-up marks and removing the backing paper as you go along. When you have reached the luff, check that the seam is fair and free of kinks and wrinkles. If you are not happy with it, take it apart, correct the faults and stick it together again.

Having read the instruction book for your machine and tried some test pieces on scrap material, there will be two adjustments you may have to make.

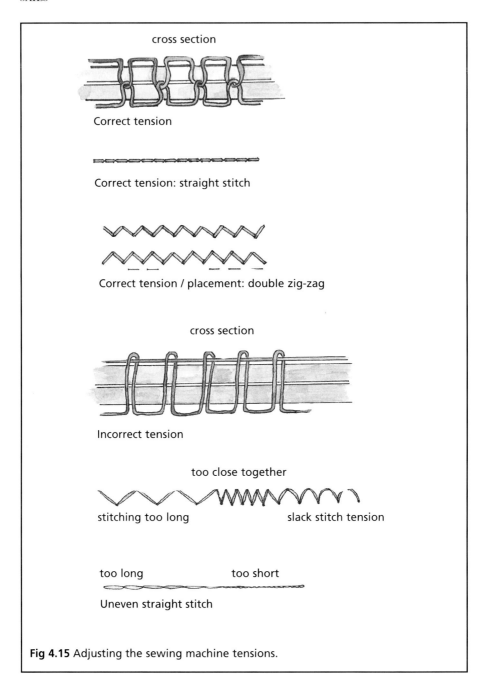

cross section

Correct tension

Correct tension: straight stitch

Correct tension / placement: double zig-zag

cross section

Incorrect tension

too close together

stitching too long   slack stitch tension

too long   too short

Uneven straight stitch

Fig 4.15 Adjusting the sewing machine tensions.

The first is the tension (Fig 4.15), which regulates where the interlocking occurs in the cloths; it should be somewhere in the middle of the sandwich, rather than on top or underneath it. The other is the stitch length. For most seams, 4–5 mm looks about right, with the zig-zags at right-angles to one another, but where a rope is to be attached, increase the length to 6–8 mm. Where you are using sticky tape, it is as well to keep a can of silicon spray handy, as the needle may tend to get clogged.

Now you can safely run the first line of stitching, keeping it close to the edge of the upper cloth (say 3 mm from it), with the leech facing away from you and leading first into the sewing machine. Working like this, with the first cloth on top of the second and to your left, and with each subsequent cloth being added from the right, ensures that only a single cloth at a time has to pass under the arm of the machine, instead of a bunch that might get jammed. Turn the cloths over and sew a line of stitching along the other edge of the seam, from luff to leech this time. Continue the routine until all the cloths are sewn together, and then lay the sail back on the floor and pricker it down above the outline markings, pulling it out firmly to remove any wrinkles, but not stretching it.

At this stage you give the sail its final shaping. Check and correct any discrepancies that may have occurred during the sticking and sewing, making sure that the edge curves are fair and agree with the design profile, and then mark and bend over the tablings where these are called for, crease them with the seam rubber (together with the patches which we'll come to in a moment) and sew them down. Don't forget to run the leechline (3 mm braided) and make sure it doesn't get caught up in the sewing. It will be attached to the headboard, emerge through a small eyelet near the clew and be secured to a mini cleat sewn to the sail. Some sailmakers like to run over the lines of stitching with the rubber to smooth them, and to finish them off by painting them on both sides with one of the proprietary sealers which penetrate and bind the stitching together as they dry.

HAND-SEWING AND THE STITCHES

Although as much of the sail as possible will be stitched on the machine, there are bound to be some parts of the work that have to be done by hand, either because it is too heavy, with too many layers of cloth (such as patches) for the machine to handle, too intricate for it, or inaccessible to it. You probably won't be able to match the dexterity and precision of a professional, but strength and an acceptable standard of neatness are quite easily achieved, provided you are patient and don't try to rush the job.

Most hand-sewing is done from above the cloth, rather than struggling to turn the work over with every stitch and push the needle through from the other side. This is the principle followed in flat seaming, the most widely used method of hand sewing panels, tablings and patches. Sit with the work across your lap and sew from bottom right to top left (Fig 4.16), with the bench hook caught in the cloth and tied off to the right, and the left hand tensioning the cloth against it. (Vice versa for left-handers.) Nudge the head of the

Fig 4.16 Sit with the work across your lap and sew from bottom right to top left.

needle into the recessed eye of the seaming palm and hold it there with the ring or forefinger while your thumb and index finger grip it firmly near the point (Fig 4.17), rotating the needle slightly anti-clockwise as you sew, in order to counteract the tendency for the thread to untwist itself as it is drawn through the cloth. Don't knot the tail end of the twine because it will prob-

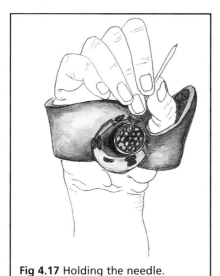

Fig 4.17 Holding the needle.

ably chafe away. Instead, leave about ½ in (1 cm) of it sticking out from the cloth and anchor it by oversewing with the next few stitches.

When flat seaming, always use the twine doubled, and start off with a length sufficient to reach from the work to your extended needle hand. Push the needle down through and then up again, all in one movement, taking care not to sew through more than the two layers of the seam. Space the stitches at 5 mm intervals (closer on light nylon) along the pencilled guideline as regularly as you can, pulling them just tight enough to sink slightly into the cloth without actually puckering it, and

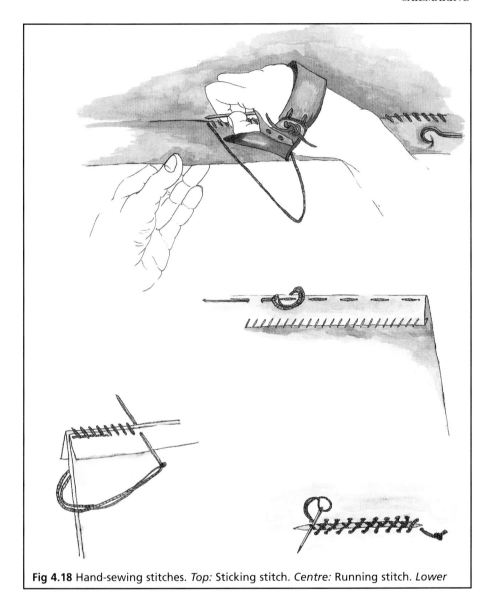

Fig 4.18 Hand-sewing stitches. *Top:* Sticking stitch. *Centre:* Running stitch. *Lower*

shifting the bench hook along as you proceed. At the end of the row, anchor the thread by passing the needle under the last few stitches and taking a final tuck under the cloth.

Next in the sewing repertoire is the sticking stitch (Fig 4.18), which can be used for tacking cloths together, instead of sticky-taping them (see below), so that they won't slide around on one another while you are trying to sew them; or to secure a luff wire to a headsail that is to be set flying, by sewing as closely as possible to the inboard side of it. (You can do this on the machine by using a piping foot.) With the needle facing away from you and pointing *along* the seam, pass it through the cloth at an angle, advance a short distance on the underside and bring it up through again. Another method of tacking is to use a running stitch, which is similar to the sticking stitch except that the needle goes through the work at right-angles, so that all the progress along the seam is made above and below it, instead of inside it. In practice, there's not a lot to choose between them if your sewing isn't particularly precise, but the running stitch tends to be the stronger.

Finally, for a row of stitches along a seam that is only visible from one side, eg when over-sewing the edge of a sail where two cloths have already been joined together, such as on a turned tabling or at the end of a batten pocket, the round stitch is simple and quick. For this it is best to work from left to right. With the bench hook pulling from your right, push the needle upwards and slightly away from you through the work, and repeat at close intervals.

PATCHES AND POCKETS

Patches (Fig 4.19) are an integral and vital part of a sail's structural system and must be fitted wherever localised stresses will occur, notably at the corners, where they are sewn on together with any tablings that run through the patch. And as with the tablings, it is essential to cut the patches so that their warp and fill match that of the sail as nearly as possible. A considerable variety of sizes, shapes and styles can be used, depending on your aesthetic taste and personal preference, the material used and the time you are prepared to spend applying them. Some are a lot more decorative and elaborate than others, but their common purpose is to transfer the loads progressively into the body panels and along the tablings.

This is done by making each patch from several different-sized layers of cloth, their outer perimeters matching that of the sail corner, their inner ones following the chosen pattern in a series of steps. These should be no closer than about $2\frac{1}{2}$ cm apart on a daysailer, 5 cm on a small cruising boat. The largest layer should be at least an inch long for every foot of sail edge ($2\frac{1}{2}$ cm in 30 cm) and with not less than two layers on either side of it – preferably three on our mainsail, and four or more on a big blue-water sail. Make each patch about 12 mm oversize all round, so that its edges can be turned under.

Opinions differ as to the best sequence for putting it all together. The simplest is to sew the largest one on first, and follow it with successively smaller layers. Some purists prefer each patch to extend into the sail less than the one outside it. A popular compromise is to start with the second largest layer, followed by the smaller ones, and finish by covering all of them with the largest. A further load-spreading precaution, if you have the time and patience, is to make each layer a different size from its partner on the opposite side of the sail. It is usually found convenient to sew the under patches on first, followed by the sail with its tabling, and then the top patches. With two, let alone three

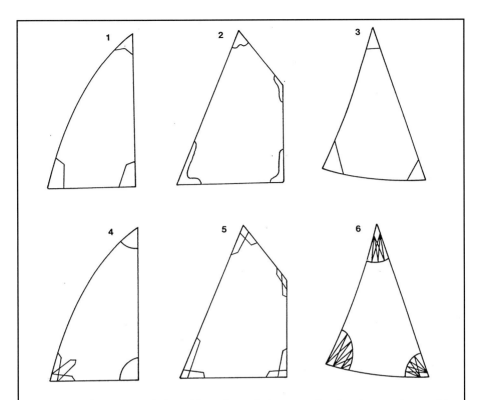

Fig 4.19 Patches. Some of the wide variety of shapes and styles that can be used to disperse the corner loads. Except on radial cuts, the cloth direction in the patches should match the weave of the sailcloth. 1 Rectangular tack and clew patches. 2 Fancy curved patches for a traditional boat. 3 Simple triangular patches. 4 Triple-finger clew patch. 5 Two-piece finger construction. 6 Radial stitching.

pieces of cloth either side of the sail, plus the tabling (or tape), hand-sewing will almost certainly be required if you don't have the luxury of an industrial machine.

Reef points, as positioned on your design plan, are constructed in similar fashion. The patches at the intermediate points, usually but not necessarily diamond shaped, are sewn either side of the sail, preferably with one slightly larger than its companion so that the stitching goes through different parts of the panel cloth. Each should have a sewn eyelet (see next page) at the centre of the diamond and a tie made up from line with a stopper knot on either side. The end patches, which take most of the strain, need to be multi-layered like those at the corners, with a heavy-duty ring worked into them.

Batten pockets (Fig 4.20) are also subjected to high stresses and must be carefully fitted. Cut the cloth for the pocket with the threadline running in the same direction as it does on the sail, and allow an additional 12 mm on all the edges so that they can be turned in when sewing. The pocket should

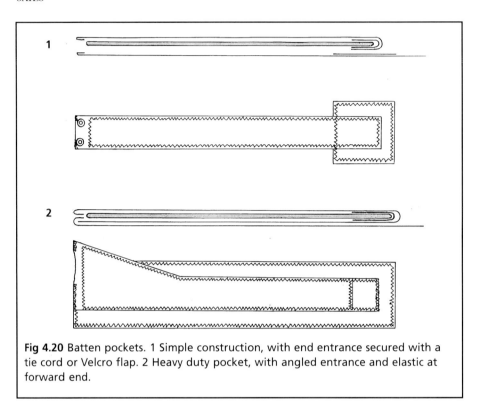

Fig 4.20 Batten pockets. 1 Simple construction, with end entrance secured with a tie cord or Velcro flap. 2 Heavy duty pocket, with angled entrance and elastic at forward end.

be large enough to accommodate the stitching as well as the batten itself, and reinforced with additional layers of cloth. Turn in a further 50 mm of cloth at the forward end, and either interpose an additional chafe patch between it and the sail – or better still, a full-length patch through which the sides of the pocket as well as the forward edge are then sewn. Finish off by round stitching both ends by hand. Some sailmakers also sew in a piece of elastic at the after end, to keep the batten pushed firmly against the leech so that it can't work loose and fall out. When sewing and oversewing the angled entrance, be careful to avoid the leech line, and should you be hand-sewing instead of machining, it's a good idea to insert a batten to prevent the needle from picking up the cloth of the pocket. Pockets for full-length battens are easily made from webbing tape, although its weave won't be consistent with that of the sail.

EYELETS, RINGS AND THIMBLES

An eyelet, as its name implies, is a very small eye, in brass for most amateurs, stainless steel for those with the necessary press. It consists of an outer ring which is pushed through a criss-cross incision in the cloth, and a mating liner which is punched into position over it. Where more strength is required, as on the reef points, the eyelet may be oversewn all round its periphery, before the liner is fitted to protect the stitching from chafe (Fig 4.21).

Eyes, which are best defined as large rings, are similarly worked into the luff and clew patches, and at the ends of each line of reef points. Their liners, known as thimbles, are then inserted and splayed out, using the appropriate punch. (Most large rings in production sails are of stainless steel and are hydraulically pressed, with no sewing: plain, but immensely strong.) Handworked rings are usually strengthened, especially the clew eye which is the most highly stressed, either by seizing to a pair of eyelets set further away from the edge of the sail so as to distribute the forces, or with one or two pieces of webbing running through the eye and sewn on in the general direction of the maximum tension.

A robust and traditional-looking alternative to a patched eye is a cringle (Fig 4.22). This is an external ring of rope, surrounding a brass or stainless thimble and attached to two eyelets in the sail.

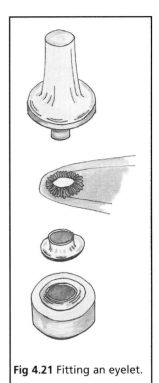

Fig 4.21 Fitting an eyelet.

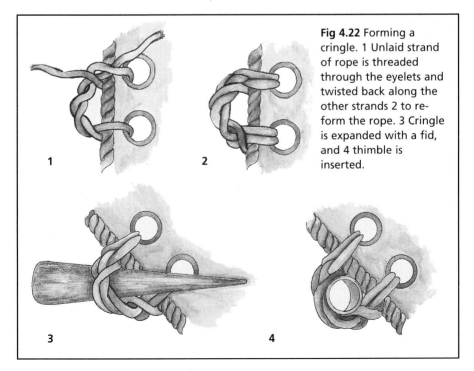

Fig 4.22 Forming a cringle. 1 Unlaid strand of rope is threaded through the eyelets and twisted back along the other strands 2 to re-form the rope. 3 Cringle is expanded with a fid, and 4 thimble is inserted.

1

2

3

4

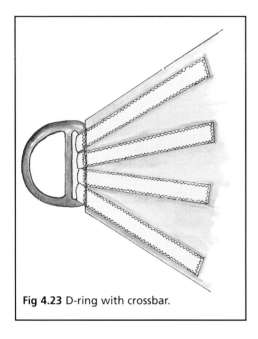

Fig 4.23 D-ring with crossbar.

To form a cringle, unlay a single strand of rope about four times as long as the circumference of the finished cringle. Thread it through one of the eyelets, leaving one end twice as long as the other, and twist them together again. Pass the longer end through the other eyelet, carefully and tightly twist it back along the others to re-form a three-strand rope, and tuck in the end as you would on a splice. The gap between the sail edge and the inside of the loop should be only *half* the finished diameter of the cringle. This is expanded by using a mallet to thump it down over a fid, which is then quickly removed before the cringle has time to shrink back, and the thimble is tapped into position.

Serving the same purpose as a patched eye or a cringle, is a stainless steel D-ring (Fig 4.23). This should be one of the types provided with a crossbar to prevent it capsizing under oblique loading. Several short lengths of webbing are passed through the ring under the crossbar, splayed out radially across the corner of the sail and sewn through to one another. By spreading the stress more evenly, this arrangement is stronger than a single large ring, though not as neat; more durable than a cringle; and easier to install than either of them. Its appearance is not to everyone's taste, but can be much improved by sewing on a leather gaiter as chafe protection.

HEADBOARDS, SLIDES AND ROPEWORK

Some blue-water voyagers prefer to fit a stout ring instead of a headboard, because these have been known to break under extreme conditions. But normally they are perfectly reliable, and act as a coat hanger in spreading the load at a Bermudan sail's skinniest corner. Made of plastics or anodised aluminium, they may either be fitted inside the sail between the top patches, pushed hard up into the pocket and sewn through pre-drilled holes; or mounted externally as a two-piece assembly, one on either side of the sail and its reinforcements, and sewn or riveted together. A large eye is then set in near the peak to accept the halyard shackle.

If you have opted for sail slides running in a track, rather than a boltrope held in a mast or foot groove, the best way to attach them is with webbing

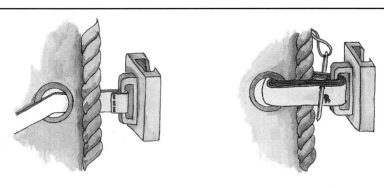

Fig 4.24 Attaching a mainsail slide with webbing tape. One end of the tape is sewn to the eye of the slide, the other end is passed several times through the sail eyelet and the slide, and all the parts of the tape are finally stitched through one another.

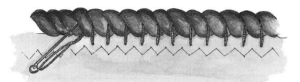

Fig 4.25 Fitting a boltrope.

tape (Fig 4.24), which is extremely hard wearing and doesn't chafe either the sail or the slides. One end of the tape is sewn to the eye of the slide, and the other passed through an eyelet in the reinforced edge of the sail and back through the slide. This is repeated three or four times, leaving enough play for the sail to swing from side to side, before the loose end is finally stitched through the six or eight parts. The sail eyelets should be placed at intervals of about a foot (30 cm) on a small sail (up to twice that on a large one), but kept far enough away from the nearest reef tack ring so that it can be pulled down past the accumulated luff slides to reach the tack hook.

There was a time when virtually all the edges of a sail were strengthened and finished by sewing them to a rope, known as a boltrope. Nowadays roping, except on traditionally rigged boats, is mostly confined to luffs and feet where they run in a grooved spar, jib luffs carried in the grooved headfoil spar used on roller reefing gear, and the occasional piece of decorative reinforcement round a clew. Wired luffs are usually still fitted to stormsails, but for everyday headsails the wire's resistance to bending makes them awkward to stow, wire splicing is labour intensive, and there is the constant threat of corrosion. So wire has been largely replaced by braided, pre-stretched polyester or low-stretch Kevlar® or Spectra® rope.

Pre-roped webbing tape is commercially available for roller headsails, with Teflon® woven in to reduce friction in the groove. However, the normal practice in making up an internal boltrope is to wrap a length of tape round the luff- or footrope, and to sew the two halves together as close to the rope as you can get. For sails of the size appropriate to a smallish cruising boat such as our 23 footer, 8 mm polyester rope and 50–75 mm tape will do nicely. If you are using the machine with a piping foot and it won't sew closely enough to the rope, lay in a light line instead and fish the rope through afterwards. Using this technique, you can also fish it around the corners, when two or more sides of the sail are to be roped, by cutting an access gap at the corner to fiddle the rope through, and sewing it up later. Alternatively, for a more traditional appearance, three-strand rope may be fitted externally. You do this by passing the needle around one strand and through the sail edge, repeating the process every strand's width further along the lay of the rope, taking great care that it doesn't twist and that both it and the sail are held taut (Fig 4.25). Nevertheless by far the simplest method for the amateur is to hand-sew the tape tightly round the rope with sticking stitches, and then to machine it to either side of the sail with two rows of zig-zag stitching. It should be finished off by tapering the ends of the rope into 'rats' tails', heat sealed with the iron.

Even though the rope is prestretched, it will probably elongate slightly under load, while the tape/sail combination will stretch quite a lot more. It is essential, however, that they remain in balance with one another. So before you start sewing, and whichever the method of attachment, each part should be hauled out, lying side by side to the sort of tension you expect from the halyard, using separate single-part tackles rigged to something solid at either end (such as a strongback across a door-way, or a tree through an open window). On a small to mid-sized sail, it is best to allow the rope to float freely inside the tabling, with just a stout multi-part seizing at the head and tack (and/or at tack and clew as the case may be). Leave several inches sticking out at each end, so that if wrinkles should appear when the tension is released, indicating that the rope is restraining the sail from developing its proper draft, it is a simple matter to cut and resew one seizing to give the sail a bit further to stretch. This procedure is not advisable, however, on any large sail, because the strain concentrated at its corners becomes very considerable in strong winds, and it would be potentially disastrous if a seizing were to pull away. So these boltropes need to be sewn in throughout their length, with the attendant care to avoid tensioning irregularities as the stitching proceeds.

FAULTS AND REMEDIES

Professional lofts usually have a test rig to check for faults in their sails, but apart from giving those you have made a preliminary examination by stringing them up horizontally in the garden, you can only do the job properly when they are set up on the boat and actually sailing. If possible, get someone else on the helm and look at the sails from a position ahead and to leeward.

The most common faults are creases. Some are impossible to avoid, particularly at the clew, and some will probably disappear after a few hours when the new cloth has settled down, so don't be in too much of a hurry to criticise your workmanship. Photograph the trouble spots, if you can, or memorise their locations, and mark them in pencil on the sail for future reference. Many of them occur because the clew, head and tack haven't been set up correctly, so try varying the halyard and outhaul tensions. You will probably be able to spot where seams or eyes have been incorrectly sewn, or where slides or hanks have been put on with uneven spacing between the sail and the spar or stay. A headboard eye not close enough to the luff or not directly below the fall of the halyard, or a headsail tack pennant out of line with the luff, will cause the sail to cant to one side and crease accordingly.

There are a number of other common problems with leeches. A slack one shows up as a crease running down the forward ends of the battens, with the roach falling away to one side; or if only the aftermost few inches of roach are slack, this section may vibrate in the wind with the characteristic drumming noise known as 'motorboating', and which can usually be dampened out with a slight adjustment to the leech line. There's also the case of the permanently hooked leech so often to be found on old sails whose leech line has been permanently tensioned, causing the cloth to stretch inside the tabling. Any of these faults can usually be cured by judiciously tightening one seam between each batten. This involves unpicking the seam in the trouble area and resewing it as a broadseam, with a 5–10 mm taper at the leech, depending on the severity of the slackness, to remove the surplus cloth. Conversely a tight leech, assuming the leech line is slack and not hooking the leech to windward, will show up as a tight line between the after ends of the battens. It is easily remedied by unpicking the seams and letting them out a few millimetres.

CARE AND REPAIR

Sails can go through hell in a single season of hard weather, but a yachtsman can minimise any damage they may sustain and prolong their life by proper handling, plus a spot of preventive maintenance from time to time, and by making immediate running repairs – homeward bounders, as they were called in the days of commercial sail. The old proverb 'a stitch in time' works well for sailors.

Deterioration of sails is usually caused by one or more of the following: flogging, mishandling, chafe, sunlight, salt and damp. Some you can't avoid entirely, but you can reduce the effects of those you can't duck.

It is not always appreciated that modern synthetic cloths, particularly those that are heavily resinated and firmly finished – let alone the laminates – are subject to work hardening. Like a sheet of metal that develops a crease and becomes brittle by being bent back and forth until it eventually fractures, the

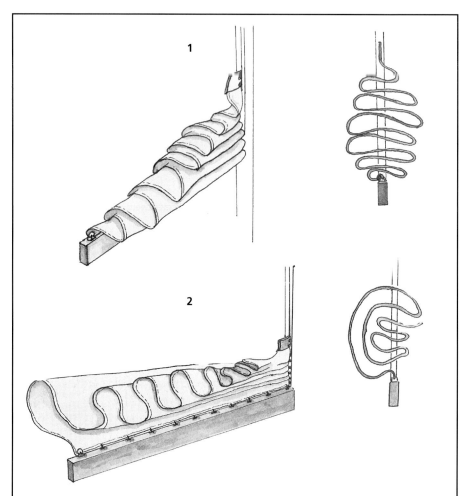

Fig 4.26 Two methods of stowing a mainsail. 1 Flaking it evenly on the boom, haul-ing the leech aft so as to avoid creasing it. 2 Pulling all the folds to one side and dumping them into the bunt before bundling the whole sausage round on top of the boom.

yarns in a sail are weakened if it is allowed to flog, leading to premature tear-ing. Flogging leeches are a common cause of this type of failure, with the breakdown usually occurring just forward of the leech tabling and clew patch-es. So before initial fluttering develops into full-blown flogging, slowly tight-en the leech line until it is just snug enough to stop the movement. In the case of a jib with a slack leech that the line cannot control without hooking it excessively, try sheeting in a degree or two to dampen the oscillation. And avoid motoring into the wind at full speed for any length of time with the main up. When battens slat to and fro, they tend to damage the cloth where they hinge at the front of their pockets.

If you have to drag sails down, pull them by the luff, which is their strongest edge. Grabbing them by the leech is certain to stretch them. Flake the main tidily on the boom (Fig 4.26), folding bights in the sail as it is lowered and at the same time hauling the leech aft to avoid any creases. If luff slides are fitted, one should be in the centre of each fold, with an even bight lying on either side of it. An alternative method of furling, only really suitable for soft fabrics, is to pull all the folds of luff to one side as the sail comes down. Then haul the upper leech aft and work your way down it towards the clew, dumping each handful into the belly of sail and folding it into itself as you go along. Finally, with the sail gathered into a sausage, bundle it round on top of the boom and lash it just firmly enough to keep it in place. Always put a sail cover on a stowed main to protect it from sunlight, or dirt carried in rain which would otherwise collect in the folds and stain them, and from bird droppings.

Headsails should never be left lashed to the guard rail after a trip, but be carefully folded and bagged (Fig 4.27). Except with a very small sail, it takes two to do the job properly, one at either side pulling out the folds to avoid

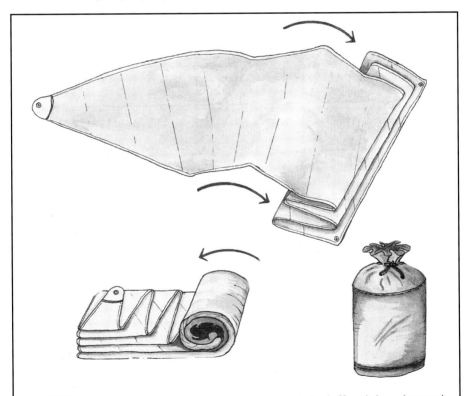

Fig 4.27 Folding a sail for bagging. Two people, one at the luff and the other at the leech, tension the sail between them to pull out the wrinkles while they flake it down. The bundle is then rolled up loosely and stowed in a slightly oversized bag.

creases and flaking them down on top of each other, starting at the foot. The whole package should then be rolled up loosely and put gently into a *large* bag, preferably three or four times the size of the rolled sail. Stuffing it down into a small bag creases the folds harshly and inevitably shortens the life of the sail. In the case of stiff, heavily resinated cloths (or laminates), the sail should be rolled up from the foot into a long sausage and stowed in a tubular bag. Nylon, on the other hand, doesn't crease much, so if the spinnaker is not kept stowed in a chute, it can be crammed into its turtle more or less any old how, provided the three corners are left accessible and clearly marked at the top of the bundle.

Whenever possible, dry the sails before they are covered or bagged, but don't be tempted to hoist them in a fresh breeze and allow them to flog. Better to lay them out on deck and tie them down while they dry out. If parts are wet with seawater, it's a good idea to rinse them out to prevent the salt from forming abrasive crystals, because these tend to cut into the cloth fibres and break down its finish. A rain shower makes a convenient alternative to a marina hosepipe; sailing in the rain is the most effective way of all to wash sails. If you get stains on them, scrub them with only a soft brush and soap or a mild detergent, so as to minimise wear on the stitching, and avoid using chemicals unless you can be sure of their effect. On the whole, they are best left to the professional cleaners. And at the end of the season, or whenever you need to dry off dinghy sails, hang them out ashore to air thoroughly, and support their weight by the luff acting as a clothes line.

The old bugbear of chafe is one that cannot be eliminated entirely, but you can avoid some of it and protect against the rest. Start by examining the sails inch by inch, if they are not new, for any signs of rubbing. Stitching and seams, and especially batten pockets, are vulnerable, as they are raised above the cloth surface. Danger spots to look for on the mainsail are where the topping lift has been allowed to rub against the leech, and wherever the body of the sail may have been in contact with shrouds, spreaders or lazyjacks. Chafe on a genoa is likely to occur while tacking, as it rolls around the spreaders, shrouds and rigging screws, and across the mast, being poked en route by stanchions, baby stay and sundry other projections. Headsails spend much of their time bellied out against the stanchions, guard rails or the pulpit; or sheeted in until they are up against a shroud or spreader on the weather side. In the case of new sails, hoist them and mark the locations of potential chafe areas as best you can.

Try to establish the cause of the chafing to see first whether it can be eliminated by re-siting any offending fittings. Apart from that, there are several protective measures that can be taken. First and foremost is to fit sacrificial patches to cover each critical area, either sewn flat on the sail, or folded in half and doubled around the foot and the leech to give protection to the edges as well as the sides of the sail. Leather gaiters can be hand-sewn round tack and clew corners where sheets are liable to damage them, and around the stitching of rings and cringles that can contact the mast, stays or shrouds. Short lengths of nylon webbing, which has a shiny finish and wears well, can be sewn to the outsides of batten pockets at potential trouble spots.

Next, go round the boat with a roll of pvc duct tape and wrap up all exposed cotter and ring pins and other sharp or protruding items – and the rigging screws too, if they are not fitted with plastic covers. The ends of spreaders must either be capped with plastic mouldings, or covered with pieces of white synthetic shag carpet with their edges stitched above and below each spreader. Parts of the shrouds themselves can be encased in split plastic hose, using the smallest size that will slide comfortably over the wire and revolve as the sail is dragged across it. (Most traditionalists prefer baggy-wrinkle, but in addition to increasing wind resistance it is liable to trap air-borne dirt and other contaminants which can accelerate sail damage.) On a long running leg, it is worth rigging a preventer to hold the boom forward and down so that it doesn't pump up and down chafing the mainsail against the shrouds, in addition to its better known duty of guarding against an accidental gybe. It consists of a tackle attached about one-third of the boom's length from the mast and stretched across to the toe rail or to a pad eye just forward of the upper shroud, with its tail led to a cleat near the cockpit. Another obvious but often overlooked precaution is to avoid dragging an unbagged sail along a non-skid deck!

When examining the sails for signs of wear and tear, make sure all the stitching is in perfect condition. If any of it is suspect, push a fine spike under it, and if it has become weakened, it will come away quite easily. Watch out for panel seaming that has been worn by a batten on the *inside* of the pocket, where it is not immediately apparent.

While at sea, adhesive sail repair tape comes in handy for get-you-home patching of tears and holes in order to stop the damage spreading, but the sail should be darned or properly repaired at the first opportunity. For small holes, tears and burns up to about 12 mm, dressmaker's over-and-under darning is adequate, but for tacking back into position any longer tears, straight or L-shaped, always use a herringbone stitch (Fig 4.18). The easier alternative of bunching the two sides together with round stitching will stretch the surrounding cloth and cause wrinkles, besides standing proud and inviting chafe. In herringboning – there are several versions, this being the simplest – all the sewing is done from one side, and should be started in sound cloth well before the tear and finished some way past it. Double the twine and either knot the bitter end or take a clove hitch round the first stitch, and proceed from left to right. Push the needle down through the slit and up through the cloth on the other side. Then bring the thread across the slit and down through the near side, up through the slit, *across the previous stitch* and down again through the slit, up through the cloth on the far side, and so on, finishing with another clove hitch after passing the needle under several of the preceding stitches. Alternate long and short stitches help to distribute the load, and draw each one just tight enough to close the slit, but not so tight as to pucker the cloth.

For patching, try to find some material identical to the sail itself and align the weave direction. When working with a synthetic cloth such as polyester, you can dispense with hems and simply hotknife the edges of the tear and the patch. But if time allows, it makes a better job to turn those of the patch under. Crease the folds with a seam rubber, hold the patch in position with double-sided sticky tape, and either machine it zig-zag or hand-sew it with small, flat seam stitches. Where a tear crosses from one panel to the next and a small narrow patch will cover it, there's no need to worry about maintaining the integrity of the original seams. But if the damage requires a long, wide patch across more than one panel, it should be made from several pieces of cloth, machined together so as to reconstruct the original panel seams, before sewing it on to the sail. In the worst case scenario, with extensive damage running along a panel for much of its length, it will probably be as well to unpick and replace the entire panel, re-creating its edge curves and tapers, and re-using its tablings and other reinforcements. But this is likely to be a lengthy task best left to the winter lay-up. Rely meanwhile on your timely taping and patching to last the season.

Taking good care of your sails is, in some respects, just as important as maintaining your car, being able to repair them even more so. With a car, if you encounter a roadside fault you can't fix, you can at least go to a garage or telephone for help, whereas at sea you are very much on your own. Nevertheless sail problems are intrinsically easier to solve. They can usually be repaired sufficiently to get you home, instead of having to rely on an auxiliary engine. Even if they or their spars should sustain serious damage, they can be jury rigged, provided you have a clear understanding of how they work, the various configurations in which they can be set and controlled, and the way each can influence the handling of the boat.

I like to think that sailing is like riding a horse. When you are able to appreciate the reasons for its behaviour and can anticipate its reactions, it becomes, in a sense, an integral part of you. The more you can develop this intimacy, the greater the pleasure that sailing will give you.

GLOSSARY

Aback A sail is aback when it is sheeted to windward and the wind comes on what should be its lee side.

Abaft nearer the stern than, further aft than, behind. As in abaft the mast.

Abeam At right angles to the fore-and-aft line of the boat.

About to go about is to tack through the wind – hence the command 'Ready about' to warn the crew.

Angle of incidence or **angle of attack.** The angle between the apparent wind and the chord of the sail.

Apparent wind The strength and direction of the wind as felt by the crew, being a combination of the true wind and the wind developed by the boat's own movement.

Aspect ratio The height of a sail (its luff length) in relation to its breadth.

Athwart Across, from side to side, as opposed to fore-and-aft.

Backstay A wire support leading aft from the mast to restrain it from falling forward.

Backwind One sail backwinds another when it deflects the airflow on to the other's lee side.

Balance A boat's ability to stay on course with the helm left free.

Barber hauler A control line from the clew of a headsail, or from a block running on its sheet, used to adjust the fullness of the sail.

Batten A flexible strip, usually made of plastic, inserted in a pocket in the leech of a sail to support the roach. Some high performance boats use full-length battens running from leech to luff.

Beam reach The point of sailing where the wind is abeam.

Bear away To turn the bows away from the wind, to alter course to leeward.

Beat To sail to windward close-hauled, as close to the wind as is practicable.

Bias The diagonal direction, at 45° to the warp and fill of a woven cloth, at which a load will stretch it most.

Bight A loop in a rope, or a coastal bay.

Block A pulley for changing the direction of pull on a rope. One or more blocks can be used to form a tackle or purchase which reduces the effort by improving the mechanical advantage.

Boom A horizontal spar to extend the foot of a sail and help to control it.

Boltrope Rope sewn along one or more edges of a sail to strengthen it and take some of the stress of the cloth when it is stretched tightly.

Brail Ropes running either side of the leech of a sail to gather it into the mast.

Bowsprit A spar projecting from the bow and from which a jib may be set. It provides a means of increasing the available sail area ahead of the mast.

Broach To slew round and luff uncontrollably broadside to wind and sea, heeling dangerously.

Broad reach The point of sailing between a beam reach and a run.

Broadseam A seam in a sail, in which the edges of neighbouring panels are cut in a convex curve, so that when they are sewn together the resulting taper in the panels forces fullness into the sail.

Bumkin A spar protruding from the stern to carry the backstay and mizzen sheet blocks.

Bunt The middle of a sail.

By the lee Running with the wind on the same side as the boom and mainsail. Easily leads to an accidental gybe.

Calendering The process of passing sailcloth between heated rollers under heavy pressure to flatten it and to make it more stable and less porous.

Camber The fore-and-aft curvature of a sail in relation to its chord.

Centre of effort The geometric point at which the wind forces on a sail, or on a combination of sails, is concentrated.

Centre of lateral resistance The geometric centre of the lateral underwater area of a hull.

Centreboard A streamlined board or plate that is lowered through a slot in the keel to provide increased lateral resistance and reduce leeway, and which can be raised to reduce the draft when sailing in shallow water.

Chord A straight line between the luff and leech of a sail.

Claw off To beat with difficulty away from a dangerous lee shore.

Clew The lower, after corner of a fore-and-aft sail, where the leech meets the foot.

Close-hauled The point of sailing where a boat is lying as close to the wind as she can without 'pinching'.

Close reach Sailing with the wind forward of the beam but not so close as to be close-hauled.

Crimp The undulation of the yarns in a woven cloth as they go over and under the crossed yarns.

Cringle A rope eye worked into the boltrope of a sail and fitted with a metal or plastic thimble.

Cunningham hole A cringle fitted a short distance above the tack, through which a line or tackle is rove to tension the luff.

Decitex Dernier. A measure of the thickness of a yarn. The higher the number, the coarser the yarn.

Downhaul A rope with which a sail or spar can be hauled down.

Draft The camber or fullness of a sail. The depth of water that a boat needs to remain afloat.

Edge curve The curvature cut into a panel of sailcloth before it is sewn up.

Euphroe A wooden block, with two or three smoothed holes instead of pulley wheels, through which are run the multi-part sheets of a Chinese junk.

Eyelet A small hole formed in a sail with a metal grommet through which a line or lacing can be passed.

Eye splice An eye formed in the end of a rope so that it can be shackled to a fitting.

Fall The hauling part of a rope or tackle.

False seam A seam made to reduce the width of a cloth by doubling it in the form of a 'Z' and sewing it down.

Fetch To reach a mark to windward without having to tack.

Fid A tapered wooden spike for opening out splices and cringles, or the lay of a rope.

Fill The yarns that run across the cloth from edge to edge.

Flake To lay a sail in folds either side of the boom. To lay a rope or chain out on deck so that it will run out easily.

Foot The lower edge of a sail.

Forestay A wire running from high on the mast to the bows or bowsprit in order to support the mast and carry a jib or genoa.

Free Not close-hauled. A boat is said to be sailing free when the wind comes from abaft the beam.

Furl To roll up or gather and lash a lowered sail.

Gaff The spar to which the head of a quadrilateral sail is attached.

Genoa A large triangular headsail extending abaft the mast.

Go about To change from one tack to another.

Gooseneck A fitting which attaches the boom to the mast, and allows it to articulate.

Gore The wedge-shaped panels of cloth in a spinnaker.

Greige Newly woven cloth before it is scoured to remove the size used to lubricate the yarns during weaving.

Grommet Originally a ring made from a single strand of rope, often worked into the boltrope. Nowadays a small grommet is referred to as an eyelet, a large one as a cringle.

Guy A rope or line used to restrain a spar such as a boom or spinnaker pole. A foreguy leads forward, an afterguy leads aft, a lazy guy is one on which there is no strain.

Gybe Jibe (US) When running, to turn the stern through the wind, bringing it across from one quarter to the other so that the boom swings across.

Halyard A line or rope used to hoist a spar, sail or flag.

Hand To lower, take in or furl a sail.

Hank A metal or nylon clip used to hold the luff of a headsail or staysail to a forestay.

Harden in To haul in a sheet so as to flatten a sail or bring it closer to the centreline of the boat.

Head The bow or stem of a boat. The top of the mast. The top edge of a four-sided sail or the top corner of a triangular one. The toilet.

Headboard A reinforcing plate sewn into the head of a triangular sail.

Headsail A general term describing any sail set forward of the mast (or foremast if there is more than one.)

Heave to A boat is hove-to by backing the headsail(s) and adjusting the mainsail and helm so that she is held quiet and steady, making almost no headway.

Hoist To haul aloft.

Horse A bar, rope or metal track on which the lower block of a mainsheet or jib boom tackle may travel athwartships.

Hounds The position where the lower shrouds and spreaders are attached. Traditionally, wooden chocks to locate the spliced eyes on the ends of the shrouds.

Jib The foremost headsail.

Kicking strap See Vang.

Lazyjacks Lines either side of a mainsail, led from the mast and under the boom, to gather in the sail as it is being lowered.

Leeboard A pivoting board, normally fitted in pairs, one on either side of a flat-bottomed boat, the leeward one being lowered to provide lateral resistance in place of a keel or centreboard.

Lee-bowing Sailing close-hauled with the tidal stream on the lee bow, so that the boat is pushed up to windward. This increases the apparent windspeed and enables the boat to point closer to the wind.

Leech The aftermost edge of a sail.

Leechline A very light line running through the tabling (hem) of the leech to prevent it from fluttering by adjusting its tension.

Lee helm The tendency of a boat to turn her bows away from the wind.

Leeward The direction in which the wind is blowing. Downwind. Opposite to windward.

Leeway The sideways drift to leeward caused by the wind.

Loose-footed A mainsail whose foot is not attached to the boom except at the clew.

Luff The forward edge of a sail.

Luff, to Sail closer to the wind. Luff up.

Mitre A central seam that roughly bisects the clew, so that the cloths run at right angles to both leech and foot.

Mizzen The after mast of a ketch or a yawl. The fore-and-aft sail set on the mizzen mast.

Offsets A table of measurements giving the co-ordinates of the various points along the edge of a sail panel to define its shape (or on the lines plan of a hull.)

Off the wind Not sailing close to the wind.

On the wind Sailing close-hauled.

Outhaul The line or tackle used to pull a sail out along a spar.

Palm A leather strap worn on the palm of the hand for thrusting a needle through sailcloth.

Parrel A strop or collar to hold the jaws of a gaff to the mast.

Peak The upper aft corner of a gaff sail where the head and leech meet. The aft end of the gaff itself.

Pinch to sail so close to the wind that the sails lose drive.

Pitch The rocking horse motion of a boat in a seaway. The distance that a propeller would advance in one revolution, assuming no slip.

Point The ability of a boat to sail close to the wind. To 'point' up is to sail closer.

Port tack Sailing with the wind blowing from the port side, mainsail across to starboard. A boat on port tack is required to keep clear of one on starboard tack.

Quarter The after side of a boat from amidships to astern.

Radial Cloth panels radiating from the clew and increasing in width towards the luff.

Rake The fore-and-aft angle of the mast or other part of a boat such as the stem, stern or rudder.

Reach A boat is reaching when she is neither close-hauled nor running. (See also close reach and broad reach.)

Reef, to To reduce the area of a sail by hauling a 'slab' down to the boom (slab, or jiffy reefing), or rolling up part of it.

Reef points A row of eyelets and ties to tie the loose folds (bunt) of a reefed sail down to its foot.

Rig The arrangement of sails and spars on a boat.

Rigging The ropes and lines that support the mast (known as the standing rigging) and those that hoist or control the spars and sails (the running rigging.)

Roach The part of the sail that extends beyond the straight line between the head and the clew. Roach is sometimes also applied to the foot.

Roband A rope band or loose-fitting loop of rope round a mast, as an alternative to lacings or hoops, to hold the luff of a mainsail to the mast.

Roping See boltrope.

Run To sail before the wind.

Runner Short for running backstay, one that can be slackened off, only the weather one being set up to support the mast from aft.

Sailmaker's yard. A unit of measurement used only in the US, where most sail-cloth originates, and amounting to 28½ in. The reason is that cotton cloth used to be woven 28½ in for sailing ships, although weight was, and still is, measured per running yard.

Scandalise To reduce the area of a mainsail by topping up the boom, or on a gaff sail by lowering the peak and tricing up the tack.

Scrim A very loose, open weave cloth sandwiched between Mylar laminates to strengthen high stress areas of a sail.

Self-tacking A headsail that automatically shifts from one side to the other when the boat is tacked, as does a mainsail.

Serve To bind the end of a rope tightly with small thread to prevent fraying. The result is known as a whipping.

Set flying A sail attached only at its head, tack and clew, the luff not secured to a stay or mast.

Sheet A rope atached to the boom or to the clew of a sail in order to harden it in or ease it out.

Shroud Those parts of the standing rigging that support the mast laterally, the cap shrouds running to the masthead and the lowers to an intermediate point where the spreaders are fitted.

Snotter A strop, usually of rope, to support the heel of a sprit or to take the thrust of a sprit boom and hold it close to the mast.

Spreaders Struts that spread the shrouds out sideways away from the mast, reducing the angle they make with the mast and hence the load on them.

Sprit A spar set diagonally across a spritsail to hold out its peak, or horizontally as a spirit boom to extend its clew.

Square rig One that carries rectangular sails suspended from yards which lie across the mast.

Standing part That part of a rope or tackle that is made fast and not hauled upon.

Starboard tack Sailing with the wind blowing from the starboard side, mainsail across to port. When two boats meet on crossing courses, the starboard tack boat has right of way.

Stay Part of the standing rigging giving fore-and-aft support to the mast.

Staysail A sail set on a stay or set flying, as distinct from those with their luffs attached to the mast. A sloop's staysail is known as a jib. Where more than one headsail is set, as on a cutter, the foremost is termed the jib. Boats with more than one mast may carry a number of staysails between the masts.

Stem The forward edge of the bow.

Strain The linear deformation of material subjected to load.

Stress The load applied to a material, divided by its cross-sectional area.

Strike-up marks Short pencil lines at intervals across the join of sail cloths laid out on the loft floor, to ensure that they match up when they are sewn together.

Tabernacle A housing on deck which carries the heel and pivot of a lowering mast.

Tabling The folded hem, or additional pieces of cloth, sewn to the edges of a sail to reinforce them.

Tack The lower forward corner of a sail.

Tack, to To go about when close-hauled, to change from one downwind tack to the other by gybing.

Tackle A purchase, with rope rove through one or more blocks to increase the mechanical advantage and hence the pulling power.

Telltales Short lengths of light material or tufts of wool fastened either side of a sail, or to the leech, to show the direction and behaviour of the airflow at that point.

Throat The upper forward corner of a gaff sail.

Topping lift An adjustable line from the mast to support the after end of the boom and to support it when the mainsail is lowered or being reefed.

Topsail A triangular sail set above the mainsail of a gaff or sprit rigged boat.

Traveller A roller- or ball-bearing car running on a track. A ring sliding on a horse or along a spar such as a bowsprit.

Vang A tackle or adjustable strut, usually running from the foot of the mast to a short distance along the boom, to pull it downwards and prevent it from lifting, and to control leech tension. A line or lines from the deck to the peak of a gaff or sprit to control its movement.

Vmg Velocity made good, being the best combination of direction and speed through the water to windward (or downwind), or actual speed over the ground towards a waypoint, using GPS.

Warp The yarns that run lengthways in a woven cloth across the fill yarns. A line used for mooring, anchoring or towing.

Wear To change tacks by turning away from the wind and gybing round.

Weather, to To be able to pass something without having to tack.

Weather helm The tendency of a boat to turn her bows to windward.

Windage Those parts of a boat exposed to the wind that contribute to the total air drag, eg superstructure, spars and rigging.

Wind-rode A boat is said to be wind-rode when lying at anchor or moored head to wind, and tide-rode when she lies to the tidal stream. It depends on which has the stronger influence.

Windward The weather side. The direction from which the wind is blowing. Towards the wind. Opposite leeward.

Wishbone A boom in two halves, outwardly curved in the shape of an airfoil, between which the sail is set.

Yard The spar carrying the head of a lateen, lug or gunter sail, or on which a squaresail is set.

INDEX

Marine Computing International Ltd
Hamble Court
Hamble Lane
Hamble
Hants
SO31 4QJ
Phone 023 8045 8047
Fax 023 8045 8057
email sales@marinecomputing.com
Website www.marinecomputing.com

USA readers: Contact Sheridan House Inc. at
154 Palisade St, Dobbs Ferry, NY 10522, USA.
Fax: (914) 693 0776

To obtain your free copy of the Sailmaster software; either post or fax us the form
attached below (US readers please use contact address above), or download it from
our website www.marinecomputing.com.
Sailmaster runs under DOS, and the minimum computer specification is: 512k free
RAM; 1Mb free disk space; EGA or VGA graphics; DOS 3.1 or later; 80 column
parallel port printer for text printout (Epson FX compatable for graphics printout).
It is supplied on a 3.5" disk, with a full manual on disk.
You receive a licensed copy of this shareware product.

MCIL can also offer the following products and services:
• mobile and satellite communications
• Weatherfax and weather satellite receiving packages
• Navigation software, electronic charts and interfacing
• Marinised computers and other marine computing hardware

Please supply me with a free copy of the Sailmaster software.
I have bought a copy of *Sails: The Way They Work* by Derek Harvey; proof of purchase
enclosed.

Name _____

Address _____

_____

_____

Phone _____

I understand that the software is supplied strictly on an 'as is' basis. No warranty is made
as to the fitness for purpose or performance of the software. User support is available
from MCIL, but may be charged for.